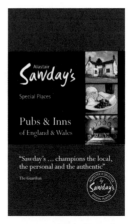

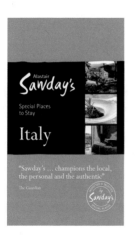

Eighteenth edition
Copyright © 2016
Alastair Sawday Publishing Co. Ltd
Published in September 2016
ISBN-13: 978-1-906136-79-6

Alastair Sawday Publishing Co. Ltd,
Merchants House, Wapping Road,
Bristol BS1 4RW, UK
Tel: +44 (0)117 204 7810
Email: info@sawdays.co.uk
Web: www.sawdays.co.uk

The Globe Pequot Press,
P. O. Box 480, Guilford,
Connecticut 06437, USA
Tel: +1 203 458 4500
Email: info@globepequot.com
Web: www.globepequot.com

Series Editor Alastair Sawday
Editor Tom Bell
Assistant to Editor Lianka Varga
Senior Picture Editor Alec Studerus
Coordinators Lianka Varga,
Sarah Barratt
Writing Tom Bell
Inspections Tom Bell

Marketing & PR
0117 204 7801
marketing@sawdays.co.uk

*We have made every effort to ensure the accuracy
of the information in this book at the time
of going to press. However, we cannot accept
any responsibility for any loss, injury or
inconvenience resulting from the use of information
contained therein.*

Production: Pagebypage Co Ltd
Maps: Maidenhead Cartographic Services
Printing: Pureprint, Uckfield
UK distribution: Travel Alliance, Bath
dmcentee@morriscontentalliance.com

Cover photo credits.
Front 1. The Bridge Inn at Ratho, entry 244 2. Cringletie House, entry 264 3. The Barn at Roundhurst, entry 191
Back: 1. Watergate Bay Hotel, entry 17   2. Houndgate Townhouse, entry 87 3. Seaham Hall, entry 89
Spine: Knockendarroch Hotel & Restaurant, entry 258

Alastair
Sawday's

Special Places
to Stay

British
Hotels & Inns

4   Contents

Two years ago we celebrated our 20th anniversary with a big dinner in Bristol. We decided to mark the occasion by handing out some awards, but with so many exceptional owners and places it was no easy task. Apart from one, that is - the award for our favourite British hotel. There really was only one contender, Langar Hall, a small and beautiful country house that sits next to a medieval church on a peaceful hill in Nottinghamshire.

It was Langar, not just because of the hotel (gorgeous), but because of its owner, Imogen Skirving, the most wonderful person you could ever hope to bump into behind a reception desk. Langar was her childhood home and she kept that feel of intimacy, then added humour, informality and good food to the mix, creating the perfect country-house hotel, a small-scale pleasure dome lost in deep country.

Photo above: Tom Germain
Photos right: Alec Studerus

In June 2016, Imogen died after being hit by a car while on holiday in Menorca. She was adored by many, a self-taught, mildly eccentric wonder of our world, who did things her own way and with great style. She represented the last wave of old-school, country-house hotel owners, who refused to yield to contemporary design or corporate ways, preferring to run their lovely boltholes as places of stylish refuge. None is better than Langar.

And so the world and his wife poured through its front door, many finding their favourite hotel and returning time and again. Actors and politicians fell in love with Imogen, as did the Test Match Special Team, for whom Langar is home when England are playing at Trent Bridge. She was one of a kind: charming, mischievous, determined, elegant, well connected, down-to-earth, full of gossip… the best company. Those who knew her fell under her spell immediately and were very glad to do so, and while she might have been small in stature, everything else about her was big, not least her heart. It is almost impossible to imagine this book without her in it.

Not that Imogen would have wanted to be sent off with a fanfare of earnest tributes. She would have preferred something a little more colourful and irreverent, so I'll leave the last word to her old friend, Henry Blofeld: 'Imogen is the most benevolent of despots. You could not wish for a more entertaining hostess.'

Alastair Sawday

Imogen Skirving
19 August 1937 – 29 June 2016

It's simple. There are no rules, no boxes to tick. We choose places that we like and are fiercely subjective in our choices. We also recognise that one person's idea of special is not necessarily someone else's so there is a huge variety of places, and prices, in this book.

Those who are familiar with our Special Places series know that we look for comfort, originality, authenticity, and reject the anonymous and the banal. The way guests are treated comes as high on our list as the setting, the architecture, the atmosphere and the food.

Inspections

We visit every place in the guide to get a feel for how both hotel and owner tick.

Photo: The Bulll, entry 196

We don't take a clipboard and we don't have a list of what is acceptable and what is not. Instead, we chat for an hour or so with the owner or manager and look round. It's all very informal, but it gives us an excellent idea of who would enjoy staying there. If the visit happens to be the last of the day, we may stay the night. Once in the book, properties are re-inspected regularly, so that we can keep things fresh and accurate.

Feedback

In between inspections we rely on feedback from our army of readers, as well as from staff members who are encouraged to visit properties across the series. This feedback is invaluable to us and we always follow up on comments.

So do tell us whether your stay has been a joy or not, if the atmosphere was great or stuffy, the owners and staff cheery or bored. The accuracy of the book depends on what you, and our inspectors, tell us. A lot of the new entries in each edition are recommended by our readers, so keep telling us about new places you've discovered too. Please use the forms on our website at www.sawdays.co.uk.

However, please do not tell us if your starter was cold, or the bedside light broken. Tell the owner, immediately, and get them to do something about it. Most owners, or staff, are more than happy to correct problems and will bend over backwards to help. Far better than bottling it up and then writing to us a week later!

Subscriptions

Owners pay to appear in this guide. Their fee goes towards the high costs of inspecting, of producing an illustrated book and of developing our website. We only include places that we find special: it is not possible for anyone to buy their way onto these pages. Nor is it possible for the owner to write their own description. We will say if the bedrooms are small, or if a main road is near. We do our best to avoid misleading people.

Disclaimer

We make no claims to pure objectivity in choosing these places. They are here simply because we like them. Our opinions and tastes are ours alone and this book is a statement of them; we hope you will share them. We have done our utmost to get our facts right but apologise unreservedly for any mistakes that may have crept in.

You should know that we don't check such things as fire alarms, swimming pool security or any other regulation with which owners of properties receiving paying guests should comply. This is the responsibility of the owners. At some of our smaller places — particularly our inns — you should request a contact number for emergencies if staff are not present overnight.

Do remember that the information in this book is a snapshot in time and may have changed since we published it; do call ahead to avoid being disappointed.

Photo: The Tommyfield, entry 130

Using this book

Finding the right place for you

All these places are special in one way or another. All have been visited and then written about honestly so that you can take what you want and leave the rest. Those of you who swear by Sawday's trust our write-ups precisely because we don't have a blanket standard; we include places simply because we like them. But we all have different priorities, so do read the descriptions carefully and pick out the places where you will be comfortable.

Maps

Each property is flagged with its entry number on the maps at the front. These maps are a great starting point for planning your trip, but please don't use them as anything other than a general guide – use a decent road map for real navigation. Most places will send you detailed instructions once you have booked your stay.

Symbols

These are explained at the very back of the book. They are based on the information given to us by the owners. However, things do change: bikes may be under repair or a new pool may have been put in. Please use the symbols as a guide rather than an absolute statement of fact and double-check anything that is important to you – owners occasionally bend their own rules, so it's worth asking if you may take your child or dog even if they don't have the symbol.

Wheelchair access ♿ – Some hotels are keen to accept wheelchair users into their hotels and have made provision for them. However, this does not mean that wheelchair users will always be met with a perfect landscape. You may encounter ramps, a shallow step, gravelled paths, alternative routes into some rooms, a bathroom (not a wet room), perhaps even a lift. In short, there may be the odd hindrance and we urge you to call and make sure you will get what you need.

Limited mobility – The limited mobility symbol 🚶 shows those places where at least one bedroom and bathroom is accessible without using stairs. The symbol is designed to satisfy those who walk slowly, with difficulty, or with the aid of a stick. A wheelchair may be able to navigate some areas, but in our opinion these places are not fully wheelchair friendly. If you use a chair for longer distances, but are not too bad over shorter distances, you'll probably be OK; again, please ring and ask. There may be a step or two, a bath

or a shower with a tray in a cubicle, a good distance between the car park and your room, slippery flagstones or a tight turn.

Children – The 🧒 symbol shows places which are happy to accept children of all ages. This does not mean that they will necessarily have cots, high chairs, etc. If an owner welcomes children but only those above a certain age, we have put these details at the end of their write-up. These houses do not have the child symbol, but even these folk may accept your younger child at quiet times. If you want to get out and about in the evenings, check when you book whether there are any babysitting services. Even very small places can sometimes organise this for you.

Pets – Our 🐕 symbol shows places which are happy to accept pets. Do let the owners know when booking that you'd like to bring your pet – particularly if it is

not the usual dog! Be realistic about your pet – if it is nervous or excitable or doesn't like the company of other dogs, people, chickens, children, then say so.

Owners' pets – The 🐈 symbol is given when the owners have their own pet on the premises. It may not be a cat! But it is there to warn you that you may be greeted by a dog, serenaded by a parrot, or indeed sat upon by a cat.

Hotel Awards

We have picked those places that deserve a special mention. Our categories are:

Hotel of the Year
Favourite newcomer;
National Treasure;
Nicely priced;
Fabulous food.

More details are given on pages 15-21 and all the award winners have been stamped.

Types of places

Hotels can vary from huge, humming and slick to those with only a few rooms that are run by owners at their own pace. In some you may not get room service or have your bags carried in and out. In smaller hotels there may be a fixed menu for dinner with very little choice, so if you have dishes that leave you cold, it's important to say so when you book your meal. If you decide to stay at an inn remember that they can be noisy, especially at weekends. If these things are important to you, then do check when you book.

Rooms

Bedrooms – These are described as double, twin, single, family or suite. A double may contain a bed which is anything from 135cm wide to 180cm wide. A twin will contain two single beds (usually 90cm wide). A suite will have a separate sitting area, but it may not be in a different room. Family rooms can vary in size, as can the number of beds they hold, so do ask. And do not assume that every bedroom has a TV.

Bathrooms – All bedrooms have their own bathrooms unless we say that they don't. If you have your own bathroom but you have to leave the room to get to it we describe it as 'separate'. There are very few places in the book that have shared bathrooms and they are usually reserved for members of the same party. Again, we state this clearly.

Meals

Breakfast is included in the room price unless otherwise stated. If only a continental breakfast is offered, we let you know.

Some places serve lunch, most do Sunday lunch (often very well-priced), the vast majority offer dinner. In some places you can content yourself with bar meals, in others you can feast on five courses. Most offer three courses for £25-£35, either table d'hôte or à la carte. Some have tasting menus, very occasionally you eat communally. Some large hotels (and some posh private houses) will bring dinner to your room if you prefer, or let you eat in the garden by candlelight. Always ask for what you want and sometimes, magically, it happens.

Prices and minimum stays

We quote the lowest price per night for two people in low season to the highest price in high season. Only a few places have designated single rooms; if no single

Photo: The William Cecil, entry 122

rooms are listed, the price we quote refers to single occupancy of a double room. In many places prices rise even higher when local events bring people flooding to the area, a point worth remembering when heading to Cheltenham for the racing or Glyndebourne for the opera.

The half-board price quoted is per person per night and includes dinner, usually three courses. Mostly you're offered a table d'hôte menu. Occasionally you eat à la carte and may find some dishes carry a small supplement. There are often great deals to be had, mostly mid-week in low season.

Most hotels do not accept one-night bookings at weekends. Small country hotels are rarely full during the week and the weekend trade keeps them going. If you ring in March for a Saturday night in July, you won't get it. If you ring at the last moment you may. Some places insist on three-night stays on bank holidays.

Photo above: The Shaven Crown, entry 155
Photo right: The Oakley Court, entry 5

Booking and cancellation

Most places ask for a deposit at the time of booking, either by cheque or card. If you cancel – depending on how much notice you give – you can lose all or part of this deposit unless your room is re-let.

It is reasonable for hotels to take a deposit to secure a booking; they have learnt that if they don't, the commitment of the guest wanes and they may fail to turn up.

Some cancellation policies are more stringent than others. It is also worth noting that some owners will take the money directly from your credit/debit card without contacting you to discuss it. So ask them to explain their cancellation policy clearly before booking so you understand exactly where you stand; it may well avoid a nasty surprise. And consider taking out travel insurance (with a cancellation clause) if you're concerned.

Arrivals and departures

Housekeeping is usually done by 2pm, and your room will usually be available by mid-afternoon. Normally you will have to wave goodbye to it between 10am and 11am. Sometimes one can pay to linger. Some inns are closed between 3pm and 6pm, so do try and agree an arrival time in advance or you may find nobody there.

Closed

When given in months this means for the whole of the month stated. So, 'Closed: November – March' means closed from 1 November to 31 March.

Sawday's British Hotel Awards

This is the time of year we throw a gong or two at some of our hotels, so here are 5 very special places that typify the Sawday ethos.

Award categories:

Hotel of the Year

Favourite newcomer

National Treasure

Nicely priced

Fabulous food

www.sawdays.co.uk/britishhotelawards

Hotel of the Year

We love small, intimate hotels and inns where the art of hospitality is practiced with flair – this wonder of our world has mastered that art in spades.

Penally Abbey, Pembrokeshire
Entry 285

www.sawdays.co.uk/britishhotelawards

Favourite newcomer

New hotels are hard to find in tough economic times, but that hasn't stopped creative owners bursting onto the scene with beautiful new places that delight us.

Coruisk House, Isle of Skye
Entry 253

National Treasure

Like a good red wine, some hotels get better with age – the Rose & Crown has a clear instinct for hospitality and has been delighting guests for years.

Rose & Crown, Durham
Entry 88

www.sawdays.co.uk/britishhotelawards

Nicely priced

There's nothing like washing up at a lovely small hotel and finding it has a lovely small price too – the Beckford Arms does that with ease.

The Beckford Arms, Wiltshire
Entry 212

Fabulous food

From hot kitchens come small miracles to delight your tastebuds and your pleasure receptors will delight in ambrosial food at the Crown & Castle.

The Crown & Castle, Suffolk
Entry 182

Photo: The Ship Inn, entry 245

Sawday's

'More than a bed
for the night…'

Britain
France
Ireland
Italy
Portugal
Spain

www.sawdays.co.uk

Self-Catering | B&B | Hotel | Pub | Treehouses, Cabins, Yurts & More

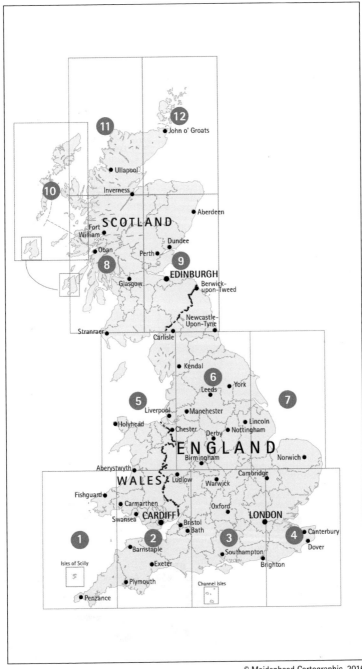

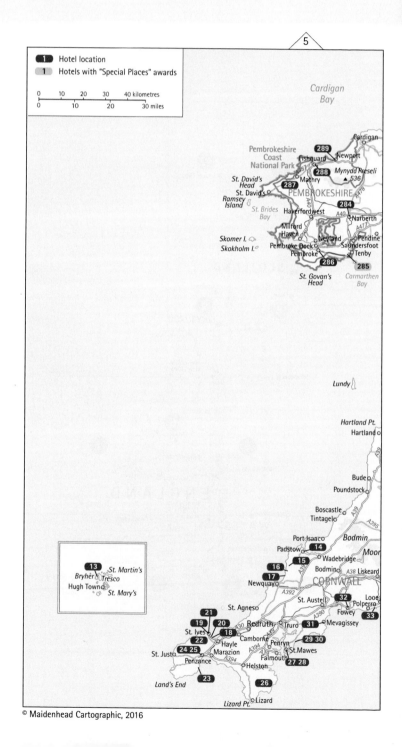

© Maidenhead Cartographic, 2016

Map 2

27

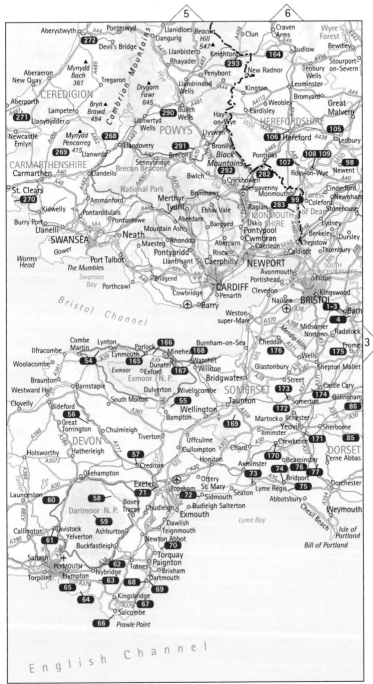

© Maidenhead Cartographic, 2016

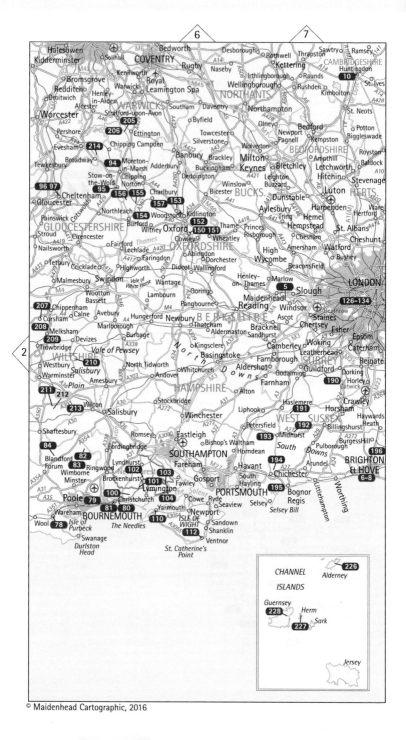

Map 4

29

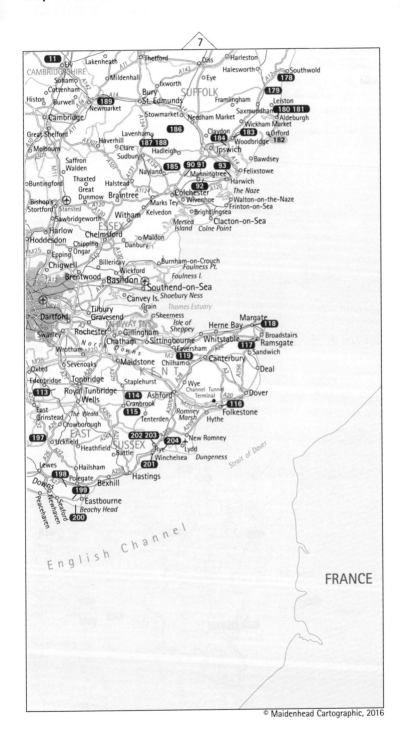

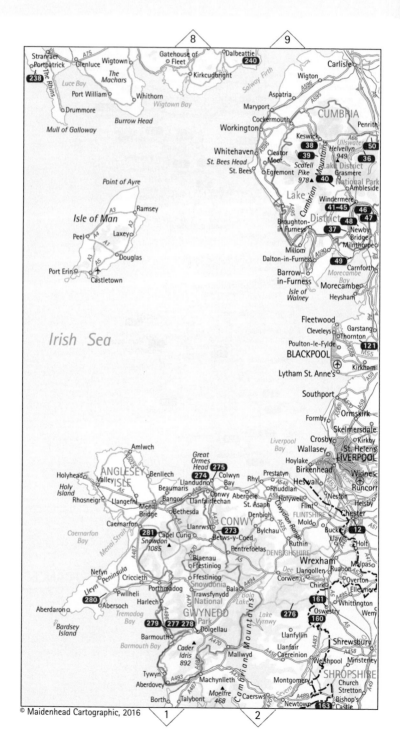

Map 6

31

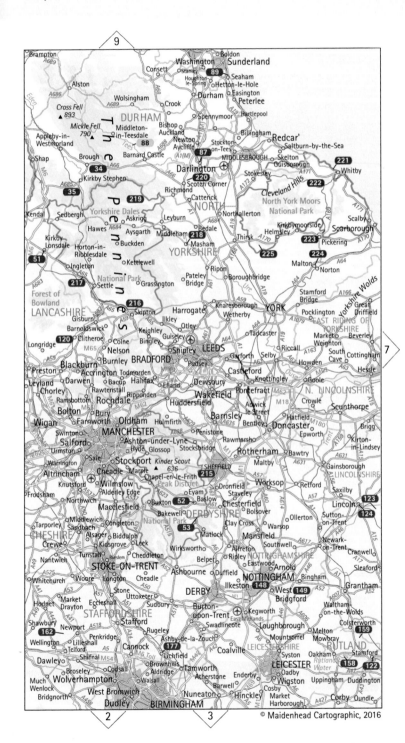

© Maidenhead Cartographic, 2016

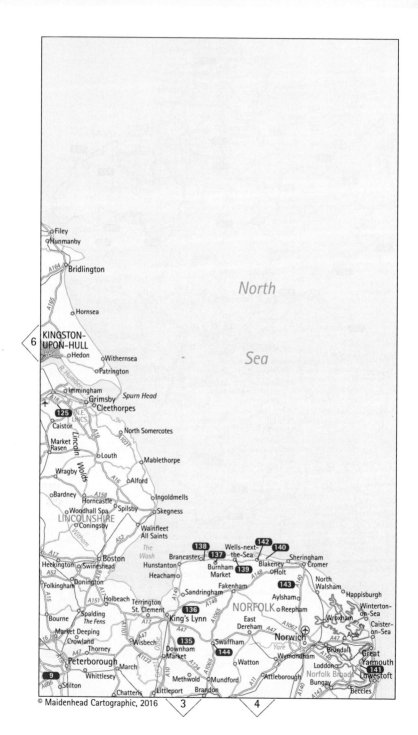

Map 8

33

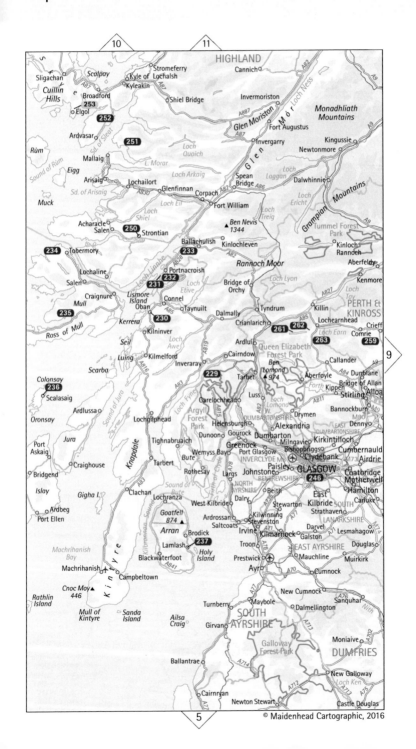

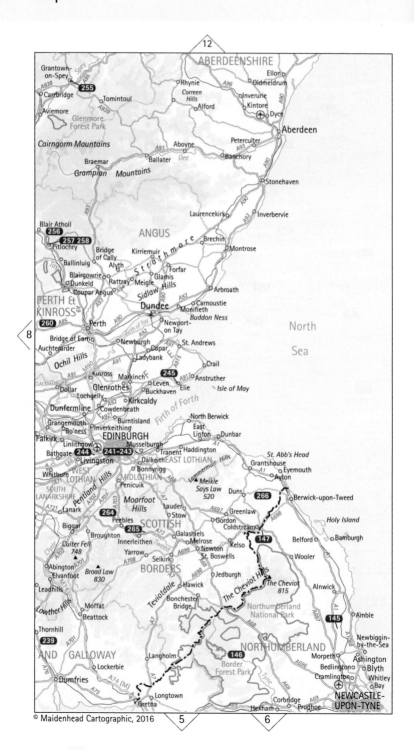

Map 10

35

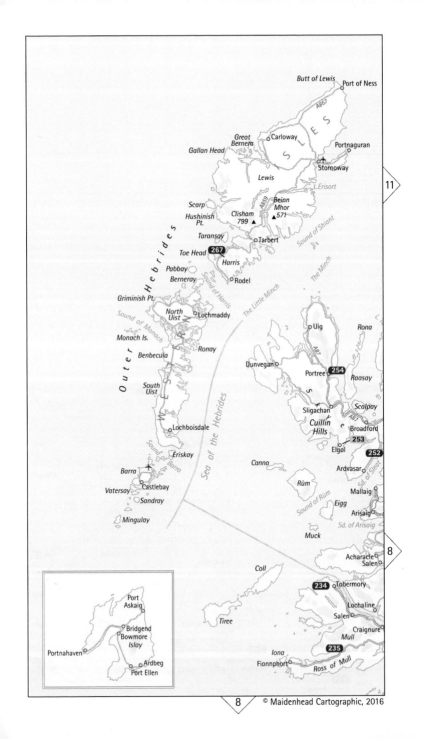

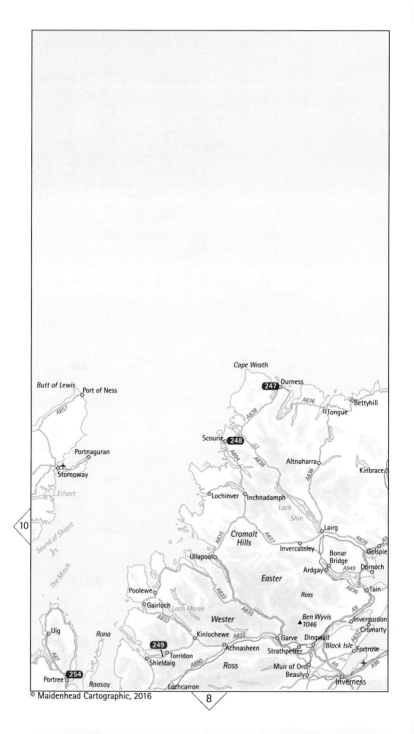

Cape Wrath

Butt of Lewis   Port of Ness

247 Durness

A836

Bettyhill

A838

Tongue

A857

Scourie 248

A894   A838   Altnaharra

A836   Kinbrace

Portnaguran

Stornoway

L.Erisort

Lochinver Inchnadamph

Loch Shin

Sound of Shiant

10

Cromalt Hills

A835   A837

Lairg

A839   A9

The Minch

Ullapool

Invercassley

Bonar Bridge   Golspie

A949   Dornoch

Ardgay

Easter

Poolewe

A832

A835   Ross

A9   Tain

A836

Gairloch   Loch Maree

Ben Wyvis
▲1046

Invergordon

L. Torridon   A832

Wester   Cromarty

Uig

Rona   Kinlochewe   A832   Garve   Dingwall   Black Isle   Fortrose

249 Torridon   Achnasheen   Strathpeffer   A9

Shieldaig   A890   Ross   Muir of Ord   A96

254   Beauly

Portree   Raasay   Lochcarron   Inverness

8

Map 12

37

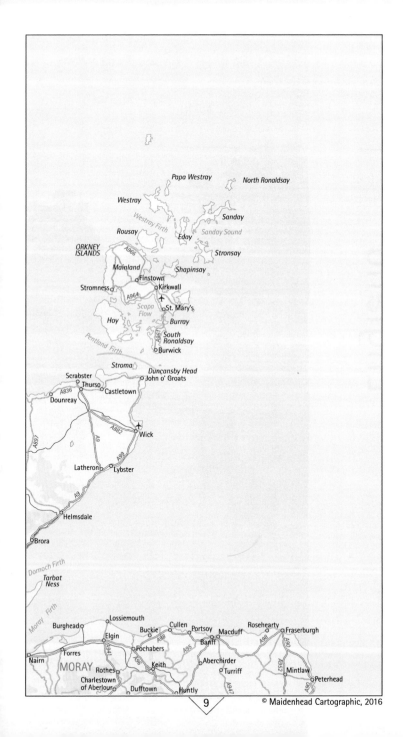

© Maidenhead Cartographic, 2016

England

Villa Magdala

Villa Magdala is one of those lovely boutique hotels that scores top marks across the board. You're pretty much in the middle of town, but hidden away on a quiet side street opposite a park. Then, there's a batch of smart bedrooms, which have style and comfort in equal measure. Add to this lovely staff on hand to book restaurants, balloon flights or day trips to Stonehenge and you have a perfect base. You're a five-minute stroll from magnificent Pulteney Bridge; the station isn't much further, so leave your car at home. You can hire bikes in town, then follow a towpath along the river out into the country. Back home, there's tea and cake on arrival, buck's fizz for breakfast, even bats and balls for children who want to go to the park. Breakfast – served in an airy dining room – is excellent: smoked salmon and free-range scrambled eggs, buttermilk pancakes, the full cooked works. Rooms vary in size, but all have excellent beds, pretty wallpaper and sparkling bathrooms. Good restaurants wait close by. Don't miss the Roman Baths or the Fashion Museum. There's off-street parking, too, a real boon. *Minimum stay: 2 nights at weekends*

Rooms	9 doubles, 11 twin/doubles: £99-£325. Singles from £89. Extra bed/sofabed available £45 per person per night.
Meals	Restaurant within 500m.
Closed	Christmas.
Directions	West into Bath on A4. Left into Cleveland Place (signed 'Through Traffic & University'). Over bridge, 2nd right and on right opposite park.

Caroline Browning
Villa Magdala
Henrietta Street, Bath, BA2 6LX

Tel	+44 (0)1225 466329
Email	enquiries@villamagdala.co.uk
Web	www.villamagdala.co.uk

Abbey Hotel

You're in the epicentre of Bath, just behind the abbey, in one of the prettiest quarters in town. Parade Gardens waits across the road, the river Avon pours over the weir at Pulteney Bridge, Bath rugby club stands on the far bank. As for the hotel, in summer you take to the terrace café for coffee and watch the world go by; in winter it turns into an après-ski bar for mince pies and mulled wine. Inside, you find contemporary art in the sitting room, wine glasses hanging from the ceiling in the stylish bar, then Chris Staines's lovely food in the theatrical restaurant, perhaps Thai mussels with lemongrass and ginger, whole roast spring chicken with herb gnocchi, salted peanut parfait with caramel popcorn and vanilla yoghurt. Smart rooms wait upstairs, where deeply comfy beds have woollen throws and colourful headboards. Some are small, others are big, all have iPads for room service, sparkling new bathrooms are beginning to emerge. Bath waits on your doorstep: rugby at the Rec, the Christmas market, all things Jane Austen. You're close to the station, too, so leave your car at home. *Minimum stay: 2 nights at weekends.*

Rooms	46 doubles, 14 twin/doubles: £105–£330.
Meals	Breakfast £15. Lunch from £7.50. Dinner, 3 courses, £30–£35. Sunday lunch from £16.
Closed	Never.
Directions	In central Bath, 100m south of the abbey, 100m west of the river Avon. Parking in Southgate car park £13 a day.

Andrew Foulkes
Abbey Hotel
North Parade, Bath, BA1 1LF

Tel	+44 (0)1225 461603
Email	reception@abbeyhotelbath.co.uk
Web	www.abbeyhotelbath.co.uk

Bath Paradise House Hotel

The view here is sublime, a wide sweep across the city that's best observed on a sunny afternoon while tucking into afternoon tea in the garden. Not that you will spend your time looking out of the windows, even if most of the rooms do have the view: what you find inside is just as special. This is a hugely welcoming house with owners and staff who go out of their way to help you make the most of Bath. Downstairs, a smart sitting room has three arched windows framing the city and an airy breakfast room with Lloyd Loom furniture. Bedrooms are lovely, even the smallest, coveted by returning guests for its doors onto the terrace. Others are more substantial, especially those with bay windows that look the right way. You'll find four-posters, beautiful fabrics, warm colours, no clutter at all. Some have vast bedheads, others travertine bathrooms; bigger rooms have sitting areas, perhaps a claw-foot bath. Menu Gordon Jones, a very short stroll, is a top spot for dinner, while the occasional peal of bells comes from a nearby church. The Thermae Spa with its rooftop pool is a must. *Minimum stay: 2 nights at weekends.*

Rooms	3 doubles, 3 twins, 4 four-posters: £120-£175. 1 family room for 3: £130-£185. Singles £75-£120.
Meals	Restaurants in Bath 0.5 miles.
Closed	Christmas Day & Boxing Day.
Directions	From train station one-way system to Churchill Bridge. A367 exit from r'bout up hill; 0.75 miles, left at Andrews estate agents. Left down hill into cul-de-sac; on left.

David & Annie Lanz
Bath Paradise House Hotel
86-88 Holloway,
Bath, BA2 4PX

Tel   +44 (0)1225 317723
Email   info@paradise-house.co.uk
Web   www.paradise-house.co.uk

Combe Grove Hotel

You spend the day in Bath looking at lots of beautiful things, then you're picked up and whisked off to this fine old house that sits on the edge of the city. It's a fantastic retreat – 70 peaceful acres of woodlands and gardens with huge views that stretch south for miles over unblemished country. Inside, you find a hotel that doubles as a contemporary art gallery. It's a work in progress and not your average hotel, rather, a place that exists to tickle your pleasure receptors, hence the muralled ceiling in the dining room, the chic bar for cool tunes and cocktails, and the outside dining terrace, where you can play boules while waiting for your dinner. Big bedrooms in the main house come with padded headboards and beautiful fabrics. Garden rooms – most with terraces or balconies – have heaps of colour and gorgeous walk-in showers. There's a spa with a pool, treatment rooms and fitness classes, all for guests to enjoy. Finally, some delicious food, perhaps beetroot with goat's cheese and candied walnuts, salmon with feta and couscous, apple beignets with cinnamon sugar. A woodland spa is coming soon. *Minimum stay: 2 nights at weekends.*

Rooms	28 doubles, 9 twin/doubles: £100-£280. 3 suites for 2: £250-£370. Singles from £90.
Meals	Lunch from £6. Dinner, 3 courses, about £35. Sunday lunch from £22. Afternoon tea from £19.95.
Closed	Never.
Directions	South from Bath on A36. Right after 4 miles at Limply Stoke traffic lights. Up hill and on left after 0.5 miles.

Neil Fincham Dukes
Combe Grove Hotel
Brasssknocker Hill,
Monkton Combe, Bath, BA2 7HU

Tel   +44 (0)1225 834644
Email   reception@combegrove.com
Web   www.combegrove.com

The Oakley Court

Now privately owned, this splendidly-intact Victorian house (with 70s wings mercifully ivy-covered) is hurling off its corporate shackles and turning itself into the friendliest of places. An enthusiastic and dedicated young team of people make sure you feel happy (and are offered food and drink) wherever you wander with your nurturing glass of bubbly: choose from the lively bar, elegant drawing and sitting rooms (with blazing fire on chilly days), a library full of interesting first editions, or sweeping lawn with deckchairs overlooking the river Thames. Children will be charmed with their own dressing gowns and cookies with milk at bedtime; dogs get treats, bustling butlers care for you. Pristine bedrooms (next for makeovers) will not raise any designer eyebrows (patterned carpets, reproduction furniture) but there are imaginative books, suggested walks/rides/runs and White Company goodies in immaculate bathrooms. Borrow a bike or wellies, hire a boat and grab a picnic, eat in Bray or just stay put and be thoroughly spoiled – fine food, honey from their own bees, homegrown veg. Ask about the horror film connections! *All rooms can sleep one child under 10.*

Rooms	81 doubles, 28 twins: £145–£400.
	9 suites for 2: £145–£400.
	Interconnecting rooms available for families.
Meals	Dinner, 3 courses, £38.
	Tasting menu, 7 courses, £65.
Closed	Never.
Directions	

Rachel Pearce
The Oakley Court
Windsor Road, Water Oakley,
Windsor, SL4 5UR

Tel	+44 (0)1753 609988
Email	reservations@oakleycourt.co.uk
Web	www.oakleycourt.co.uk

Artist Residence Brighton

At the top of a square, looking down to the sea, a cute hotel with an arty vibe. You're bang in the middle of Brighton with all the stuff you'd want on your doorstep: galleries, bars, the pier and the Brighton Pavilion. As for the hotel, good food, great staff, relaxed informality and a playful style are the hallmarks here. You get stripped boards, exposed brick walls, then an old garage door that slides back to reveal a chic restaurant with an open kitchen on display. In typical AR style, it's now one of the best places to eat in Brighton – delicious tasting menus that get you talking as well as eating. You'll find cool art, the odd wall clad in corrugated iron, even an ornamental drainpipe! Bedrooms come in different styles. Some have Pop Art murals, others come in Regency colours, a new batch are super-cool with baths in the room. Most have small, stylish shower rooms, one has a decked terrace. There's a quirky bar for cocktails, a ping pong table that doubles as a boardroom, then lunch in the front restaurant with views through big windows down to the sea. The beach waits below. *Minimum stay: 2 nights at weekends.*

Rooms	12 doubles, 5 twins: £95–£310.
	1 suite for 6: £300–£360.
	5 triples: £150–£250.
Meals	Breakfast £2.50–£8. Lunch from £7.
	Dinner, 4 courses, about £30.
	Restaurants within 500m.
Closed	Never.
Directions	A23 south into Brighton. Right at pier along seafront. Right after 1 mile into Regency Square. Hotel in northeast corner. Car park below square.

Charlie & Justin Salisbury
Artist Residence Brighton
33 Regency Square,
Brighton, BN1 2GG

Tel   +44 (0)1273 324302
Email   brighton@artistresidence.co.uk
Web   www.artistresidencebrighton.co.uk

brightonwave

A small, friendly, boutique B&B hotel in the epicentre of trendy Brighton. The beach and the pier are a two-minute walk, the bars and restaurants of St James Street are around the corner. An open-plan sitting room/dining room comes in cool colours with big suede sofas, fairy lights in the fireplace and ever-changing art on the walls. Bedrooms at the front are big and fancy, with huge padded headboards that fill the wall and deluge showers in sandstone bathrooms. Those at the back may be smaller, but so is their price and they come with spotless compact showers; if you're out more than in, why worry? All rooms have fat duvets, white linen, flat-screen TVs and DVD/CD players; the lower-ground king-size has its own whirlpool bath and garden. Richard and Simon are easy-going and happy for guests to chill drinks in the kitchen (there are corkscrews in all the rooms). Breakfast, served late at weekends, offers pancakes, the full English or sautéed tarragon mushrooms on toast. Good food waits on your doorstep: Riddle and Finns, The Salt Rooms, an Italian restaurant up the road. Fabulous Brighton waits. *Minimum stay: 2 nights at weekends.*

Rooms	3 doubles, 4 twin/doubles, 1 four-poster: £95–£185. Singles £74–£79.
Meals	Restaurants nearby.
Closed	1 week over Christmas & 2 weeks in January.
Directions	A23 to Brighton Pier roundabout at seafront; left towards Marina; 5th street on left. On-street parking vouchers £9 for 24 hours.

	Richard Adams & Simon Throp
	brightonwave
	10 Madeira Place,
	Brighton, BN2 1TN
Tel	+44 (0)1273 676794
Email	info@brightonwave.co.uk
Web	www.brightonwave.co.uk

Drakes

Drakes has the lot: cool rooms, a funky bar, big sea views, one of the best restaurants in town. It stands across the road from the beach, with the famous pier a three-minute walk and the big wheel even closer. Inside, a chic style has conquered all corners. Bedrooms are exemplary. Eleven have free-standing baths in the room, all have waffle bathrobes and White Company lotions, but what impresses most is the detail and workmanship. Handmade beds rest on carpets that are changed every year, contemporary plaster mouldings curl around ceilings like mountain terraces, Vi-Spring mattresses, wrapped in the crispest linen, are piled high with pillows. Don't worry if you can't afford the best rooms; others may be smaller and those at the back have city views, but all are fantastic and the attic rooms are as cute as could be. As for the food, it's some of the best in town, perhaps cauliflower soup with a smoked quail egg, honey-glazed duck with cassis sauce, pears poached in sweet wine with a chocolate and hazelnut mousse. The Lanes are close and packed with hip shops. Don't miss the Royal Pavilion.

Rooms	16 doubles, 1 twin/double: £120–£290.
	1 suite for 2: £300–£360.
	2 singles: £120–£160.
	Dinner, B&B from £92.50 p.p.
	Extra bed/sofabed available £25 p.p.p.n.
Meals	Breakfast £7.50–£15.
	Lunch, 2-3 courses, £20–£25.
	Dinner, 2-3 courses, £32.50–£45.
	Chef's Taster Menu, 5 courses, £60.
Closed	Never.
Directions	M23 & A23 into Brighton. At seafront, with pier in front, turn left up the hill. Drakes on left after 300 yds.

Richard Hayes
Drakes
43-44 Marine Parade,
Brighton, BN2 1PE

Tel	+44 (0)1273 696934
Email	info@drakesofbrighton.com
Web	www.drakesofbrighton.com

The Crown Inn

A thatched inn built of mellow stone that stands on the green in this pretty village. Paths lead out into open country and you can follow the river up to Fotheringhay, where Mary Queen of Scots lost her head. Back at the pub, warm interiors mix style and tradition to great effect. The bar has stone walls, ancient beams, flagstone floors and a roaring fire; in summer you decant onto the terrace and sip a pint of Black Sheep while watching village life pass by. Back inside, a beautiful new restaurant has recently appeared with golden stone walls, pale olive panelling and some very good food, anything from glazed ham and local eggs to oxtail lasagne, saddle of venison, sticky toffee tart with toffee sauce. You can also eat in the sitting-room bar on smart armchairs in front of another fire. Stylish bedrooms – some in the main house, others off the courtyard – are all different. You'll find smart colours, chic wallpapers, excellent bathrooms and good art. The bar hosts quiz nights, live music and the odd game of rugby on the telly, while on May Day there's a hog roast for the village fête.

Rooms	6 doubles with sofabeds, 2 twin/doubles: £120-£180. Singles from £55. £30 per child.
Meals	Lunch & dinner £5-£25. Not Sun eve. Restaurant closed first week January.
Closed	Replaced.
Directions	A1(M), junc. 17, then A605 west for 3 miles. Right on B671 for Elton. In village left, signed Nassington.

Marcus Lamb
The Crown Inn
8 Duck Street, Elton,
Peterborough, PE8 6RQ

Tel	+44 (0)1832 280232
Email	inncrown@googlemail.com
Web	www.thecrowninn.org

The Old Bridge Hotel

This lovely hotel, the best in town, mixes old-fashioned hospitality with contemporary flair, a template of excellence for others to follow. It's a big hit with the locals, who come for the food (delicious), the wines (exceptional) and the stylish interiors. Ladies lunch, businessmen chatter, kind staff weave through the throng. You can eat wherever you want: in the muralled restaurant; from a sofa in the lounge; or sitting in a winged armchair in front of the fire in the bar. You feast on anything from homemade soups to rack of lamb (starters are available all day), while breakfast is served in a panelled morning room with Buddha in the fireplace. It's all the work of owners John and Julia Hoskins. Julia's beautiful bedrooms have warm colours, fine fabrics, crisp linen and padded bedheads. One has a mirrored four-poster, several have vast bathrooms, others overlook the river Ouse. All have posh TVs, power showers and bathrobes. John, a Master of Wine, has a wine shop in reception, where you can taste before you buy. The A14 passes at the back, but it doesn't matter a jot. Cambridge is close.

Rooms	18 doubles, 1 twin, 3 four-posters: £125-£230. 2 singles: £99. Dinner, B&B £90-£130 p.p.
Meals	Lunch & dinner £5-£35.
Closed	Never.
Directions	A1, then A14 into Huntingdon. Hotel on southwest flank of one-way system that circles town.

John & Julia Hoskins
The Old Bridge Hotel
1 High Street,
Huntingdon, PE29 3TQ

Tel	+44 (0)1480 424300
Email	oldbridge@huntsbridge.co.uk
Web	www.huntsbridge.com

The Anchor Inn

A 1650s ale house on Chatteris Fen. The New Bedford rivers streams past outside; it was cut from the soil by the pub's first residents, Scottish prisoners of war brought in by Cromwell to dig the dykes that drain the Fens. These days, cosy interiors wait: low beamed ceilings, timber-framed walls, raw dark panelling, terracotta-tiled floors. A wood-burner warms the bar, so stop for a pint of cask ale, then spin into the restaurant for a good meal – hand-dressed crabs from Cromer in spring, asparagus and Bottisham hams in summer, wild duck from the marshes in winter. Four spotless bedrooms above the shop are just the ticket, not overly posh, just comfy and colourful with crisp linen, smart carpets, pretty throws and wicker armchairs. Three rooms have river views, the suites have sofa beds in their sitting rooms, a couple have new bathrooms, two above the restaurant get a little noise. Sleep with the window open and you'll be woken by the dawn chorus. Footpaths flank the water; stroll down and spot mallards, whooper swans, even the odd seal – the river is tidal to the Wash. Don't miss Ely.

Rooms	1 double, 1 twin/double: £80–£99. 2 suites for 2: £115–£155. Singles from £59.50. Extra bed £20.
Meals	Lunch, 2 courses, £13.95. Dinner, 3 courses, £25–£35. Sunday lunch from £12.95.
Closed	Never.
Directions	From Ely A142 west. In Sutton left on B1381 for Earith. Right in southern Sutton, signed Sutton Gault. 1 mile north on left at bridge.

Majiec Bilewski
The Anchor Inn
Bury Lane,
Sutton Gault, Ely, CB6 2BD

Tel	+44 (0)1353 778537
Email	anchorinn@popmail.bta.com
Web	www.anchorsuttongault.co.uk

Edgar House

Edgar House is one of those wonderful places that mixes the informality of a boutique B&B with the luxury of a five-star hotel. It sits peacefully on the River Dee, its garden bounded by the city's Roman wall. Inside, the restaurant doubles as a library, the sitting room comes with a smouldering fire, doors lead onto the garden for afternoon tea in the sun. Back inside, all sorts of unexpected delights wait: an honesty bar in a telephone box, a mini-cinema for a movie or two, then a grand staircase that sweeps you up to flawless rooms. Expect gorgeous beds wrapped in crisp linen, beautiful fabrics and lots of colour, then sofas and interactive TVs. Two rooms have balconies, two have terraces, all but one have river views. Magnificent bathrooms with walk-in showers come as standard; some have a double-ended bath, too, while the suite has a copper bath in the room. Drop down to the river, feed the ducks, check out the cathedral and the mediaeval quarter. Dinner is the final treat, perhaps wood pigeon with wild redcurrants, sea bass with a saffron broth, chocolate and orange fondant. *Children over 14 welcome.*

Rooms	6 doubles: £199–£249. 1 suite for 2: £219–£239. Dinner, B&B from £135 p.p.
Meals	Lunch from £9. Dinner (not Mon) £35; 7-course tasting menu £55. Sunday lunch from £18. Afternoon tea £19.75.
Closed	Never.
Directions	North into Chester on A483. Over bridge, then right with main flow at r'bout. 2nd right onto Lower Bridge Street. 2nd left into Duke Road. Right into car park after Recorder's Office. keep right and on left.

Tim Mills & Mike Stephen
Edgar House
22 City Walls,
Chester, CH1 1SB

Tel	+44 (0)1244 347007
Email	hello@edgarhouse.co.uk
Web	www.edgarhouse.co.uk

Hell Bay

Ship-wrecked sailors would refuse rescue from this chic island bolthole. It's a castaway's dream with sandy beaches, pretty coves and this wonderfully spoiling hotel. It's a friendly place with lovely staff who look after you with great warmth. As for the unremitting luxuries, you'll find a convivial bar for games and island ales, a sun-trapping terrace for afternoon tea, and a smart restaurant for the best food on the Scillies, perhaps tandoori scallops, wild sea bass, prune and Armagnac soufflé with Earl Grey ice cream. Airy bedrooms have a beach-house feel with seaside colours, wicker sofas, robes in sparkling bathrooms, then a terrace or balcony with big sea views. There's a swimming pool with sun loungers and a treatment room, and the impossibly popular Crab Shack for seafood delights in summer. The hotel is very family friendly; children can gather eggs from the coop and have them cooked for breakfast, there's a mini-golf course, a games room, babysitters are on hand. Elsewhere: other islands to explore, kayaks to hire, gardens to visit. Dogs are very welcome. A honeymooner's heaven. *Under 2s free.*

Rooms	25 suites for 2: £250–£640 Price includes dinner for 2. Singles from £160.
Meals	Lunch from £6.95. Dinner included; non-residents £45.
Closed	November to mid-March.
Directions	Ship from Penzance, or fly to St Mary's from Exeter, Newquay or Land's End; boat transfer to Bryher.

Philip Callan
Hell Bay
Bryher, Isles of Scilly, TR23 0PR
Tel   +44 (0)1720 422947
Email   contactus@hellbay.co.uk
Web   www.hellbay.co.uk

The Seafood Restaurant

In 1975 a young chef called Rick Stein opened a restaurant in Padstow. These days he has four more as well as a deli, a pâtisserie, a seafood cookery school and 40 beautiful bedrooms. Despite this success, his homespun philosophy has never wavered: buy the freshest seafood from fisherman on the quay, then cook it simply and eat it with friends. It is a viewpoint half the country seems to share – the Seafood Restaurant is now a place of pilgrimage – so come to discover the Cornish coast, walk on the cliffs, paddle in the estuary, then drop into this lively restaurant for a fabulous meal, perhaps black risotto with Cornish cuttlefish, grilled Padstow lobster with fine herbs, hot chocolate fondant with toasted marshmallow ice cream. Book in for the night and a table in the restaurant is yours, though flawless bedrooms are hard to leave. They are scattered about town, some above the restaurant, others at the bistro or just around the corner at St Petroc's House. All are immaculate. Expect the best fabrics, Vi-Spring mattresses, stunning bathrooms, the odd terrace with estuary views. *Minimum stay: 2 nights at weekends*

Rooms	32 doubles, 8 twin/doubles: £110–£330.
Meals	Lunch £38.50.
	Dinner £58.50.
Closed	Christmas Day & Boxing Day.
Directions	A39, then A389 to Padstow. Follow signs to centre; restaurant on left opposite harbour car park.

Jill & Rick Stein
The Seafood Restaurant
Riverside, Padstow, PL28 8BY

Tel	+44 (0)1841 532700
Email	reservations@rickstein.com
Web	www.rickstein.com/stay

Bedruthan Hotel & Spa

Bedruthan has the lot – stunning sea views, a couple of swimming pools, a spa with treatment rooms, then sitting rooms and restaurants galore. The most recent addition is a sensory spa garden offering seven steps to heaven: a salt scrub; a sauna; a cold bucket shower; a dip in the hot tub; a wet scrub; a visit to the sky garden; a second bite at the hot tub. Adults get the run of the place in school time, then children come in the holidays and slide down zip wires or sign up to surf school. Qualified staff look after younger children, who can paint, play, or jump into a cage of coloured balls while their parents snooze on sunbeds by the pool. There's a wood burner in the quiet sitting room, a cocktail bar that opens onto a terrace, then stylish bedrooms with retro colours and sparkling bathrooms. Some have separate rooms for children, others have terraces or sea views, a few overlook the car park. Younger children have early suppers, adults return later for a slap-up meal, perhaps guinea fowl, whole lemon sole, chilled strawberry soup with prosecco sorbet. The beach is a short stroll.

Rooms	38 twin/doubles: £135-£270.
	27 suites for 4: £205-£490.
	30 family rooms for 4: £175-£305.
	6 singles: £75-£125.
	Dinner, B&B from £95 p.p.
Meals	Lunch from £7. Dinner £30-£35.
	Sunday lunch from £15.
Closed	Christmas & 3 weeks in January.
Directions	On B3276 in Mawgan Porth.

Janie White
Bedruthan Hotel & Spa
Mawgan Porth,
Newquay, TR8 4BU
Tel   +44 (0)1637 860860
Email   stay@bedruthan.com
Web   www.bedruthan.com

The Scarlet

The Scarlet does what few others can – this may be a super-cool design hotel with one of the loveliest spas in the land, but the service here is fantastic: friendly, attentive, ready to help. As for the hotel, it sits above the sea with a vast wall of glass in reception to frame the view. Outside, you'll find a hot tub in the garden from which you can stargaze at night; inside, there's a stylish restaurant that opens onto a decked terrace, where you scoff delicious Cornish food while gazing out to sea. Elsewhere, an open fire in the sitting room, a pool table in the library, then a cool bar for Cornish wines and ales. Exceptional bedrooms all have sea views, then balconies or terraces, private gardens or viewing pods. Expect organic cotton, oak floors from sustainable forests, perhaps a free-standing bath or a huge walk-in shower. As for the spa, you get tented treatment rooms, chill-out pods that hang from the ceiling, and a couple of swimming pools flanked by sunbeds. Finally, the hotel is green to its core, with a biomass boiler, solar panels and state-of-the-art insulation.
Minimum stay: 2 nights at weekends. Dogs welcome.

Rooms	21 doubles, 8 twin/doubles: £195–£405.
	8 suites for 2: £270–£460.
	Dinner, B&B from £127.50 p.p.
Meals	Lunch, 3 courses, £22.50.
	Dinner, 3 courses, £42.50.
Closed	4 January–12 February.
Directions	North from Newquay on B3276 to
	Mawgan Porth. Signed left in village
	halfway up hill.

Meeche Hood
The Scarlet
Tredragon Road,
Mawgan Porth, TR8 4DQ

Tel	+44 (0)1637 861800
Email	stay@scarlethotel.co.uk
Web	www.scarlethotel.co.uk

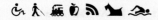

Watergate Bay Hotel

Watergate Bay is one of those lovely Cornish landscapes where nature rules the roost, a world of sand, sea and sky and nothing but. The few buildings that have taken root here don't qualify as a village and have no name, they're just chattels of the beach, which runs for a mile and is one of the best in Cornwall. The hotel sits directly above, making the most of the view, with walls of glass in the café/bar, a smart terrace strewn with sun loungers, a swimming pool that looks out to sea. Outside, the hotel's surf school will kit you out to ride the waves; you can kite surf and paddle board, too, while beach polo and music festivals come in summer. As for the hotel, it mixes cool design with an informal vibe. Coastal light floods the café, there's a cute sitting room with an open fire, then treatment rooms and a hot tub in the spa. Airy bedrooms – some with sea views, others with balconies – have seaside colours and chic bathrooms. As for the food, you can eat in the café or the grill, or walk 50 paces to the Beach Hut for a burger, or try Jamie Oliver's Fifteen. A great family hotel.

Rooms	47 twin/doubles: £160-£345.
	2 suites for 2, 20 suites for 4: £255-£495.
	Singles £120-£268.
	Dinner, B&B £160-£335 p.p.
Meals	Lunch from £5.75.
	Dinner, 3 courses, about £35.
Closed	Never.
Directions	Leave A30 at Indian Queens and follow signs past Newquay Airport. Left at the T-junction and hotel in village.

Mark Williams
Watergate Bay Hotel
On the Beach,
Watergate Bay, TR8 4AA
Tel   +44 (0)1637 860543
Email   reservations@watergatebay.co.uk
Web   www.watergatebay.co.uk

Boskerris Hotel

Marianne and Jonathan's lovely hotel has stylish interiors and big views of ocean and headland. It's a family affair – friendly, welcoming, a great little base. In summer, you can sink into sofas on the decked terrace and gaze out to sea. Godrevy Lighthouse twinkles to the right, St Ives slips into the sea on the left, the sands of Carbis Bay and Lelant shimmer between. Inside, white walls and big mirrors soak up the light. You get painted floorboards and fat sofas in the sitting room, then delicious breakfasts and big views in the dining room. Airy bedrooms are coolly uncluttered, with padded headboards, seaside colours, smart TVs and coffee machines. Eleven have the view, all have fancy bathrooms, some with deep baths and deluge showers. You'll find White Company lotions and Designers Guild fabrics, while in one room you can soak in the bath whilst gazing out to sea. Staff are kind, nothing is too much trouble. A coastal path leads down to St Ives (20 mins), mazy streets snake past beaches and up to the Tate. Dinner is available at night, or you could head into town. *Children over 7 welcome.*

Rooms	10 doubles, 3 twins: £125–£255. 1 family room for 4: £190–£240. 1 triple: £165–£200. Singles from £93.50.
Meals	Dinner, 3 courses, about £30.
Closed	Mid-Nov to late February.
Directions	A30 past Hayle, then A3074 for St Ives. After 3 miles pass sign for Carbis Bay, then third right into Boskerris Road. Down hill, on left.

Jonathan & Marianne Bassett
Boskerris Hotel
Boskerris Road,
Carbis Bay, St Ives, TR26 2NQ

Tel	+44 (0)1736 795295
Email	reservations@boskerrishotel.co.uk
Web	www.boskerrishotel.co.uk

Blue Hayes Private Hotel

The view from the terrace is magical, a clean sweep across the bay to St Ives. You breakfast here in good weather in the shade of a Monterey pine, as if transported back to the French Riviera circa 1950. As for the hotel, it's an unadulterated treat, mostly due to Malcolm, whose limitless generosity is stamped over every square inch. Few hotels close for four months to redecorate every winter, but that's the way things are done here – this may explain why so many guests book for the following year when checking out. The house shines in ivory white with the occasional dash of colour from carpets and curtains. A wall of glass in the bar weatherproofs the view. Big rooms are gorgeous, two with balconies, one with a terrace, all with sparkling bathrooms. Light suppers are on hand, though a short stroll into town leads to dozens of restaurants; Alfresco on the harbour is excellent and torches are provided for the journey back. Penzance, Zennor, Tate St Ives and a host of beaches are all close. There's folk and jazz for the September festival, a great time to visit. A true one-off. *Children over 10 welcome.*

Rooms	4 doubles: £190–£230.
	1 suite for 2: £250–£270.
	1 triple: £200–£230.
	Singles £130–£150.
Meals	Packed lunch by arrangement.
	Light suppers from £12.
	Restaurants within walking distance.
Closed	November – February.
Directions	A30, then A3074 to St Ives. Through Lelant & Carbis Bay, over mini-r'bout (Tesco on left) and down hill. On right immed. after garage on right.

Malcolm Herring
Blue Hayes Private Hotel
Trelyon Avenue,
St Ives, TR26 2AD

Tel	+44 (0)1736 797129
Email	info@bluehayes.co.uk
Web	www.bluehayes.co.uk

Primrose Valley Hotel

This Edwardian villa above Portminster Beach had seen better days, but Natasha and Mihaka like a challenge, so they bought it, closed it and spent five months renovating from top to toe. The results are gorgeous, a chic new world with airy interiors that swim in seaside light. You're at the bottom of the hill, about 200 metres back from the beach. Bedrooms have a deliciously simple style: off whites, smart fabrics, colourful local art. Those at the front have sea views, four have balconies, one at the back has its own deck. You'll find rugs on wood floors, stylish furniture, perhaps wooden planks covering one wall. Sparkling bathrooms have power showers, the odd claw-foot bath, then robes and REN oils. Downstairs, a big open-plan room at the front has sofas and armchairs on one side, then tables for yummy breakfasts on the other, but sneak round the back and find a cocktail bar, not a bad spot to recuperate after a hard day on the beach. Light bites are on tap, but good restaurants wait in town, a five-minute stroll. Don't miss Tate St Ives or the Barbara Hepworth Museum. *Minimum stay: 2 nights at weekends.*

Rooms	4 doubles, 3 twin/doubles: £110–£195. 2 suites for 2: £180–£195. Singles from £125.
Meals	Bar snacks & platters from £5. Restaurants 500m.
Closed	1 December to 10 February.
Directions	A30, then A3074 for St Ives. Downhill for town. Slow down at sign indicating Visitor Parking and Restricted Zone, then immediately right down Primrose Valley. Under bridge; left; back under bridge; hotel to the left.

Natasha & Mihaka MacGreggor
Primrose Valley Hotel
Primrose Valley,
St Ives, TR26 2ED
Tel   +44 (0)1736 794939
Email   info@primroseonline.co.uk
Web   www.primroseonline.co.uk

Trevose Harbour House

This super-chic B&B started life in the 1850s as a fisherman's cottage. These days it's a small-scale version of a design hotel, pristine from top to toe. It's all the result of an 18-month renovation and it sits in the old town, a two-minute stroll from the beach. Inside, form and function rule the roost: everything is beautiful, nothing superfluous. Interiors come in blue and white with fresh flowers, local art, beautiful ceramics, and umbrellas in case it rains. Downstairs is open-plan – a small sitting room with an honesty bar concealed in a '50s dresser on one side, on the other a dining room where you sit at Ercol tables and tuck into an excellent breakfast under hanging lamps. Rooms have Hypnos beds, crisp linen, beautiful fabrics and impeccably upholstered armchairs. Three have sea views, all have smart TVs, coffee machines and hot-water bottles. Bathrooms are flawless: underfloor heating, walk-in showers, white robes and Neal's Yard oils, perhaps a claw-foot bath. Outside, labyrinthine lanes lead to the harbour, sandy beaches, art galleries and lots of delicious restaurants. Dreamy. *Minimum stay: 2 nights. Children over 12 welcome.*

Rooms	5 doubles: £155–£245.
	1 suite for 2: £235–£275.
	Singles from £145.
Meals	Restaurants within 500 meters.
Closed	Mid-November to mid-March
Directions	A30 west, then A3074 for St Ives. Park in station car park above beach (£7.50 for 24 hours). At car park entrance take steps down to the Warren. House on left after 300m.

Angela & Olivier Noverraz
Trevose Harbour House
22 The Warren,
St Ives, TR26 2EA

Tel	+44 (0)1736 793267
Email	hi@trevosehouse.co.uk
Web	trevosehouse.co.uk

The Gurnard's Head

This quirky inn is one of the best, the sort of place you'd hope to find at the end of the road. Outside, the wild west coast weaves up to St Ives; secret beaches appear at low tide, cliffs tumble down to the water, wild flowers streak the land pink in summer. Inside, it's earthy, warm, stylish and friendly, with rustic interiors, colour-washed walls, stripped wooden floors and fires at both ends of the bar. Logs are piled high in an alcove, maps and art hang on the walls, books fill every shelf; if you pick one up and don't finish it, take it home and post it back. Cosy rooms have warm colours and the odd antique, then Vi-Spring mattresses, crisp white linen, colourful throws and Roberts radios. Downstairs, you can scoff delicious food in the bar, the restaurant or out in the garden in good weather. Tasty snacks wait – pork pies, crab claws, half a pint of Atlantic prawns – as does more substantial fare, maybe grilled sardines, Cornish lamb with root vegetables, roasted apples and pears. Picnics can be arranged, there's bluegrass folk music in the bar most weeks. Dogs are very welcome.

Rooms	3 doubles, 4 twin/doubles: £115–£180. Dinner, B&B from £82.50 p.p.
Meals	Lunch from £12. Dinner, 3 courses, £25–£35. Sunday lunch from £13.
Closed	Christmas.
Directions	On B3306 between St Ives & St Just, 2 miles west of Zennor, at head of Treen village.

Charles & Edmund Inkin
The Gurnard's Head
Zennor,
St Ives, TR26 3DE

Tel	+44 (0)1736 796928
Email	enquiries@gurnardshead.co.uk
Web	www.gurnardshead.co.uk

The Old Coastguard

The Old Coastguard stands on the water in one of Cornwall's loveliest coastal villages. It's a super spot and rather peaceful – very little has happened here since the Spanish sacked the place in 1595. It's owned by Edmund and Charles Inkin, brothers who are past masters at running lovely small hotels; warm colours, attractive prices, great food and kind staff are their hallmarks. Downstairs, the airy bar and the dining room come together as one, the open plan informality creating a great space to hang out. You get smart rustic tables, earthy colours, local ales and local art, then wooden floors and a crackling fire. Drop down a few steps to find a bank of sofas and a wall of glass framing sea views; in summer, doors open onto a decked terrace, a lush lawn, then the coastal path weaving down to the small harbour. Bedrooms hit the spot: warm colours, excellent beds, robes in fine bathrooms, books everywhere. Most have the view, eight have balconies. Don't miss dinner: salt and pepper monkfish, fish stew with mussels, chocolate mousse with tonka bean ice cream. Dogs are very welcome.

Rooms	10 doubles, 3 twin/doubles: £135-£210. 1 suite for 2: £175-£225. 1 family room for 4: £190-£240. Dinner, B&B from £94 p.p.
Meals	Lunch from £6. Dinner, 3 courses, about £30. Sunday lunch from £12.50.
Closed	1 week in early January.
Directions	Take coastal road west from Penzance, through Newlyn and on to Mousehole. Hotel on left after car park.

Charles & Edmund Inkin
The Old Coastguard
The Parade, Mousehole,
Penzance, TR19 6PR

Tel	+44 (0)1736 731222
Email	bookings@oldcoastguardhotel.co.uk
Web	www.oldcoastguardhotel.co.uk

Artist Residence Penzance

Distinctly hip, deliciously quirky and overflowing with colour and style, this groovy little bolthole is hard to beat. The house dates to 1600 and stands on the ley line that connects St Michael's Mount to Stonehenge. You're in the old town, a stone's throw from the harbour. It's a very friendly place, open all day, with staff who stop to chat and help. Interiors overflow with originality and flair: the restaurant has walls of wood and pop art, there's a wood-burner in a stylish sitting-room bar, then a lovely garden for ping pong, table football, the odd summer barbecue and a beach-hut bar. Bedrooms come in different shapes and sizes. Lots have brightly colourful murals, most have compact bathrooms, two new rooms have claw-foot baths and walk-in showers, while the family room has a fridge and spacious apartments have fully equipped kitchens. All have good beds, white linen and toppers for a good night's sleep. You get American pancakes, local eggs and homemade granola at breakfast, perhaps chilli squid or pulled pork with apple ketchup for dinner. Don't miss St Michael's Mount. *Minimum stay: 2 nights at weekends in summer.*

Rooms	12 doubles, 2 twin/doubles: £75–£180.
	1 family room: £110–£235.
	2 triples: £125–£200.
	2 apartments for 4: £190–£280.
	Singles £75–£125.
Meals	Lunch & dinner from £6;
	3 courses £20–£25.
	Pub/restaurant across the road.
Closed	Never.
Directions	A30 into Penzance. Follow signs to town centre; up main street; left at top; keep left and on right after 200m.

Charlie & Justin Salisbury
Artist Residence Penzance
20 Chapel Street,
Penzance, TR18 4AW

Tel	+44 (0)1736 365664
Email	penzance@artistresidence.co.uk
Web	www.artistresidencecornwall.co.uk

Chapel House

Everything here is beautiful – a stunning Georgian house; views over town that stretch out to sea; bedrooms and bathrooms to rival those in the best designer hotels. All of which would be blossom in the wind without Susan, whose instinct to go the extra mile knows no restraint – this is not just a gorgeous house, but a friendly one, too. Outside, smart red bricks give some idea of the grandeur within, but step inside and find a contemporary wonderland that took two years to refurbish. The hall is home to works from the Newlyn School of Art, the double sitting room has high ceilings, an open fire and a baby grand piano, doors lead onto a balcony and down to a courtyard garden, a peaceful retreat in summer. Bedrooms are hard to fault: white walls soak up the light; handmade beds give a fine night's sleep; super-chic wet rooms have fabulous showers. One has a wood-burner in the room, another a bath under a glass roof that slides open. There's much more: delicious kitchen suppers at weekends; cooking demonstrations with local chefs; great restaurants along the road. The magical west coast waits.

Rooms	6 doubles: £150-£200. Singles from £100. Extra beds for babies to 12-year-olds free; 12+ £10.
Meals	Kitchen suppers on Friday/Saturday £22-£25 (or on request during week). Sunday lunch from £14.50.
Closed	Rarely.
Directions	Along harbourside with sea on left. Opp. docks, right into Quay St. Up hill; on right opp. St Mary's Church. Parking can be tricky.

Susan Stuart
Chapel House
Chapel Street,
Penzance, TR18 4AQ
Tel   +44 (0)1736 362024
Email   hello@chapelhousepz.co.uk
Web   chapelhousepz.co.uk

Bay Hotel

The Bay Hotel sits under a vast Cornish sky with views to the front of nothing but sea – unless you count the beach at low tide, where buckets and spades are mandatory. Outside, the lawn rolls down to the water. In summer it's sprinkled with deckchairs and loungers, so grab a book or snooze in the sun and listen to the sounds of the seaside. Airy interiors are just the ticket: stylish and homely with lots of comfort. The view follows you around, keeping your eyes glued to the horizon. There are flowers everywhere, cavernous sofas, a small bar for pre-dinner drinks. Bedrooms vary in size, one has its own balcony, all have sea views (some from the side). Expect tongue-and-groove panelling, coastal colours, super bathrooms and smart TVs. As for the food, lobsters come courtesy of the next door neighbour, while the steak and kidney pie never leaves the menu. Try moules marinière, sea bass with samphire, lemon and caper butter, Grand Marnier crème brûlée. Harbour cruises often bump into dolphins, seals, even basking sharks. You're on the coastal path, so bring your boots, but don't miss afternoon tea. *Minimum stay: 2 nights at weekends. Children over 4 welcome. Pets by arrangement.*

Rooms	6 doubles, 5 twin/doubles: £140–£280. 3 suites for 2: £250–£310. Price includes dinner for 2. Singles from £105.
Meals	Lunch from £6. Dinner included; non-residents £34.95.
Closed	November–February.
Directions	A3083 south from Helston, then left onto B3293 for St Keverne. Right for Coverack after 8 miles. Down hill, right at sea, second on right.

Ric, Gina & Zoe House
Bay Hotel
North Corner, Coverack,
Helston, TR12 6TF

Tel	+44 (0)1326 280464
Email	enquiries@thebayhotel.co.uk
Web	www.thebayhotel.co.uk

The St Mawes Hotel

Seaside chic, a relaxed feel and some lovely rooms are the hallmarks of this small hotel that stands on the water with big views out to sea. Outside, pavement tables are popular with people watchers, though those in the know head upstairs to the balcony, an unbeatable spot on a good day. Inside, you'll find sofas in front of the fire in the bar, then rugs on stripped boards in the colourful first-floor dining room. The food is delicious, the best local produce cooked simply, perhaps calamari with lemon mayonnaise, a crispy goat's cheese pizza, peanut butter brownie with vanilla ice cream. Beautiful bedrooms are scattered about, some with beautiful timber frames. Those at the front have watery views, all have chic fabrics, colourful art, the best beds, then robes and walk-in showers; a couple have baths, too. You'll find driftwood art scattered about, well-kept ales waiting at the bar and a small cinema for films. The harbour stands directly outside, so hire kayaks and explore the bay. Don't miss the castle or cricket on the beach. The coastal path starts at the front door. *Minimum stay: 2 nights at weekends.*

Rooms	7 twin/doubles: £130–£285. Cots/children in parents' room from £25.
Meals	Continental breakfast included, full English £8. Lunch from £6.50. Dinner, 3 courses, £25–£30.
Closed	Never.
Directions	The hotel is on the seafront in the town. Parking available opposite in public car park (£6 a day in high season, free in low season).

Ben Bass
The St Mawes Hotel
Harbourside,
St Mawes, TR2 5DW

Tel	+44 (0)1326 270170
Email	stay@stmaweshotel.com
Web	www.stmaweshotel.co.uk

The Idle Rocks

A stunning hotel, bang on the water, in one of Cornwall's prettiest seaside towns. The terrace is a delight, a place to linger in the sun, with waves lapping directly below and sail boats cruising beyond. Fisherman land their lobsters at the quay, boat taxis whizz you off to sandy beaches, you can hire kayaks and explore the bay. As for Idle Rocks, a recent renovation has turned it into one of Cornwall's coolest boltholes. Chic interiors flood with light, beautiful rooms have stunning bathrooms, delicious food comes from the hills and the water around you. You'll find sofas in front of the sitting room fire, lamps that hang above the bar, walls of glass in the restaurant that open onto the terrace. Uncluttered bedrooms, most with sea views, have whitewashed walls, fine local art, padded window seats, then big beds wrapped in crisp white linen. Bathrooms are just as good, some with claw-foot baths, others with walk-in showers, all with robes and aromatherapy oils. Don't miss dinner, perhaps scallop and lobster ravioli, Cornish hogget with carrots, poached figs with Earl Grey sorbet. Magical. *Minimum stay: 2 nights at weekends.*

Rooms	10 doubles, 5 twin/doubles, 1 twin: £150-£350. 3 suites for 2: £260-£380. 1 family room for 4: £320-£450. Cots/children in parents' room from £25.
Meals	Lunch from £8; set menu £27.50-£35. Dinner, à la carte, £40-£45.
Closed	3-17 January.
Directions	Leave A390 between St Austell and Truro for St Mawes on A3078. Drop into village and on left by water.

Paul Goodwin
The Idle Rocks
Harbourside, 1 Tredenham Road,
St Mawes, TR2 5AN

Tel	+44 (0)1326 270270
Email	info@idlerocks.com
Web	www.idlerocks.com

Driftwood Hotel

The position here is hard to beat. Views head out to sea, the coastal path sweeps you away, six acres of beautiful gardens drop down to a private beach. As for Driftwood, Cape Cod meets Cape Cornwall, with chic, airy interiors at every turn. The sitting room is stuffed with beautiful things – fat armchairs, deep sofas, driftwood lamps, a smouldering fire – while big windows pull in the view. In summer, doors open onto a decked terrace for breakfast and lunch in the sun. Bedrooms are gorgeous (all but one have sea views), some big, others smaller, one in a cabin halfway down the cliff with its own terrace. All have the same clipped elegance: warm colours, big beds, white linen, wicker chairs. There are Roberts radios on bedside tables, cotton robes in excellent bathrooms. Drop down to the dining room for a Michelin-starred dinner, perhaps lemon sole with crystallised ginger, local lamb with candied pine nuts, spiced pineapple with lemongrass and lime. There are high teas for children, hampers for beach picnics and rucksacks for walkers. On clear nights the sky is full of stars. Brilliant. *Minimum stay: 2 nights at weekends.*

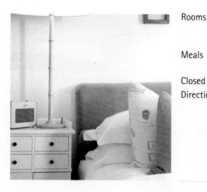

Rooms	13 doubles, 1 twin: £180–£270. 1 cabin for 4: £225–£255. Dinner, B&B from £122.50 p.p.
Meals	Dinner £50 (inc. in room price in low season). Tasting menu £80.
Closed	Early December to early February.
Directions	From St Austell, A390 west. Left on B3287 for St Mawes; left at Tregony on A3078 for approx. 7 miles. Signed left down lane.

Paul & Fiona Robinson
Driftwood Hotel
Rosevine,
Portscatho, Truro, TR2 5EW

Tel	+44 (0)1872 580644
Email	info@driftwoodhotel.co.uk
Web	www.driftwoodhotel.co.uk

The Rosevine

A small, family bolthole on the Roseland Peninsula with views that tumble across trim lawns and splash into the sea. Tim and Hazel welcome children with open arms and have created a small oasis where guests of all ages can have great fun. There's a playroom for kids (Xbox, plasma screen, DVDs and toys), an indoor pool, and a beach at the bottom of the lane. Children's teas are on hand, as are cots and highchairs, while babysitters can be arranged. Parents don't fare badly either: an elegant sitting room with sofas in front of the wood-burner; sea views and Lloyd Loom furniture in a light-filled restaurant; sun loungers scattered about a semi-tropical garden. Suites and apartments come with small kitchenettes (fridge, sink, dishwasher, microwave combi-oven); you can self-cater, eat in the restaurant or mix and match (there's a deli menu for posh takeaways). Some rooms are open-plan, others have separate bedrooms for children, those on the ground floor open onto terraces. Expect uncluttered interiors, flat-screen TVs, crisp linen and robes in good bathrooms. Eight have a balcony or terrace. St Mawes is close. *Minimum stay: 3 nights in high season. Pets by arrangement.*

Rooms	7 studios for 3: £200–£270.
	4 suites, 4 apartments for 4: £250–£450.
Meals	Lunch from £8. Dinner, 3 courses, about £30.
Closed	January.
Directions	From A390 south for St Mawes on A3078. Signed left after 8 miles. Right at bottom of road; just above beach.

Martin Nicholas
The Rosevine
Rosevine,
Portscatho, Truro, TR2 5EW

Tel	+44 (0)1872 580206
Email	info@rosevine.co.uk
Web	www.rosevine.co.uk

Trevalsa Court Hotel

Trevalsa stands at the top of the cliff with rather good sea views. In summer, the sitting room decants into the garden, with deckchairs and sun loungers sprinkled about. You can nip down to a sandy beach or pick up Cornwall's coastal path, which passes at the end of the garden; turn left for cliff walks or right for Mevagissey, a cute old fishing village. Don't dally too long. Trevalsa is a seaside treat: friendly, stylish, gently spoiling. Inside, the view is weatherproofed by an enormous mullioned window in the beautiful sitting room, a great place to watch the elements spin by. Elsewhere, you'll find a small bar with colourful art, then a panelled dining room for tasty food, perhaps mussels steamed in Cornish cider, lamb cutlets with root vegetables, chocolate fondant with basil ice-cream. Lovely bedrooms have warm colours, pretty fabrics, padded headboards and the odd wall of paper. Most have sea views, bigger rooms have sofas, the family suite has its own terrace, all have excellent bathrooms. Breakfast is served on the terrace in summer, the Lost Gardens of Heligan are close.

Rooms	7 doubles, 3 twin/doubles, 2 twins: £120–£260. 1 suite for 4: £200–£385. 2 singles: £60–£105. Dinner, B&B £85–£158 p.p. Extra bed/sofabed available £20–£60 p.p.p.n.
Meals	Dinner £30.
Closed	20 November to 10 February; Easter.
Directions	B3273 from St Austell signed Mevagissey, through Pentewan to top of the hill, left at the x-roads, over mini r'bout. Hotel on left, signed.

Susan & John Gladwin
Trevalsa Court Hotel
School Hill, Mevagissey,
St Austell, PL26 6TH

Tel	+44 (0)1726 842468
Email	stay@trevalsa-hotel.co.uk
Web	www.trevalsa-hotel.co.uk

The Old Quay House Hotel

You drop down the hill, weave through narrow lanes, then pull up at this boutique hotel which started life as a seaman's mission. It's a lovely spot, with the estuary lapping behind the house and a waterside terrace for summer dining; at breakfast you can watch local boats zipping past. Inside, stylish bedrooms have goose down duvets, colourful fabrics and smart wicker furniture, then lovely bathrooms with white robes, the odd claw-foot tub, perhaps a walk-in shower. Most rooms look the right way, eight have balconies (some tiny), the view from the penthouse suite is hard to beat. Downstairs, good food waits in the restaurant, so slink onto the terrace for a cocktail, then dig into some excellent local fare, perhaps oysters with red wine shallots, lobster thermidor with salad and fries, espresso crème brûlée with cinnamon beignets. Fowey is enchanting, bustles with life and fills with sailors for the August Regatta. If you want to escape, you can take the ferry across to Polruan where Daphne du Maurier lived, then walk over to spectacular Lantic Bay for a picnic lunch on the beach. *Minimum stay: 2 nights at weekends in high season.*

Rooms	5 doubles, 5 twin/doubles: £145-£285. 1 suite for 2: £335. Singles from £105.
Meals	Lunch about £15, Easter-October. Dinner £30-£37.50.
Closed	Rarely.
Directions	Entering Fowey, follow one-way system past church. Hotel on right where road at narrowest point, next to Lloyds Bank. Nearest car park 800 yds.

Martin Nicholas
The Old Quay House Hotel
28 Fore Street,
Fowey, PL23 1AQ

Tel	+44 (0)1726 833302
Email	info@theoldquayhouse.com
Web	www.theoldquayhouse.com

Talland Bay Hotel

The position here is magical. First you plunge down rollercoaster lanes leaving the world behind, then you arrive at this lovely hotel and find a rather good view – a vast carpet of sea that shoots off to the horizon. Pine trees stand guard on one side, an old church crowns a hill on the other, then two acres of lawns roll down to a ha-ha before the land tumbles down to the bay. In summer, loungers and croquet hoops appear on the lawn, and you can nip down to a beach café for lunch by the water. Back at the hotel there's a conservatory brasserie, a sitting room bar and a roaring fire in the half-panelled dining room. You'll find art on the walls, polished flagstones, a terrace for afternoon tea. Follow the coastal path over the hill, then return for a good dinner, perhaps roasted scallops with caramelised orange, loin of venison with chestnut purée, lemongrass panna cotta with peach sorbet. Bedrooms have warm colours, vast beds, beautiful linen, the odd panelled wall. One has a balcony, a couple open onto terraces, all have lovely bathrooms. Gardens, beaches and the coastal path wait. *Pets by arrangement.*

Rooms	15 twin/doubles: £120–£240.
	4 suites for 2: £200–£280.
	3 cottages for 2: £160–£240.
	Dinner, B&B £95–£180 p.p.
Meals	Lunch from £5.50.
	Sunday lunch £21.50–£25.
	Afternoon tea from £6.
	Dinner, brasserie from £12.95;
	restaurant £36–£42.
Closed	Never.
Directions	From Looe A387 for Polperro. Ignore
	1st sign to Talland. After 2 miles, left
	at x-roads; follow signs.

Stephen Waite
Talland Bay Hotel
Porthallow,
Looe, PL13 2JB
Tel   +44 (0)1503 272667
Email   info@tallandbayhotel.co.uk
Web   www.tallandbayhotel.co.uk

Augill Castle

Simon and Wendy's folly castle may look rather grand, but inside is a wonderfully informal world – no uniforms, no rules, just a place to kick off your shoes and relax. Follow your nose and find sofas in front of the fire in the hall, a grand piano in the music room, an honesty bar that opens onto a terrace. Fancy getting married in a castle? They'll do that too. Breakfast is served communally in a vast dining room under a wildly ornate ceiling – local bacon, eggs from resident hens, homemade breads and jams. Elsewhere, panelled walls, roaring fires, books, art and antiques. Bedrooms are deliciously different. Some are enormous, one has a wardrobe in the turret, you'll find big bathrooms, bold colours and vintage luggage. Cottages have extra space for families and if you decide to bring the children, there's lots for them to do too – dressing up boxes, five acres of gardens with a treehouse and a playground, even a cinema in the old potting shed. The Dales and the Lakes are close for spectacular walking and cycling, but sybarites may just want to stay put.
Minimum stay: 2 nights at weekends.

Rooms	8 doubles, 2 four-posters: £140–£180. 1 suite for 2: £200–£240. 6 cottages for 4: £200–£280. Singles from £100.
Meals	Dinner, 2-3 courses, £20–£25. Private dining available for 6+ from £30 p.p. Supper platter £15. Afternoon tea £18. Children's high tea £10.
Closed	Never.
Directions	M6 junc. 38; A685 through Kirkby Stephen. Before Brough right for South Stainmore; signed on left in 1 mile. Kirkby Stephen station 3 miles.

Simon & Wendy Bennett
Augill Castle
South Stainmore,
Kirkby Stephen, CA17 4DE

Tel	+44 (0)17683 41937
Email	enquiries@stayinacastle.com
Web	www.stayinacastle.com

Entry 34   Map 6

The Black Swan

A lovely small hotel in the middle of a pretty village that's surrounded by blistering country. It's all things to all men: a smart restaurant, a lively bar, a village shop; they even hold a music festival here in September. A stream runs through the big garden, where you can eat in good weather; free-range hens live in one corner. Inside, chic country interiors fit the mood perfectly. You get fresh flowers, tartan carpets, games and books galore. There's a bar for local ales, a sitting-room bar with an open fire, but the hub of the hotel is the bar in the middle, where village life gathers. You can eat wherever you want – there's an airy restaurant, too – so dig into delicious country fare, with meat from the hills around you, perhaps a tasty home-made soup, Galloway beef and root vegetable stew, sticky toffee pudding with vanilla ice cream. Pretty bedrooms are fantastic for the money. Expect warm colours, beautiful linen, smart furniture, super bathrooms; one suite has a wood-burner. Stunning walking waits, the Lakes and Dales are close, children and dogs are welcome. A very happy place.

Rooms	10 twin/doubles: £80–£100. 5 suites for 2: £115–£130. Singles from £65.
Meals	Lunch from £4.50. Dinner, 3 courses, £25–£30.
Closed	Never.
Directions	Off A685 between M6 junc. 38 & A66 at Brough.

Louise Dinnes
The Black Swan
Ravenstonedale,
Kirkby Stephen, CA17 4NG

Tel	+44 (0)15396 23204
Email	enquiries@blackswanhotel.com
Web	www.blackswanhotel.com

Howtown Hotel

Welcome to Howtown, a world lost in time on a lane that goes nowhere on the quiet side of Ullswater. The position here is heavenly – water, mountain, field and sky – one of the best in the Lakes. The house sits in its own hamlet, dates to 1640, and has been welcoming guests for 114 years, a licensed farmhouse that has passed though five generations of the same family, who still run sheep and cattle on 400 acres of Lakeland fell. Inside, the past lives on: a panelled bar, William Morris wallpaper, smouldering coal fires, wall clocks and lots of brass. Homely bedrooms upstairs have simple pleasures: good beds, sheets and blankets, toile throws, fabulous views. Most are en suite, three have bathrooms one step across the landing. Dinner is old-school – you're summonsed by a gong – then served at oak tables with a beautiful dresser at one end of the dining room. There's a set menu, perhaps vegetable soup, roast lamb, then Howtown's famous sherry trifle; delicious sandwiches are available at lunch. David has an amphibious car for the odd lake cruise. Walking starts from the front door. Matchless. *No email – phone enquiries only.*

Rooms	8 doubles; 3 twin/doubles, each with separate bathroom: £178.
	1 single sharing shower room: £89.
	All room prices include dinner.
	2 self-catering cottages for 5, 2 for 7: £450–£700 per week.
Meals	Lunch (cold table) £14.
	Dinner included in room price; non-residents £25. Sunday lunch £16.
Closed	1st Sunday in November to mid-March.
Directions	South from Pooley Bridge with Ullswater on right. Hotel on left after 4 miles.

Jacquie & David Baldry
Howtown Hotel
Ullswater,
 Penrith, CA10 2ND
Tel   +44 (0)17684 86514
Web   www.howtown-hotel.co.uk

The Swan Hotel & Spa

The Swan – once a 17th-century monastic farmhouse – stands on the river Leven, a wide sweep of water that pours out of Windermere on its way to Morecambe Bay. It's a lovely spot and the hotel makes good use of it – a 50-metre terrace runs along it on its way to an ancient packhorse bridge. Interiors pack a designer punch – this is a stylish hotel with an informal vibe and kind staff on hand to help. Potter about and find lots of colour, striking wallpapers, then sofas in front of open fires. You'll find sitting rooms scattered here and there, a lively bar for a pint of ale, a stylish brasserie for tasty food. There's a spa that's hard to miss – the swimming pool shimmers behind a wall of glass in reception. Treatment rooms, a sauna and steam room and a gym all wait, as does a juice bar. Airy bedrooms have comfy beds, crisp white linen, padded bedheads and smart TVs. Some have river views, family suites have bunk beds for children. Back downstairs, dig into tasty food in the bar or brasserie, perhaps Persian salt cod fritters, a posh burger, chocolate brownie with peanut mousse. Brilliant.

Rooms	13 doubles, 30 twin/doubles: £99-£234. 8 suites for 4: £189-£329.
Meals	Lunch from £5.95. Bar meals from £9.95. Dinner, 3 courses, £25-£35. Sunday lunch from £13.95.
Closed	Never.
Directions	M6 junc. 36, then A590 west. Into Newby Bridge. Over roundabout, then 1st right for hotel.

	Sarah Gibbs
	The Swan Hotel & Spa
	Newby Bridge, LA12 8NB
Tel	+44 (0)15395 31681
Email	reservations@swanhotel.com
Web	www.swanhotel.com

The Cottage in the Wood

A great little base for the northern Lakes with lots of style, super food and owners who go the extra mile. You're on the side of Whinlatter Pass with big views east to a chain of Lakeland peaks. Outside, the terrace looks the right way, a great spot for a drink in summer. Inside, chic interiors are just the ticket: an airy sitting room, a fire that burns on both sides, books and games to keep you amused, windows galore in the restaurant. Nicely priced bedrooms have white walls to soak up the light and sparkling bathrooms for a good wallow. One in the eaves has a claw-foot bath, four have mountain views, one has a fabulous bathroom and opens onto its own terrace. There's lots to do – lakes to visit, hills to climb, cycle trails to follow. Whatever you do, come home to some lovely local food, perhaps Curthwaite goat's curd with beetroot and rocket, Herdwick hogget with garlic dumplings, passion fruit soufflé with mango ice-cream. There's a drying room for walkers, secure storage for bikes, a burn that tumbles down the hill. Starry skies on clear nights will amaze you. Brilliant. *Minimum stay: 2 nights at weekends.*

Rooms	6 doubles, 2 twin/doubles: £110–£175. 1 suite for 2: £190–£215. Singles £88–£96.
Meals	Lunch from £14.95. Dinner £36–£55. Not Sunday eve. Sunday lunch £25.
Closed	January. Mondays.
Directions	M6 junc. 40, A66 west to Braithwaite, then B5292 for Lorton. On right after 2.5 miles (before visitor centre).

Kath & Liam Berney
The Cottage in the Wood
Braithwaite, Keswick, CA12 5TW

Tel	+44 (0)17687 78409
Email	relax@thecottageinthewood.co.uk
Web	www.thecottageinthewood.co.uk

Borrowdale Gates

If you want deep peace, spectacular landscapes and a slice of luxury in a stylish hotel, you'll find it here. This is Borrowdale, an unchanged corner of the rural idyll, 'the loveliest square mile in Lakeland' to quote Alfred Wainwright. High peaks encircle you, sheep graze the fields, the river Derwent potters past. The view from the top of High Seat is one of the best in the Lakes, with Derwentwater sparkling under a vast sky. Lowland walking is equally impressive: long or short, high or low, Borrowdale delivers. At the end of the day roll back to this lovely hotel. Big windows downstairs frame majestic views. You get binoculars, the daily papers, afternoon tea in front of roaring fires or out on the terrace in summer. Bedrooms are great value for money, with warm colours, super beds, smart bathrooms, a sofa if there's room. Some open onto terraces, several have small balconies, all have the view. As for the restaurant, a wall of glass looks out over the village and beyond, a fine spot for a good meal, perhaps hand-dived scallops, fell-bred lamb, lemon tart with cassis sorbet.
Minimum stay: 2 nights at weekends; 3 nights on Bank Holidays. Pets by arrangement.

Rooms	18 twin/doubles: £190-£220.
	3 suites for 2: £224-£310.
	4 singles: £95-£110.
	All room prices include dinner.
Meals	Light lunches from £8.
	Dinner for non-residents £30-£41.
Closed	5-19 January.
Directions	M6 to Penrith, A66 to Keswick, then B5289 south for 4 miles. Right at humpback bridge, through Grange, hotel on right.

Colin Harrison
Borrowdale Gates
Grange-in-Borrowdale,
Keswick, CA12 5UQ

Tel   +44 (0)17687 77204
Email   hotel@borrowdale-gates.com
Web   www.borrowdale-gates.com

The Eltermere Inn

This gorgeous Lakeland inn, once a Georgian farmhouse, seems lost to the world, yet it's only a couple of miles from Grasmere. In summer you sit in the peaceful garden with local sheep for company and dig into afternoon tea; in winter you order a pint at the bar, then roast away in front of the fire. You're in an unblemished village that stands back from the water in the shade of forested hills. Inside, beautiful interiors are part country house, part village inn. There's a grand piano in the dining room, ancient slate floors in the bar, then big sofas and lovely art in the airy sitting room. Upstairs, stylish rooms have warm colours, local wool carpets, big beds and Mulberry fabrics. Some have padded window seats, others are open to the eaves, all have excellent bathrooms; those at the front have views of lake and mountain. Downstairs, you find the sort of food you hanker for after a day in the hills, perhaps bouillabaisse, steak and kidney pie, banana gingerbread with toffee sauce. Walks start from the front door, there's croquet on the lawn, they even grow their own vegetables. *Minimum stay: 2 nights at weekends.*

Rooms	12 twin/doubles: £140-£275. Singles from £125. Extra bed/sofabed £40 p.p.p.n.
Meals	Lunch from £5.50. Dinner, set menu £18.50-£28.50; 3 courses à la carte £30-£35. Afternoon tea from £13.25.
Closed	Christmas.
Directions	West from Ambleside for 3 miles on A593, then right for Eltermere. On right in village.

Mark & Ruth Jones
The Eltermere Inn
Elterwater,
Ambleside, LA22 9HY

Tel	+44 (0)15394 37207
Email	info@eltermere.co.uk
Web	www.eltermere.co.uk

Miller Howe Hotel & Restaurant

The view is breathtaking, a clean sweep over Windermere to the majestic Langdale Pikes. As for Miller Howe, this Edwardian country house was made famous by TV chef John Tovey in the 1970s. These days the atmosphere is nicely relaxed. Interiors flood with light, contemporary art mixes with period features, and you can grab the daily papers, then sink into a sofa and roast away in front of the fire. You'll find vintage wallpapers, the odd bust, beautiful fabrics, original wood floors. There's a cute little bar, a conservatory for afternoon tea, then a terrace for drinks in summer, with five acres of beautiful gardens rolling down towards the lake. Back inside, spin into the dining room, where walls of glass frame the view. Menus offer local delights, perhaps Cartmel venison, Cumbrian pork with a cider jus, ginger panna cotta with roast pineapple. Bedrooms vary in size, but all are individually designed with smart fabrics, period furniture and posh TVs. Some have balconies with big lake views, cottage suites in the garden offer sublime peace. Don't miss sunset. *Minimum stay: 2 nights at weekends. Pets are allowed in 2 bedrooms.*

Rooms	5 doubles, 7 twin/doubles: £170-£240. 3 suites for 2: £170-£270. Dinner, B&B from £105 p.p.
Meals	Lunch from £8.95. Dinner, 4 courses, £47.50. Sunday lunch £30.
Closed	Rarely.
Directions	From Kendal A591 to Windermere. Left at mini-r'bout onto A592 for Bowness; 0.25 miles on right.

Helen & Martin Ainscough
Miller Howe Hotel & Restaurant
Rayrigg Road,
Windermere, LA23 1EY
Tel   +44 (0)15394 42536
Email   info@millerhowe.com
Web   www.millerhowe.com

Cedar Manor Hotel

A small country house on the edge of Windermere with good prices, pretty interiors and delicious food. Jonathan and Caroline love their world and can't stop spending money on it. They recently added a smart terrace at the front, turned the office into another sitting room, and put in a couple of fancy bathrooms. This 17th-century house was once home to a retired vicar, hence the ecclesiastic windows. Outside, an ancient cedar of Lebanon shades the lawn. Inside, cool colours and an easy style flow throughout. The big sitting room doubles as the bar and comes in browns and creams with sofas and local art. Bedrooms – some warmly traditional, others nicely contemporary – have Zoffany fabrics, Lloyd Loom wicker and flat-screen TVs; most have fancy bathrooms, some have big views, the bathroom in the coach-house suite is out of this world. You eat in a pretty dining room with views to the front or on the terrace in good weather, perhaps goat's cheese with a red pepper mousse, local lamb with tarragon gnocchi, warm chocolate fudge cake with real-ale ice cream. All things Windermere are on your doorstep. *Minimum stay: 2 nights at weekends.*

Rooms	7 doubles, 1 twin: £135–£195.
	2 suites for 2: £225–£425.
	Singles from £105.
Meals	Dinner £32.95–£39.95.
Closed	Rarely.
Directions	From Windermere A591 east out of town for Kendal; hotel on right, next to church, before railway station.

Jonathan & Caroline Kaye
Cedar Manor Hotel
Ambleside Road,
Windermere, LA23 1AX

Tel	+44 (0)15394 43192
Email	info@cedarmanor.co.uk
Web	www.cedarmanor.co.uk

Jerichos

A friendly B&B hotel with attractive prices in the middle of Windermere. Step inside and find airy interiors with stripped wood floors and a splash of colour on the walls. There's a sitting room with a couple of baby chesterfields, then a pretty dining room where you breakfast on homemade bread and local eggs, perhaps a grilled kipper or smoked salmon and scrambled eggs. Spotless bedrooms offer a night or two of affordable luxury. Those on the first floor have high ceilings, you get leather bedheads, comfy armchairs, white duvets and excellent bathrooms. Most have fancy showers, all come with iPod docks, a wall of paper and Lakeland art. Good restaurants wait on your doorstep – Hooked for fish. Francine's for tasty bistro fare, Wild & Co. for a good steak – the sort of stuff you want after a day in the hills. As for Windermere, the Lake is a short stroll, a good way to round off breakfast. You can hire kayaks, learn to sail, take a cruise. There are mountain bike trails and the odd hill to climb, too. The station is close, so come by train; from London it's faster than by car. *Minimum stay: 2 nights at weekends, 3 nights on bank holiday weekends.*

Rooms	8 doubles: £120–£145. 2 singles: £75.
Meals	Restaurants nearby.
Closed	Last 3 weeks in January.
Directions	A591 from Kendal to Windermere. Pass train station, don't turn left into town, rather next left 200 yards on. First right and on right after 500m.

Chris & Jo Blaydes
Jerichos
College Road,
Windermere, LA23 1BX

Tel	+44 (0)15394 42522
Email	info@jerichos.co.uk
Web	www.jerichos.co.uk

Linthwaite House

It's not just the view that makes Linthwaite so special, though Windermere sparkling half a mile below with a chain of peaks rising beyond does grab your attention. There's loads to enjoy here – 14 acres of gardens and grounds, a fantastic terrace for sunny days and interiors that go out of their way to pamper your pleasure receptors. The house itself is beautiful, one of those grand Lakeland Arts & Crafts wonders, with original woodwork and windows in all the right places. Logs are piled high by the front door, fires smoulder, sofas wait in the conservatory sitting room, where big views loom. Country-house bedrooms are coolly uncluttered with warm colours, chic fabrics, hi-tech gadgetry, fabulous bathrooms. Those at the front have lake views, a couple have hot tubs, you can stargaze from one of the suites. Downstairs, ambrosial food waits in the dining rooms (one is decorated with nothing but mirrors), perhaps seared tuna with pickled ginger, chargrilled pigeon with beetroot purée, caramelised banana tart with peanut butter ice-cream. Sunbeds wait on the terrace. Fabulous. *Minimum stay: 2 nights at weekends.*

Rooms	21 doubles, 5 twin/doubles: £240–£454. 4 suites for 2: £492–£684. Price includes dinner for 2.
Meals	Lunch from £14.95. Dinner for non-residents £58.
Closed	Rarely.
Directions	M6 junc. 36. Take A590 north, then A591 for Windermere. Left at r'bout onto B5284. Past golf course and hotel signed left after 1 mile.

Andy Nicholson
Linthwaite House
Crook Road, Bowness-on-Windermere,
Windermere, LA23 3JA

Tel	+44 (0)15394 88600
Email	stay@linthwaitehouse.com
Web	www.linthwaitehouse.com

Gilpin Hotel

Gilpin is one of the loveliest places to stay in the country, simple as that. It's a family affair and delivers at every turn, its staff delightful, its food divine, its interiors a treasure trove of beautiful things. It is one of those rare places that never stands still and recent additions include five stunning spa chalets above a small lake and a second restaurant serving pan-Asian food. Despite all this, it remains an English country-house hotel. A cool elegance flows throughout with smouldering fires, Zoffany wallpapers, gilded mirrors, flowers everywhere. An elegant sitting room runs into a chic bar, where doors open onto a terrace for Pimm's in the sun; magnolia trees, cherry blossom and a copper beech wait in the 20-acre garden. Bedrooms are divine: crisp linen, smart fabrics, robes in beautiful bathrooms. The garden suites have hot tubs, the spa suites have saunas, too. As for the food, it's all whisked up by Hrishikesh Desai (who won Chefs On Trial to land his job), perhaps chilli-glazed lobster, spring lamb with masala sauce, Yorkshire rhubarb with Bergamot panna cotta. *Special rates for 3 or more nights. Minimum stay: 2 nights at weekends.*

Rooms	8 doubles, 12 twin/doubles: £335-£385. 6 suites for 2: £385-£535. 5 suites for 2 (spa lodges on the lake): £635. Price includes dinner for 2.
Meals	Dinner included; non-residents £65. Lunch from £6.50. Sunday lunch £35. Afternoon tea from £22.50.
Closed	Never.
Directions	M6 junc 36, A591 north, then B5284 west for Bowness. On right after 5 miles.

John, Christine, Barnaby & Zoe Cunliffe
Gilpin Hotel
Crook Road, Bowness-on-Windermere,
Windermere, LA23 3NE

Tel	+44 (0)15394 88818
Email	hotel@thegilpin.co.uk
Web	www.thegilpin.co.uk

Gilpin Lake House & Spa

Every now and then you bump into a hotel that knocks your socks off, and Gilpin Lake House does just that. This is an extraordinary little place – a tiny spa hotel with only six rooms, luxury and intimacy entwined. It sits away from the crowds, lost in the hills, surrounded by acres of peaceful woodland. A swimming pool in the house opens onto a terrace, where you can flop on sun loungers and gaze down on the lake. Elsewhere, beautiful gardens, a rowing boat, and a second hot tub overlooking fells. There's a treatment room in a cabin that sits above the lake, then a snug boathouse with a deck on the water. As for the house, you'll find sofas in front of a wood-burner in the sitting room, then lake views, books galore and beautiful art. Spoiling rooms have fabulous beds, sofas and armchairs, beautiful fabrics, bathrooms that don't hold back. Breakfast is served wherever you want: in your room, on the terrace, in the conservatory. There's a chauffeur to whizz you up to their sister hotel for dinner (included in the price). Come with friends and take the whole place. Out of this world. *Min. stay: 2 nights at weekends, 3 on bank holidays & Easter. Children over 7 welcome.*

Rooms	6 twin/doubles: £495-£605. Price includes dinner for 2 at Gilpin Hotel, chauffeur included!
Meals	Dinner included; non-residents £65. Afternoon tea from £22.50.
Closed	Never.
Directions	B5284 west for Bowness. Left at Wild Boar pub, right through village and straight ahead for 2 miles. Keep right at fork and on left.

John, Christine, Barnaby & Zoe Cunliffe
Gilpin Lake House & Spa
Crook, Windermere, LA8 8LN

Tel	+44 (0)15394 88818
Email	hotel@thegilpin.co.uk
Web	www.thegilpin.co.uk/lake-house

The Punch Bowl Inn

You're in the hills above Windermere in a pretty village encircled by lanes that defeat most tourists. It's a lovely spot, deeply rural, with ten-mile views down the valley and a church that stands next door; bell ringers practise on Friday mornings, the occasional bride glides out in summer. Yet while the Punch Bowl sits lost to the world, it is actually a deliciously funky inn. Rescued from neglect and renovated in great style, it now sparkles with a stylish mix of old and new. Outside, honeysuckle and roses ramble on stone walls. Inside, a clipped elegance runs throughout, with Farrow & Ball colours, rugs on wood floors and sofas in front of the wood-burner. Scott Fairweather's ambrosial food is a big draw, perhaps Lancashire cheese soufflé, loin of rabbit with crayfish mousse, pear soufflé and pecan ice-cream. Chic bedrooms are lovely, too, all with beautiful linen, pretty fabrics and Roberts radios, while fabulous bathrooms have double-ended baths, separate showers and white robes. Four have the view, the suite is enormous, weekday prices are tempting. There's a terrace for lunch in the sun, too.

Rooms	5 doubles, 1 twin/double, 2 four-posters: £105–£235. 1 suite for 2: £180–£305. Singles from £80.
Meals	Lunch from £5. Dinner, 3 courses, £30–£35.
Closed	Never.
Directions	M6 junc. 36, then A590 for Newby Bridge. Right onto A5074, then right for Crosthwaite after 3 miles. Pub on southern flank of village, next to church.

Richard Rose
The Punch Bowl Inn
Crosthwaite,
Kendal, LA8 8HR

Tel	+44 (0)15395 68237
Email	info@the-punchbowl.co.uk
Web	www.the-punchbowl.co.uk

The Masons Arms

The Masons is a Lakeland institution, an ancient inn lost in blissful country above Witherslack. You're on the side of a hill with 15-mile views across sheep-strewn fields to Scout Scar; in summer, pub life decants onto a spectacular terrace – a sitting room in the sun – where window boxes and flowerbeds tumble with colour. The inn dates from the 16th century and is impossibly pretty. The bar is gorgeous, with low ceilings, wavy beams, flagged floors and roaring fires, then splendid local ales to quench your thirst. Rustic elegance upstairs comes courtesy of stripped floors, country rugs and red walls in the first-floor dining room, so grab a window seat for fabulous views and dig into fine, local fare, perhaps cheese soufflé, haunch of venison, toffee and banana sundae. Apartments (stylish and cosy) and cottages (off the courtyard, great for families) are a steal. All come with good kitchens – you can cook your own breakfast or have it in the pub. You'll find comfy beds and a chic country style, while several have private terraces. There's jazz on Sundays in summer. Cartmel Priory is close. *Minimum stay: 2 nights at weekends. Travel cots / extra beds from £10.*

Rooms	5 apartments for 2: £85-£140.
	1 self-catering cottage for 2-4,
	1 self-catering for 2-6: £110-£175.
Meals	Breakfast & lunch from £4.95.
	Bar meals from £9.95.
	Dinner, 3 courses, £25-£30.
	Sunday lunch from £12.95.
Closed	Never.
Directions	M6 junc. 36; A590 west, then A592 north. 1st right after Fell Foot Park. Straight ahead for 2.5 miles. On left after sharp right-hand turn.

John & Diane Taylor
The Masons Arms
Strawberry Bank, Cartmel Fell,
Grange-over-Sands, LA11 6NW

Tel   +44 (0)15395 68486
Email   info@masonsarmsstrawberrybank.co.uk
Web   www.masonsarmsstrawberrybank.co.uk

Aynsome Manor Hotel

A small country house with a big heart. It may not be the grandest place in the book but the welcome is genuine, the peace is intoxicating and the value unmistakable. From the front, a long sweep across open meadows leads south to Cartmel and its priory, a view that has changed little in 800 years. The house, a mere pup by comparison, dates to 1512. Step in to find red armchairs, a grandfather clock and a coal fire in the hall. There's a small bar for a dram at the front and a cantilever staircase with cupola dome that sweeps you up to a first-floor drawing room, where panelled windows frame the view. Downstairs, you eat under a wildly ornate ceiling with Georgian colours and old portraits on the walls. You get lovely country cooking, too: French onion soup, roast leg of Cumbrian lamb, rich chocolate mousse served with white chocolate sauce. Bedrooms are simple, spotless, cosy and colourful. Some have views over the fields, one may be haunted, all have good bathrooms. Staff are lovely, nothing is too much trouble, kippers with lemon at breakfast are a treat. Windermere and Coniston are close.

Rooms	5 doubles, 4 twins, 1 four-poster: £90–£125. 2 family rooms for 4: £90–£150. Dinner, B&B from £75 p.p.
Meals	Packed lunches by arrangement £9.50. Dinner, 4 courses, £33.
Closed	Christmas.
Directions	From M6 junc. 36 take A590 for Barrow. At top of Lindale Hill follow signs left to Cartmel. Hotel on right 3 miles from A590.

Christopher & Andrea Varley
Aynsome Manor Hotel
Aynsome Lane, Cartmel,
Grange-over-Sands, LA11 6HH

Tel	+44 (0)15395 36653
Email	aynsomemanor@btconnect.com
Web	www.aynsomemanorhotel.co.uk

Askham Hall

Despite its grandeur – this is a Grade I-listed manor house with a 12th-century peel tower – Charlie runs Askham with huge informality and you're encouraged to kick off your shoes and treat the place as home. It's not a hotel, more a restaurant with fancy rooms, but there's lots to keep you amused: contemporary art and open fires, a beautiful drawing room with an honesty bar, a small spa with an outdoor pool, then gardens that open to the public and a café for pizza at lunch. The hall sits in 40 acres of prime Cumbrian grazing land between Ullswater and the Eden Valley with paths that follow the river below into glorious parkland. It's all part of the Lowther estate, where Charlie rears his own meat for Richard Swale's kitchen. And the restaurant lies at the heart of Askham, its seasonal food a big draw, perhaps slow-cooked duck with fig and walnut, Lowther venison with parmesan gnocchi, buttermilk panna cotta with sorrel sorbet. Chic bedrooms have a contemporary country-house style: some vast, one with a tented bathroom, others have views to Knipe Scar. Home-laid duck eggs wait at breakfast, too.

Rooms	11 twin/doubles: £150–£260. 4 suites for 2: £250–£320. Singles £138. Dinner, B&B from £125 p.p. Extra bed/sofabed available £30 p.p.p.n.
Meals	Lunch from £9. Dinner, 3 courses, £50. 5-course tasting menu £65.
Closed	Sundays & Mondays. January to early February.
Directions	M6, junc. 39, then A6 north. Askham signed left after 7 miles. In village.

Charlie Lowther
Askham Hall
Askham, CA10 2PF
Tel   +44 (0)1931 712350
Email   enquiries@askhamhall.co.uk
Web   www.askhamhall.co.uk

The Sun Inn

This lovely old inn sits between the Dales and the Lakes in an ancient market town, one of the prettiest in the north. It backs onto St Mary's churchyard, where wild flowers flourish, and on the far side you'll find 'the fairest view in England', to quote John Ruskin. Herons fish the river Lune, lambs graze the fells beyond, a vast sky hangs above. Turner came to paint it in 1825 and benches wait for those who want to linger. As for the Sun, it does what good inns do – looks after you in style. There's lots of pretty old stuff – stone walls, rosewood panelling, wood-burners working overtime – and it's all kept spic and span, with warm colours, fresh flowers and the daily papers on hand. You find leather banquettes, local art and chairs in the dining room from Cunard's Mauretania, so eat in style, perhaps suckling pig, sea trout with mussel cream, chocolate and walnut tart. Bedrooms upstairs are stylishly uncluttered with warm colours, smart fabrics, stone walls and robes in good bathrooms. Car park permits come with your room and can be used far and wide. Market day is Thursday. *Minimum stay: 2 nights at weekends.*

Rooms	9 doubles, 2 twin/doubles: £135–£189. Dinner, B&B from £88 p.p. Singles from £82. Extra beds £20.
Meals	Lunch from £4.50. Dinner £28–£34.
Closed	Christmas.
Directions	M6 junc. 36, then A65 for 5 miles following signs for Kirkby Lonsdale. In town centre.

Mark & Lucy Fuller
The Sun Inn
6 Market Street, Kirkby Lonsdale,
Carnforth, LA6 2AU

Tel	+44 (0)15242 71965
Email	email@sun-inn.info
Web	www.sun-inn.info

Cavendish Hotel

The Cavendish has impeccable credentials. It stands on the Chatsworth Estate, is owned by the Duke and Duchess of Devonshire, and Chatsworth House itself stands a mile or two across the fields from this smart hotel. All of which means you can rise leisurely, have a good breakfast, then follow paths across to one of Britain's loveliest houses; fine gardens and a jaw-dropping art collection wait. As for the hotel, it has a warm country-house feel: sofas in front of the fire in the sitting room; art from the 'big house' on the walls; afternoon tea served on the lawn in summer. Bedrooms mix pretty florals with period colours and smart fabrics. None are small, all but one have country views, some are rather swanky. You get robes in excellent bathrooms, a sofa if there's room, crisp linen on comfy beds. Downstairs you can eat in the Garden Room or out on its terrace (more informal, lovely views) or in the elegant restaurant, perhaps hand-dived scallops, haunch of venison, Granny Smith apple crumble. Outside, the Peak District waits for walkers, while fishing can be arranged.

Rooms	20 doubles, 2 twins: £189–£219.
	1 suite for 2: £300.
	1 family room for 4: £169–£219.
	Singles from £133.
Meals	Continental breakfast £9.70,
	full English £18.90. Lunch from £6.
	Dinner £30–£45.
Closed	Never.
Directions	M1 junc. 29, A617 to Chesterfield,
	A619 to Baslow. On left in village.

Philip Joseph
Cavendish Hotel
Church Lane, Baslow,
Bakewell, DE45 1SP

Tel	+44 (0)1246 582311
Email	info@cavendish-hotel.net
Web	www.cavendish-hotel.net

The Peacock at Rowsley

The Peacock sits between two fine houses, Haddon Hall and Chatsworth House. You can follow rivers up to each – the Derwent to Chatsworth, the Wye to the hall – both a stroll through beautiful parkland. As for the hotel, it was built in 1652 and was home to the steward of Haddon. Inside, old and new mix gracefully: mullioned windows, hessian rugs, aristocratic art, then striking colours that give a contemporary feel. You'll find Mouseman tables and chairs in the restaurant, where French windows open onto the terrace. Elsewhere, a fire smoulders in the bar every day, the daily papers wait in the sitting room, the garden lawn runs down to the river. Stylish bedrooms have crisp linen, good beds, Farrow & Ball colours, the odd antique; one has a bed from Belvoir Castle. Good food waits in the restaurant, with meat and game from the estate, perhaps venison terrine, roast partridge, Bakewell Tart with buttermilk ice cream. There's afternoon tea in the garden in summer and you can fish both rivers, with day tickets available from reception. Guests also receive a discount on entry to Haddon Hall. *Minimum stay: 2 nights at weekends.*

Rooms	10 doubles, 2 four-posters: £190-£290. 1 suite for 2: £230-£290. 2 singles: £120-£135.
Meals	Lunch from £4.50. Dinner £60. Sunday lunch £22.50-£29.50.
Closed	Rarely.
Directions	A6 north through Matlock, then to Rowsley. On right in village.

Laura Ball
The Peacock at Rowsley
Bakewell Road, Rowsley,
Matlock, DE4 2EB

Tel	+44 (0)1629 733518
Email	reception@thepeacockatrowsley.com
Web	www.thepeacockatrowsley.com

The Old Rectory Hotel Exmoor

A gorgeous small hotel in the hills above the Exmoor coast. The road from Lynton is a great way in, through woods that cling to a hill with the sea below. As for the Old Rectory, it's a mini Gidleigh Park, charming from top to toe. Three acres of spectacular gardens wrap around you, only birdsong disturbs you, though Exmoor deer occasionally come to drink from the pond. Inside, Huw and Sam continue to lavish love and money in all the right places. Their most recent addition is a beautiful orangery with smart sofas and warm colours then doors onto the garden for afternoon tea in the sun. Interiors are lovely: Farrow & Ball colours, the odd stone wall, a cute little sitting room, fresh flowers and books everywhere. Bedrooms are just as good with big beds, crisp linen, cool colours and beautiful bathrooms. You'll find digital radios, flat-screen TVs and the odd leather sofa, too. Spin into the restaurant for an excellent meal, perhaps Ilfracombe crab, Exmoor duck, strawberry champagne trifle. Afternoon tea 'on the house' is served in the garden in good weather.

Rooms	3 doubles, 4 twin/doubles: £185–£230. 4 suites for 2: £245–£270. Price includes dinner for 2.
Meals	4-course dinner included in price; non-residents £35.
Closed	November–March.
Directions	M5 junc. 27, A361 to South Molton, then A399 north. Right at Blackmoor Gate onto A39 for Lynton. Left after 3 miles, signed Martinhoe. In village, next to church.

Huw Rees & Sam Prosser
The Old Rectory Hotel Exmoor
Martinhoe, Parracombe,
Barnstable, EX31 4QT

Tel   +44 (0)1598 763368
Email   info@oldrectoryhotel.co.uk
Web   www.oldrectoryhotel.co.uk

Loyton Lodge

You get the impression the tiny lanes that wrap around this small estate act as a sort of fortification, one designed to confuse invaders and protect this patch of heaven. And heaven it is – 280 acres of rolling hills and ancient woodland, with wild flowers, pristine rivers, strutting pheasants and the odd red deer commuting across the fields. It's England circa 1964 with nothing but birdsong to break the peace and glorious walks that start at the front door. As for Loyton, it's a great little base for a night or two deep in the hills. It mixes contemporary interiors with an old-school feel – roaring fires, comfy sofas, wonderful art, even a snooker room. Bedrooms have warm colours and smart fabrics, perhaps a sleigh bed or a claw-foot bath, then books and robes and crisp white linen. Breakfast is a treat – bacon and sausages from home-reared pigs, eggs from estate hens – and there's dinner by arrangement, perhaps local asparagus, lemon sole, walnut and fruit crumble. Take the whole house and bring the family or come for the odd night of live jazz. Exmoor waits, as do good local restaurants.

Rooms	7 doubles, 2 twin/doubles, 1 twin: £95-£130. Singles from £80. Extra beds £20 (under 12s free).
Meals	Dinner, 3 courses, about £30, by arrangement.
Closed	Rarely.
Directions	A396 north from Tiverton to Bampton, then right onto B3227. After 1 mile, left for Loyton. Over x-roads, left at hill. Lodge on right after 0.5 mile.

Isobel, Sally & Angus Barnes
Loyton Lodge
Morebath,
Tiverton, EX16 9AS
Tel   +44 (0)1398 331051
Email thelodge@loyton.com
Web   www.loyton.com

Northcote Manor

A small country-house hotel built on the site of a 15th-century monastery. Those who want peace in deep country will find it here. You wind up a one-mile drive, through a wood that bursts with colour in spring, then emerge onto a lush plateau of rolling hills; the view from the croquet lawn drifts east for ten miles. As for the house, wisteria wanders along old stone walls, while the odd open fire smoulders within. There's an airy hall that doubles as the bar, a country-house drawing room that floods with light, and a sitting room where you gather for pre-dinner drinks. Super food waits in a lovely dining room, steps lead down to a pretty conservatory, doors open onto a gravelled terrace for summer breakfasts with lovely views. Bedrooms are no less appealing – more traditional in the main house, more contemporary in the garden rooms. Expect padded bedheads, mahogany dressers, flat-screen TVs, silky throws. You can walk your socks off, then come home for a good meal, perhaps white Cornish crab, local lamb, strawberry soufflé with vanilla ice-cream. Exmoor and North Devon's coasts are close.

Rooms	9 twin/doubles, 7 suites for 2: £170–£280. Singles from £120. Dinner, B&B from £130 p.p. Extra bed/sofabed available £15–£25 p.p.p.n.
Meals	Light dishes from £6.50. Lunch £22.50–£25.50. Dinner, 3 courses, £45. Tasting menu £90. Sunday lunch from £28.50.
Closed	Never.
Directions	M5 junc. 27, A361 to S. Molton. Fork left onto B3227; left on A377 for Exeter. Entrance 4.1 miles on right, signed.

Richie Herkes
Northcote Manor
Burrington,
Umberleigh, EX37 9LZ

Tel	+44 (0)1769 560501
Email	rest@northcotemanor.co.uk
Web	www.northcotemanor.co.uk

The Lamb Inn

This 16th-century inn is adored by locals and visitors alike. It's a proper inn in the old tradition with gorgeous rooms and the odd touch of scruffiness to add authenticity to its earthy bones. It stands on a cobbled walkway in a village lost down tiny lanes, and those lucky enough to chance upon it leave reluctantly. Inside there are beams, but they are not sandblasted, red carpets with a little swirl, sofas in front of an open fire. Boarded menus trumpet irresistible food – carrot and orange soup, haunch of venison with a port jus, an excellent rhubarb crumble. You can eat wherever you want: in the bar, in the fancy restaurant, or out in the walled garden in good weather. There's a cobbled terrace, a skittle alley, maps for walkers and well-kept ales. Upstairs, seven rooms have a chic country style. Two have baths in the room, those in the barn have painted stone walls, the suite has a wood-burner and a private terrace. All are lovely with comfy beds, white linen, good power showers and flat-screen TVs. Kind staff chat with ease. Dartmoor waits, but you may well linger. Brilliant.

Rooms	5 doubles, 1 twin/double: £69–£130. 1 suite for 3: £150.
Meals	Lunch from £9. Dinner, 3 courses, £20–£30. Sunday lunch from £8.90.
Closed	Rarely.
Directions	A377 north from Exeter. 1st right in Crediton, left, signed Sandford. 1 mile up & in village.

Mark Hildyard & Katharine Lightfoot
The Lamb Inn
Sandford,
Crediton, EX17 4LW
Tel   +44 (0)1363 773676
Email   thelambinn@gmail.com
Web   www.lambinnsandford.co.uk

Mill End

Mill End sits on the Two Moors Way, flanked on one side by the river Teign, as good a spot as any on Dartmoor. It's a firm favourite with walkers, foodies and dogs – your pooch is extremely welcome here. Outside, birds sing, rabbits hop, and mere mortals sit in the colourful garden digging into afternoon tea. Interiors are being refurbished by new owners. You'll find timber frames, nooks and crannies, pretty art and games galore. There's a small bar for pre-dinner drinks, comfy sofas in front of an open fire, then a stylish restaurant for good food, perhaps Brixham scallops, pork with a spiced jus, orange meringue tart. Bedrooms are 'mid-refurb'. Two in the house have a lovely new feel, the suites (one with a big balcony) are as smart as ever, and new rooms in what was the owner's cottage have warm colours, big beds and hill views; one has a terrace, another a balcony. Other rooms await their turn, some of which are dog friendly. There's high tea for children, then porridge for breakfast. Castle Drogo, Fernworthy Resevoir and Buckland Abbey – home to Sir Francis Drake – all wait nearby.

Rooms	10 doubles, 2 twin/doubles, 3 twins: £125–£165. 5 suites for 2: £145–£215. Singles from £75. Extra beds from £25.
Meals	Lunch from £6. Dinner, 3 courses, about £30. Sunday lunch £22–£26.
Closed	Rarely.
Directions	M5, then A30 to Whiddon Down. South on A382, through Sandy Park, over small bridge and on right.

Tara & Nick Culverhouse
Mill End
Chagford,
Newton Abbot, TQ13 8JN

Tel	+44 (0)1647 432282
Email	info@millendhotel.com
Web	www.millendhotel.com

Lydgate House Hotel

You're in 36 acres of heaven, so come for the wonder of Dartmoor: deer and badger, fox and pheasant, kingfisher and woodpecker all live here. A 30-minute circular walk takes you over the East Dart river, up to a meadow where rare orchids flourish, then back down to a 12th-century clapper bridge. Herons dive in the river, you may spot them from the conservatory as you dig into your locally cured bacon and eggs. The house is a nourishing stream of homely comforts: a drying room for walkers, deep white sofas, walls of books, a wood-burner in the sitting room. Karen cooks the sort of food you'd hope for after a day on the moors, perhaps mushroom and ricotta ravioli, roast partridge with a port and damson jus, plum and almond tart with clotted cream. Homely bedrooms are warm and cosseting with crisp florals and comfy beds. Two are big and have claw-foot baths, all have a nice price. There's breakfast on the terrace in good weather and a stone cottage for six if you want to look after yourselves. Fabulous walks start from the front door, while Castle Drogo and Buckland Abbey are close. *Discounts for stays of 3 or more nights.*

Rooms	5 doubles: £95-£132.
	2 singles: £49-£60.
	Cottage: £430-£1,075 per week.
Meals	Dinner, 2-3 courses £22.95-£27.50
	(not Sunday & Monday).
Closed	January.
Directions	From Exeter A30 west to Whiddon Down, A382 south to Moretonhampstead, B3212 west to Postbridge. In village, left at pub. House signed straight ahead.

	Stephen & Karen Horn
	Lydgate House Hotel
	Postbridge,
	Yelverton, PL20 6TJ
Tel	+44 (0)1822 880209
Email	info@lydgatehouse.co.uk
Web	www.lydgatehouse.co.uk

Lewtrenchard Manor

A magnificent Jacobean mansion, a wormhole back to the 16th century. Inside, the full aristocratic monty is on display: a spectacular hall with a cavernous fireplace, a dazzling ballroom with extraordinary plasterwork. There are priest holes, oak panelling, oils by the score. Best of all is the 1602 gallery with its stunning ceiling and grand piano, while *Onward Christian Soldiers* was written in the library. Bedrooms are large. Some are grandly traditional (the four-poster belonged to Queen Henrietta Maria, wife of Charles I); others are more contemporary with airy colours and modern bathrooms. All have jugs of iced water, garden flowers and bathrobes. Delicious food waits downstairs – perhaps smoked haddock risotto, thyme-roasted Lewdown venison, salted caramel and chocolate delice with banana ice cream; there's a chef's table, too, where you watch the kitchen at work on a bank of TVs. Outside, a beautiful courtyard that's home to an ancient wisteria, a Gertrude Jekyll parterre garden, and an avenue of beech trees that makes you feel you're in a Hardy novel. Dartmoor is close. *Minimum stay: 2 nights at weekends*

Rooms	4 doubles, 6 twin/doubles: £175–£230. 4 suites for 2: £230–£245. Singles from £120. Dinner, B&B from £132.50 p.p.
Meals	Lunch: bar meals from £5.50; restaurant from £19.50. Dinner, 3 courses, £49.50. Children over seven welcome in restaurant.
Closed	Rarely.
Directions	From Exeter, exit A30 for A386. At T-junc., right, then 1st left for Lewdown. After 6 miles, left for Lewtrenchard. Keep left, house on left after 0.5 miles.

Sue, James, Duncan & Joan Murray
Lewtrenchard Manor
Lewdown,
Okehampton, EX20 4PN

Tel	+44 (0)1566 783222
Email	info@lewtrenchard.co.uk
Web	www.lewtrenchard.co.uk

The Horn of Plenty

The Horn of Plenty is one of those clever hotels that has survived the test of time by constantly improving itself. This latest addition is six gorgeous new rooms, four of which have terraces or balconies that give 40-mile views over the Tamar Valley. Potter about outside and find six acres of gardens, then a path that leads down through bluebell woods to the river. Inside, beautiful simplicity abounds: stripped floors, gilt mirrors, fine art, fresh flowers everywhere. Bedrooms in the main house come in country-house style, those in the garden have a contemporary feel. All have smart colours, big comfy beds, perhaps a claw-foot bath or a ceiling open to the rafters; ten have a terrace or a balcony. Despite all this, the food remains the big draw, so come to eat well, perhaps beetroot mousse with goat's cheese parfait, grilled duck with chicory and orange, chocolate cannelloni with banana sorbet; views of the Tamar snaking through the hills are included in the price. Afternoon tea is served on the patio in summer. Tavistock, Dartmoor and the Eden Project are close.

Rooms	16 twin/doubles: £110–£245. Singles from £100. Dinner, B&B from £135 p.p. Extra bed/sofabed available £25 p.p.p.n.
Meals	Lunch from £19.50. Dinner, 3 courses, £49.50. Tasting menu £65.
Closed	Never.
Directions	West from Tavistock on A390 following signs to Callington. Right after 3 miles at Gulworthy Cross. Signed left after 0.75 miles.

Julie Leivers & Damien Pease
The Horn of Plenty
Gulworthy, Tavistock, PL19 8JD
Tel   +44 (0)1822 832528
Email   enquiries@thehornofplenty.co.uk
Web   www.thehornofplenty.co.uk

Glazebrook House Hotel

The front door at Glazebrook House could well be a rip in the space-time continuum. Outside, English decorum reigns; inside, a wonderland for your senses waits. You don't really find a hotel, more a contemporary art installation that you get to live in for a day or two. It's a reinvention of a 19th-century collector's house and it overflows with beautiful things: pink flamingos, enormous chandeliers, ancient maps, a bust of the queen with a halo instead of a crown. Downstairs, there's a dinosaur in the library, a tasting room for wine and whisky, a red-marbled bar with sofas and armchairs, then doors onto a terrace for afternoon tea. Bedrooms come fully loaded: vast beds, the loveliest linen, bold colours, quirky art. You get iPads, smart TVs and bulging minibars 'on the house'. Black marble bathrooms are faultless: expect walk-in showers, fluffy robes, perhaps a free-standing bath. Tasty bistro food waits downstairs, maybe goat's cheese fritters, fillet of brill, rhubarb and blueberry crumble. The A38 passes close by; you only hear it outside, you won't know it's there at night. Dartmoor waits.

Rooms	6 doubles, 1 twin: £179–£239. 1 single: £139–£159.
Meals	Lunch from £6. Dinner, 3 courses, about £35.
Closed	Rarely.
Directions	From Exeter, A38 to Plymouth. Signed Avonwick/South Brent. Follow South Brent and hotel signs. Pass London Inn on right, second right to Glazebrook House.

Pieter & Fran Hamman
Glazebrook House Hotel
South Brent, TQ10 9JE
Tel   +44 (0)1364 73322
Email enquiries@glazebrookhouse.com
Web   www.glazebrookhouse.com

Plantation House

This lovely small hotel delivers what so many of us want: a warm welcome, lovely food, rooms that spoil us rotten. Downstairs, a fire smoulders in the sitting-room bar; upstairs, fine Georgian windows frame views of hill and forest. Stylish bedrooms are full of comforts. They come with excellent bathrooms, lovely beds, crisp linen and warm colours. You get padded bedheads, sound systems, bowls of fruit, white robes to pad about in. Back downstairs, you'll succumb to a pre-dinner drink – in front of the fire in the bar in winter, out on the pretty terrace in summer. As for Richard's food, it bursts with flavour, so expect to eat well, perhaps Thai-style sea bass with ginger and lemongrass, local lamb with a Merlot jus, chocolate terrine with hazelnut ice cream. Soft fruits, vegetables and potatoes come from the garden in summer, as do home-laid eggs at breakfast. The river Erme passes across the road – follow it down to the sea and discover wonderful Wonwell Beach. There's lots to see around you: Dartmoor to the north, Totnes, Dartmouth, Salcombe and Slapton Sands to the south. Brilliant.

Rooms	5 doubles, 1 twin: £125–£185. 1 suite for 2: £195–£230. 1 single: £75–£80.
Meals	Dinner, 5 courses, from £36.
Closed	Never.
Directions	A38, then A3121 for Ermington. In village on western fringe.

Richard Hendey
Plantation House
Totnes Road,
Ermington, Ivybridge, PL21 9NS

Tel	+44 (0)1548 831100
Email	info@plantationhousehotel.co.uk
Web	www.plantationhousehotel.co.uk

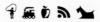

Burgh Island Hotel

Burgh is unique – grand English Art Deco trapped in aspic. Noël Coward loved it, Agatha Christie wrote here. It's much more than a hotel – you come to join a cast of players – so bring your pearls and come for cocktails under a stained-glass dome. By day you lie on steamers in the garden, watch gulls wheeling above, dip your toes into Mermaid's pool or try your hand at a game of croquet. At night you dress for dinner, sip vermouth in a palm-fringed bar, then shuffle off to the ballroom and dine on delicious organic food while the sounds of swing and jazz fill the air. Follow your nose and find flowers in vases four-feet high, bronze ladies thrusting globes into the sky, walls clad in vitrolite, a 14th-century smugglers inn. Art Deco bedrooms are the real thing: Bakelite telephones, ancient radios, bowls of fruit, panelled walls. Some have claw-foot baths, others have balconies, the Beach House suite juts out over rocks. There's snooker, tennis, massage, a sauna. You're on an island, so sweep across the sands at low tide or hitch a ride on the sea tractor. *Minimum stay: 2 nights at weekends.*

Rooms	10 doubles, 3 twin/doubles: £400-£430. 12 suites for 2: £485-£640. Price includes dinner for 2.
Meals	Lunch from £13.50. Dinner included; non-residents £60. Sunday lunch £48. 24-hour residents' menu from £10.50.
Closed	Rarely.
Directions	Drive to Bigbury-on-Sea. At high tide you are transported by sea tractor, at low tide by Landrover. Walking across the beach takes 3 minutes. Eco-taxis can be arranged.

Deborah Clark & Tony Orchard
Burgh Island Hotel
Burgh Island, Bigbury-on-Sea,
Kingsbridge, TQ7 4BG
Tel   +44 (0)1548 810514
Email   reception@burghisland.com
Web   www.burghisland.com

The Henley Hotel

A small house above the sea with fabulous views, super bedrooms and some of the loveliest food in Devon. Despite these credentials, it's Martyn and Petra who shine most brightly, their kind, generous approach making this a memorable place to stay. Warm interiors have wooden floors, Lloyd Loom furniture, the odd potted palm, then big windows to frame the view. Below, the Avon estuary slips gracefully out to sea. At high tide surfers ride the waves, at low tide you can walk on the sands. There's a pretty garden with a path tumbling down to the beach, binoculars in each room, a wood-burner in the snug and good books everywhere. Bedrooms are a steal (one is huge). Expect warm colours, crisp linen, tongue-and-groove panelling and robes in super little bathrooms. As for Martyn's table d'hôte dinners, expect to eat very well. Fish comes daily from Kingsbridge market, you might find grilled figs with goat's cheese and Parma ham, roast monkfish with a lobster sauce, then hot chocolate soufflé with fresh raspberries. Gorgeous Devon is all around. Better than the Ritz! *German spoken. Minimum stay: 2 nights at weekends.*

Rooms	2 doubles, 2 twin/doubles: £120–£137. 1 suite for 2: £150. Singles from £85. Dinner, B&B £87–£97 p.p. (2 night minimum).
Meals	Dinner £36.
Closed	November–March.
Directions	From A38, A3121 to Modbury, then B3392 to Bigbury-on-Sea. Hotel on left as road slopes down to sea.

Martyn Scarterfield & Petra Lampe
The Henley Hotel
Folly Hill, Bigbury-on-Sea,
Kingsbridge, TQ7 4AR

Tel	+44 (0)1548 810240
Email	thehenleyhotel@btconnect.com
Web	www.thehenleyhotel.co.uk

South Sands Hotel

Two coves west from the bustle of town, this smart hotel stands above the beach with views of water, hill and sky. Interiors have a New England feel — seaside colours, softly painted wood, walls of glass that bring in the view. Doors in the restaurant open onto a decked terrace, where at high tide the beach disappears and the sea laps against the wall below. Pull yourself away to walk in the hills, sail on the water, hire a kayak or try your hand at paddle boarding. If that sounds too energetic, then drop down to the beach for family fun. Children are very welcome and you'll find beach towels, buckets and spades, even crabbing nets for excursions to rock pools. Back at the hotel, you dine on lovely local food, perhaps Salcombe crab cakes with foraged leaves, moorland beef with a red wine sauce, chocolate fondant with pistachio ice cream. Rooms at the front have watery views, a couple have terraces, all have comfy beds, a smart style and swish bathrooms. One has 'his and hers' claw-foot baths that look out to sea, while the family suites have kitchens and separate bedrooms for kids. Brilliant. *Minimum stay: 2 nights at weekends*

Rooms	16 doubles, 6 twin/doubles: £170-£385. 5 suites for 4: £340-£475.
Meals	Lunch from £17.95. Dinner £15.95-£40.
Closed	Rarely.
Directions	A381 to Salcombe, then signed right to South Sands. Follow road down hill, then along water. On left.

	Antoine Gay
	South Sands Hotel
	Bolt Head,
	Salcombe, TQ8 8LL
Tel	+44 (0)1548 859000
Email	enquiries@southsands.com
Web	www.southsands.com

Seabreeze

A 16th-century teahouse with rooms on Slapton Sands: only in England. The sea laps ten paces from the front door, the hills of Devon soar behind, three miles of beach shoot off before your eyes. Seabreeze is a treat: cute, relaxed, a slice of old-world magic. Inside, you find Carol and Bonni baking the old-fashioned way, and it's all delicious: hot scones, Victoria sponge, banana and chocolate chip brownies. The tearoom itself – white walls, pretty art, tables topped with maps – is warmed by a wood-burner in winter. In summer you decamp onto the terrace, where sea and sky fuse. Bedrooms are lovely with seaside colours, jars of driftwood and a warm, cosy feel; you can lie in bed and look out to sea from those at the front. Outside, there's lots to do: buckets and spades on the beach, cliff-top walks to local pubs, a huge lake for migratory birds, kayaks for intrepid adventures. Breakfast sets you up for the day (the bacon sandwich is a thing of rare beauty). Local restaurants wait at night: Start Bay Inn in the village, Church House Inn up the road.
Minimum stay: 2 nights at weekends in high season.

Rooms	2 doubles, 1 twin/double: £80–£140. Singles from £70.
Meals	Lunch from £5. Restaurants in village.
Closed	Never.
Directions	A379 south from Dartmouth to Torcross. House on seafront in village.

Carol Simmons & Bonni Lincoln
Seabreeze
Torcross,
Kingsbridge, TQ7 2TQ

Tel	+44 (0)1548 580697
Email	info@seabreezebreaks.com
Web	www.seabreezebreaks.com

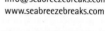

Bayards Cove Inn

In 1620 the Mayflower stopped in Bayards Cove before sailing for America. It docked just outside this cool little inn, one of the oldest buildings in Dartmouth. But if its timber frames are ancient, then its jaunty interiors are the polar opposite with a warm contemporary feel that spreads itself far and wide. Once inside you realise you're in a small and quirky café/restaurant that does a good line in world wines and local ale. You also realise you've landed in heaven and soon you're planning an invasion of one of the bay windows, where you can sink into comfy armchairs and survey life inside and out. Interiors have warm colours, low beams, white stone walls and ancient wood everywhere. There are fairy lights, too, a bar weighted down by freshly baked cakes, and cool tunes afloat in the air. Cosy rooms have timber frames, padded bedheads, pretty fabrics, comfy beds. Most have compact shower rooms, but you won't mind for a minute; some have views of the water or wildly wonky floors. There's great food, perhaps crispy squid, moules frites, local ice creams. Dartmouth waits at the front door. *Minimum stay: 2 nights at weekends. Pets by arrangement.*

Rooms	4 doubles, 1 twin/double: £90–£155.
	1 suite for 2: £130–£180.
	1 family room for 4: £110–£160.
	Singles £95–£150.
Meals	Lunch from £5.95. Dinner from £9.95
	(not Mon-Wed off season).
Closed	Never.
Directions	In Dartmouth south along sea front
	for lower ferry. Follow road right for
	200m and on left at T-junction.

Charlie & Zuzana Deuchar
Bayards Cove Inn
Lower Street,
Dartmouth, TQ6 9AN

Tel	+44 (0)1803 839278
Email	bayardscove@gmail.com
Web	www.bayardscoveinn.co.uk

Nonsuch House

You're halfway up the hill with unbeatable views over the Dart estuary. Yachts zip about, ferries cross to Dartmouth, big boats glide past out at sea. Wherever you go, the view follows you around – the terrace for tea in summer, the conservatory for lovely food, the four big bedrooms that spoil you rotten. One opens onto a small terrace, all have binoculars to scan the high seas. You'll find big comfy beds, warm colours and seaside art. There are robes in good bathrooms and Bramley oils, too. Kit and Penny are great fun and look after you in style. Kit, an ex-hotelier, cooks lovely dinners four nights a week (BYO). The best local produce makes it to your plate, perhaps hand-dived scallops, Blackawton lamb, Dartmouth lobster, homemade truffles; in winter you retire to the sitting room for coffee in front of an open fire. There's lots to do in the area. Ferries whizz you across to Dartmouth, you can walk to the castle, learn to paddleboard, take boat trips up to Totnes, or follow the coastal path. Mitch Tonks at the Seahorse is a great spot for dinner on Kit's nights off. *Min stay: 2 nights at weekends. Over 10s welcome. Stay for 3 nights or more midweek, £120 per night.*

Rooms	1 double, 3 twin/doubles: £130–£185. Singles from £90. Extra beds £40.
Meals	Dinner, 3 courses, £39.50 (not Tues/Wed/Sat). BYO. Pub/restaurant 5-minute walk & short boat trip.
Closed	Rarely.
Directions	2 miles before Brixham on A3022, A379. Right at r'bout, 100yds on fork left (B3205) downhill, through woods, left up Higher Contour Rd, down Ridley Hill. At hairpin bend. Parking nearby.

Kit & Penny Noble
Nonsuch House
Church Hill, Kingswear,
Dartmouth, TQ6 0BX

Tel	+44 (0)1803 752829
Email	enquiries@nonsuch-house.co.uk
Web	www.nonsuch-house.co.uk

The Cary Arms at Babbacombe Bay

The Cary Arms is a chic little inn that hovers above Babbacombe Bay with huge views of sea and sky. But it's not like other inns. Its determination to spend money creating the lap of luxury is matchless, which explains the spectacular new suites and beach huts that have recently taken root in the garden. Walls of glass frame the views, bedrooms look out to sea, bathrooms with walk-in showers are hard to beat. Best of all is your terrace, metres from crystal clear waters, with views that stretch for miles; don't expect to move too far. As for the inn, you can eat fresh seafood on terraces that drop downhill towards a small jetty, where locals fish. The pub has six moorings in the bay, you can charter a boat and explore the coast. Inside, you find stone walls, wooden floors and a fire that burns every day. Rooms in the main house have a New England style, all but one with a private terrace or balcony. You get fabulous beds, super bathrooms (one has a claw-foot bath that looks out to sea). Finally, you can snorkel and kayak, there's a treatment room, and a small spa with an infinity pool is on its way. *Minimum stay in cottages: 2 nights.*

Rooms	7 doubles: £195–£295. 9 suites for 2, 1 suite for 4: £375–£475. 1 family room for 4: £395. 3 cottages for 6-9: from £550; £2,750–£3,250 per week. Extra bed/sofabed available £25 p.p.p.n. Dogs £20 per night.
Meals	Lunch from £7.95. Dinner £25–£35.
Closed	Never.
Directions	From Teignmouth south on A379; 5 miles to St Marychurch, thro' lights, left into Babbacombe Downs Rd. Follow road right; left downhill.

Felicia Crosby
The Cary Arms at Babbacombe Bay
Beach Road, Babbacombe,
Torquay, TQ1 3LX

Tel	+44 (0)1803 327110
Email	enquiries@caryarms.co.uk
Web	www.caryarms.co.uk

Southernhay House

A beautiful small hotel on the loveliest square in town, a short stroll from the cathedral. The house dates to 1805 and was built for a major returning from the Raj. These days, it mixes quirky design with all the comforts you'd expect of a small, city hotel. It's central, welcoming, the rooms are lovely, the dining room serves great bistro food and there's a chic bar for cocktails or a pint of local ale. Downstairs, French windows at the back of the house draw you onto a small terrace, where you can eat in good weather, perhaps mussels in a white wine sauce, bangers and mash with a rich gravy, chocolate fondant with vanilla ice cream. Potter about and find electric blue sofas, 50s starlets framed on the wall, old style radiators and beautiful art. Stylish bedrooms wait upstairs – some are bigger, all are lovely. Expect bold colours, sumptuous fabrics, Indian art, hi-tech gadgetry. Cool bathrooms come as standard, bigger rooms have free-standing baths. Exeter has lots to offer: Roman walls, a 12th-century cathedral, the imperious Royal Albert Memorial Museum & Art Gallery. Topsham is close for river walks.

Rooms	10 doubles: £150–£240.
Meals	Lunch from £6.50.
	Dinner, 3 courses, about £30.
	Afternoon tea from £19.50.
Closed	Never.
Directions	M5, junction 29, then B3183 west into city. Left at T-junction. At one-way system, circle round and as if coming back to where you started and Sourthenhay East is on your left.

Deborah Clark & Tony Orchard
Southernhay House
36 Southernhay East,
Exeter, EX1 1NX

Tel	+44 (0)1392 435324
Email	home@southernhayhouse.com
Web	www.southernhayhouse.com

Sidmouth Harbour Hotel

This lovely spa hotel sits above the town with huge views across Lyme Bay towards Portland Bill. It's a great spot with a terrace that has addictive qualities when the sun shines and a beautiful restaurant with walls of glass to weatherproof the view. You're 200 metres away from two sandy beaches, perfect for sunny days, but the hotel has lots to stop you wandering: a couple of swimming pools, five treatment rooms, a steam room and a sauna. Potter about and find a white marble bar, coastal art in the airy sitting room, then a stylish restaurant, where a vast Chesterfield sofa runs along six tables. Bedrooms are scattered about, some in the main house, others in the courtyard, but all have the same cool style: seaside colours, blond wood furniture, robes for excellent bathrooms, padded headboards and crisp white linen. Several in the main house have sea views, some have balconies, too. By day you take to the coastal path, spin down to the town, or bask on the beach. By night you return for a slap-up meal; start with crab chowder, follow with roast chicken and top it all off with chocolate tart and vanilla ice cream. *Min. stay: 2 nights at weekends (April-October).*

Rooms	48 twin/doubles: £170–£350. 7 singles: £105–£185. Price includes dinner.	
Meals	Lunch from £6.50. Dinner, 3 courses, included in room price; non-residents about £30. Sunday lunch from £17.95. Afternoon tea from £16.50.	
Closed	Never.	
Directions	South from Honiton on A375 into Sidmouth. Right at seafront and hotel on right after 600m.	

	Ken Cumming Sidmouth Harbour Hotel The Westcliff, Manor Road, Sidmouth, EX10 8RU
Tel	+44 (0)1395 513252
Email	sidmouth@harbourhotels.co.uk
Web	www.sidmouth-harbour-hotel.co.uk

Alexandra Hotel & Restaurant

This is a lovely hotel with a rather good view, a clean sweep up the Jurassic coast all the way along Chesil Beach and round to Portland Bill. It sits high on the hill with one foot in town and the other paddling in the water. Directly below, the Cobb curls into the sea, the very spot where Meryl Streep withstood crashing waves in *The French Lieutenant's Woman*. Outside, there's a sun-trapping garden, where guests fall asleep in deckchairs in summer, book in hand. Inside, an easy elegance flows. You get stripped wood floors, windows everywhere, an airy bar for pre-dinner drinks, an attractive sitting room with lots of books. There are two restaurants: a beautiful dining room that could double as a ballroom, then a conservatory brasserie that opens onto a terrace for lunch in summer; both provide tasty, local sustenance, perhaps Lyme Bay scallops, pork belly with cavolo nero, lemon posset with poached fruits. Bedrooms, most with sea views, hit the spot. Expect cool colours, comfy beds, padded headboards, robes in lovely bathrooms. Lyme, the beach, and the fossil-ridden coast, all wait. *Pets by arrangement.*

Rooms	19 twin/doubles: £180–£325.
	3 family rooms for 4: £303–£319.
	2 singles: £95–£130.
	1 apartment for 6: £365.
Meals	Lunch from £9.90.
	Dinner, 3 courses, about £35.
	Sunday lunch from £23.
	Afternoon tea from £7.50.
Closed	January–3 Feb 2017.
Directions	In Lyme Regis up hill on high street; keep left at bend; on left after 200m.

Mr & Mrs Haskins
Alexandra Hotel & Restaurant
Pound Street, Lyme Regis, DT7 3HZ

Tel	+44 (0)1297 442010
Email	enquiries@hotelalexandra.co.uk
Web	www.hotelalexandra.co.uk

The Bull Hotel

The Bull was Dorset's first boutique hotel, a cool little place with lovely staff, an informal vibe, tasty food and lots of colour. It was bought by Fullers in 2014, who immediately poured in a small fortune to make it even better. The results are dreamy – airy interiors, big art, some fancy new bathrooms and a chic new restaurant. It remains as friendly as ever and draws a local crowd, who come for coffee and cake, a cool bar that rocks at weekends, even a masked ball on New Year's Eve, all of which makes it a lot of fun for guests passing through. Downstairs, you'll find an open fire, stripped wood floors and a pint of London Pride in the bar; in summer, life decants onto a flower-filled courtyard. Colourful bedrooms – all different – have lots of style: beautiful beds, pashmina throws, chic wallpapers, perhaps a bath at the foot of your bed. Some have sofas, family rooms have bunk beds for kids. You get digital radios, flat-screen TVs, then cool bathrooms, some with big power showers. Don't miss the food, perhaps Portland crab, Dorset lamb, coconut panna cotta. Chesil Beach is close. *Minimum stay: 2 nights at weekends.*

Rooms	10 doubles, 1 twin, 3 four-posters: £100-£220. 1 suite for 2: £235-£265. 3 family rooms for 4: £220-£245. 1 single: £90-£115.
Meals	Lunch, 2 courses, from £12. Dinner, 3 courses, around £35. Sunday lunch £19.
Closed	Never.
Directions	On main street in town. Car park at rear.

Ali Pember
The Bull Hotel
34 East Street, Bridport, DT6 3LF
Tel   +44 (0)1308 422878
Email   info@thebullhotel.co.uk
Web   www.thebullhotel.co.uk

The Seaside Boarding House, Restaurant & Bar

You pop up the hill, come to the end of the road, then follow a track along the cliff and down to this lovely and bright small hotel. Rolling hills shoot north towards Dorchester, while the view east follows Chesil Beach, a mere 20 miles round to Portland Bill. The Boarding House's natural beauty comes courtesy of a recent facelift, proving conclusively that cosmetic surgery works! Outside, there's a dining terrace overlooking the sea, then paths that drop down to the beach. Inside, walls of glass flood big rooms with seaside light. There's a bar for cocktails and afternoon tea, a library with books and games for rainy days, then a restaurant for delicious food: perhaps cheese soufflé, whole lemon sole and chocolate and hazelnut delice. Upstairs bedrooms all have sea views and mix period furniture (some from HMS Windsor) with 21st-century design: beautiful beds, Zoffany colours, rugs on wood floors, cushioned window seats. Bathrooms have white robes and vintage tiles, then a big shower, a claw-foot bath, or both. The coastal path passes directly outside, so bring your walking boots. Brilliant. *Minimum stay: 2 nights at weekends.*

Rooms	8 doubles: £180-£235. Dinner, B&B from £120 p.p.
Meals	Lunch from £14. Dinner, 3 courses, about £30. Sunday lunch £25-£30. Afternoon tea from £10.
Closed	Never.
Directions	East from Bridport on B3157. Downhill into Burton Bradstock; right at garage on left-hand bend; up hill to end of road. On left down track.

	Mary-Lou Sturridge
	The Seaside Boarding House, Restaurant & Bar
	Cliff Road, Burton Bradstock, DT6 4RB
Tel	+44 (0)1308 897205
Email	info@theseasideboardinghouse.com
Web	theseasideboardinghouse.com

BridgeHouse Hotel

Beaminster – or Emminster in Thomas Hardy's *Tess* – sits in a lush Dorset valley. From the hills above, you drop through glorious country, rolling down to this old market town, where the church tower soars towards heaven. As for this lovely hotel, it's a 13th-century priest's house and comes with original trimmings: stone flags, mullioned windows, old beams and huge inglenooks. It's intimate, friendly and deeply comfortable, with something beautiful at every turn. There are rugs on parquet flooring, a beamed bar with an open fire, a splendid dining room with Georgian panelling and a Robert Adam's fireplace. Beautiful lighting sets the mood for excellent food, perhaps Witchampton snails, an imperious steak and kidney pie, pear and rosemary tarte tatin. Rooms in the main house are bigger and smarter, those in the coach house are simpler and less expensive; all are pretty with chic fabrics, crisp linen, flat-screen TVs and stylish bathrooms. Breakfast is served in the conservatory, so watch the gardener potter about as you scoff your bacon and eggs. Chesil Beach at West Bay is close. *Minimum stay: 2 nights at weekends.*

Rooms	6 doubles, 3 twin/doubles, 2 four-posters, 2 family rooms for 4: £95-£200. Dinner, B&B £82.50-£145 p.p. (obligatory on Fridays & Saturdays from April to September). Extra beds: children under 17 £25; adults £35-£50.
Meals	Lunch from £8.50. Dinner, 3 courses, £25-£35.
Closed	Never.
Directions	From Yeovil A30 west; A3066 for Bridport to Beaminster. Hotel at far end of town as road bends to right.

Mark & Jo Donovan
BridgeHouse Hotel
3 Prout Bridge,
Beaminster, DT8 3AY

Tel	+44 (0)1308 862200
Email	enquiries@bridge-house.co.uk
Web	www.bridge-house.co.uk

The Greyhound

It's hard to fault this little inn. It sits in one of Dorset's loveliest villages, lost in a lush valley with country views that shoot uphill. Outside, there's a colourful terrace that draws a crowd in summer. Inside, cool, rustic interiors mix old and new to great effect. You find stone walls, old flagstones, gilt mirrors and a wood-burner to keep things cosy. There's a lively locals' bar where you can grab a pint of real ale, then a cosy little restaurant where you dig into delicious food. The feel throughout is informal and you can eat wherever you want, so spin onto the terrace in good weather and try seared scallops, boeuf bourguignon, sticky toffee pudding. Six lovely rooms wait in an old skittle alley. They're not huge, but nor is their price, and what they lack in space, they make up for in comfort and style, with crisp linen, airy colours and pretty furniture. There's a DVD library, too, and Wellington boots if you want to walk. The Cerne Abbas giant is close, while the coast is on your doorstep: Lyme Regis for fossil hunters, West Bay for fine walking and fabulous Chesil Beach. *Minimum stay: 2 nights on bank holidays.*

Rooms	5 doubles, 1 twin: £89-£99. Singles from £69.
Meals	Lunch from £5.50. Dinner, 3 courses, about £30 (not Sunday evening).
Closed	Rarely.
Directions	South from Sherborne on A352. Right after 12 miles, signed Sydling St Nicholas. In village.

Matthew Martinez
The Greyhound
26 High Street, Sydling St Nicholas,
Dorchester, DT2 9PD

Tel   +44 (0)1300 341303
Email   info@dorsetgreyhound.co.uk
Web   www.dorsetgreyhound.co.uk

The Priory Hotel

The lawns of this 16th-century priory run down to the river Frome. Boats float past, an old church rises behind, a gorgeous garden filled with colour wraps around you. As for this lovely country house, you'll find a grand piano in the drawing room, a first-floor sitting room with garden views, and a stone-vaulted dining room in the old cellar. Best of all is the terrace, where you can sit in the sun and watch the river pass – a perfect spot for lunch in summer. Bedrooms in the main house come in different sizes, some cosy in the eaves, others grandly adorned in reds and golds. You get Zoffany fabrics, padded window seats, bowls of fruit, the odd sofa. Eight have river views, others look onto the garden or church. Chic bathrooms – some dazzlingly contemporary – all come with white robes. Rooms in the boathouse, a 16th-century clay barn, are lavish, with oak panelling, stone walls and sublime views. Outside, climbing roses, a duck pond, and banks of daffs and snowdrops in spring. Corfe Castle and Studland Bay are close. A slice of old England with delicious food to boot. *Minimum stay: 2 nights at weekends. Over 14s welcome.*

Rooms	12 twin/doubles: £220–£320.
	5 suites for 2: £350–£380.
Meals	Lunch from £14.95.
	Dinner, 3 courses, £47.50.
Closed	Never.
Directions	West from Poole on A35, then A351 for Wareham and B3075 into town. Through lights, 1st left, right out of square, then keep left. Entrance on left beyond church.

Jeremy Merchant
The Priory Hotel
Church Green,
Wareham, BH20 4ND

Tel   +44 (0)1929 551666
Email   reservations@theprioryhotel.co.uk
Web   www.theprioryhotel.co.uk

Urban Beach Hotel

A quirky little place close to the beach with cool interiors and a happy buzz in the bar. Mark and Fiona have a great way of doing things: they employ a Head of Happy and go out of their way to help their lovely staff flourish. It works brilliantly, if you stay it's hard not to notice a difference. Inside, the bar/restaurant is the hub of the house. Surf movies play silently, a couple of surf boards hang on the walls, you get big circular leather booths, then driftwood lamps and a house guitar. There's a table of cakes, a bar for cocktails, candle lanterns scattered about, the daily papers and a few cool tunes. Bedrooms upstairs are nicely priced, some bigger than others, but even the smaller rooms are lovely with warm colours, crisp linen and excellent bathrooms. A decked terrace outside is popular for summer barbecues, but the beach waits at the end of the road, seven miles of sand with a surf shop on the way down. Urban Reef, Mark & Fiona's sister restaurant, has a balcony and terrace overlooking the sea; they'll book you in for dinner, you can even have your breakfast there. *Minimum stay: 2 nights at weekends (3 nights bank holidays).*

Rooms	9 doubles, 1 twin/double: £97–£180.
	2 singles: £72.
Meals	Lunch & dinner £5–£25.
Closed	Never.
Directions	South from Ringwood on A338; left for Boscombe (east of centre). Over railway, right onto Centenary Way. Keep with the flow (left, then right) to join Christchurch Rd; 2nd left (St John's Rd); 2nd left.

Mark & Fiona Cribb
Urban Beach Hotel
23 Argyll Road,
Bournemouth, BH5 1EB

Tel	+44 (0)1202 301509
Email	reception@urbanbeach.co.uk
Web	www.urbanbeach.co.uk

Captain's Club Hotel and Spa

The Captain's Club stands on the banks on the Stour, where a tiny ferry potters along the river dodging swans and ducks. In summer, you decant onto its lovely terrace and watch river life pass by. Inside, walls of glass weatherproof the view. The sprawling bar fills with light and comes with deep sofas, the daily papers and a grand piano. It's smart, stylish and very informal, with live music at weekends. The hotel also has its own boat, so you can take to the high seas and spin over to the Isle of Wight or Brownsea Island. Back on dry land uncluttered bedrooms have river views, low-slung beds, crisp white linen, neutral colours and excellent bathrooms. None are small, some are huge with separate sitting rooms, apartments have more than one bedroom, so perfect for families and friends. There's a spa, too, with a hydrotherapy pool, a sauna and four treatment rooms. Lovely food is on tap all day in the bar, while the mirrored restaurant ensures everyone has the view. Lobster, Dorset crab, sea bass and a good steak all wait. Christchurch is a short walk upstream. Brilliant. *Minimum stay: 2 nights at weekends.*

Rooms	17 doubles: £199–£259.
	12 apartments for 2-6: £289–£649.
Meals	Bar meals all day from £6.
	Lunch from £15. Dinner £30–£35.
Closed	Never.
Directions	M27/A31 west, then A338/B3073 south into Christchurch. At A35 (lights at big r'bout) follow one-way system left. Double back after 100m. Cross r'bout heading west and 1st left into Sopers Lane. Signed left.

Timothy Lloyd & Robert Wilson
Captain's Club Hotel and Spa
Wick Ferry, Wick Lane,
Christchurch, BH23 1HU

Tel	+44 (0)1202 475111
Email	reservations@captainsclubhotel.com
Web	www.captainsclubhotel.com

The Kings

This is one of those lovely places that delivers what many of us want: lots of style, delicious food, happy staff, attractive prices. The setting is just as good, a slice of Georgian England, with the river Stour to the left, the ruined castle to the right and the old bowling green in between. A riverside path leads down to Christchurch Quay, and another to the gardens at the priory – blissful stuff. As for the hotel, you'll find a cool new bar with big orange armchairs, green leather bar stools and candles everywhere at night – not a bad spot for champagne cocktails. Comfy bedrooms have lots of style: smart colours, fine beds, good bathrooms, perhaps a sofa if there's room. Three overlook the front, those in the eaves have a cute, cosy feel. Back downstairs you find the big draw – excellent food in the candlelit restaurant. Try Dorset cheddar soufflé, turbot with garlic and thyme, lemon meringues with limoncello. It's all local with menus from an amazing £15. Lobster nights bring in the locals, the Christchurch Food Festival comes in May with stalls on the bowling green. Perfect. *Minimum stay: 2 nights at weekends.*

Rooms	14 doubles, 6 twins: £99–£199.
Meals	Lunch from £6.50.
	Dinner, 3 courses: set menu £18.50;
	à la carte about £30.
	Sunday lunch from £15.
Closed	Never.
Directions	West into Christchurch on A35. 2nd left onto High Street, then left at roundabout into Castle Street. On left after 200m. Parking on right in lay-by.

Lukasz Dwornik
The Kings
18 Castle Street,
Christchurch, BH23 1DT

Tel	+44 (0)1202 588933
Email	kings@harbourhotels.co.uk
Web	www.thekings-christchurch.co.uk

10 Castle Street

It may have a humble address, but that is the only humble feature you will find at 10 Castle Street, a stunning Queen Anne mansion that sits in 27 acres of idyllic gardens and parkland. Inside, you discover the re-invention of the English country-house hotel. As tradition demands, it is privately owned and has the feel of home, albeit a deliciously grand one that doubles as a contemporary art gallery. You'll find an elegant drawing room that opens onto a terrace; Ionic columns in the airy bar; a dining room with French windows that frame garden views; a first-floor, sitting-room bar that has the feel of a gentleman's club. Outside, the terrace overlooks a fine English garden, with its trim lawns, wild flowers and an avenue of lime trees. Bedrooms have cool colours, chic fabrics, crisp linen and smart bathrooms; some are huge with garden views, a couple are tiny, but good for a night. Don't miss the food, perhaps Scottish langoustines, haunch of venison, orange and cardamom crème brûlée. There's a bakery, a smokehouse, a cinema and a kitchen garden, with a spa coming in 2017. Out of this world.

Rooms	9 doubles: £165–£350. Extra bed/sofabed available £40 p.p.p.n.
Meals	Lunch from £15. Dinner, 3 courses, about £40. Sunday lunch from £24. Afternoon tea from £19.50.
Closed	Never.
Directions	North from A31 onto A338. Left in Fordingbridge onto B3078. On left after 5 miles in village.

Alexander & Gretchen Boon
10 Castle Street
Cranborne, BH21 5PZ
Tel   +44 (0)1725 551133
Email   enquiries@10castlestreet.com
Web   www.10castlestreet.com

La Fosse at Cranborne

This is a lovely restaurant with rooms in a pretty Dorset village – small and friendly, nicely homespun, owner-run and owner-cooked. Emmanuelle and Mark love their world, it's a way of life and they share it with guests happily and generously. Downstairs, there's a smart sitting room with stripped floors and maps for walkers. Upstairs, a clutch of pretty bedrooms wait with warm colours, attractive fabrics, comfy beds and spotless bathrooms. They're very well priced, so splash out on the bigger rooms and find a sofa or a separate sitting room. Not that you'll linger long. Mark's food is the big draw, much of it sourced within 20 miles. You eat in a pretty dining room with an open fire roaring beyond a couple of sofas. It's delicious stuff, perhaps game terrine with ale chutney, slow-cooked lamb with village vegetables, then pears poached in sloe gin with chocolate ice cream. Best of all is the cheese board, a tasting menu of ten local cheeses – utterly irresistible. You can walk it all off a few miles west at Hambledon Hill (a prehistoric hill fort) with big country views. Brilliant. *Minimum stay: 2 nights at weekends.*

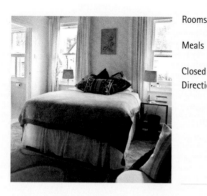

Rooms	3 doubles, 2 twin/doubles: £99–£120. 1 suite for 2: £165.
Meals	Dinner, 3 courses, £27.50. Not Sunday.
Closed	Never.
Directions	A338 to Fordingbridge, then B3078 into Cranborne. Right at village shop and on right.

Emmanuelle & Mark Hartstone
La Fosse at Cranborne
The Square, Cranborne,
Wimborne, BH21 5PR
Tel   +44 (0)1725 517604
Email   lafossemail@gmail.com
Web   www.la-fosse.com

Castleman Hotel & Restaurant

It's a little like stepping into the pages of a Hardy novel: an untouched corner of rural Dorset, a 400-year-old bailiff's house, sheep grazing in lush fields, a rich cast of characters pottering about. The Castleman – part country house, part restaurant with rooms – is a true one-off: quirky, intimate, defiantly English (you'll think you've landed in Ambridge). It pays no heed to prevailing fashions, not least because the locals would revolt if it did. Barbara runs the place in great style. Touches of grandeur are hard to miss: a panelled hall, art from Chettle House, a magnificent Jacobean ceiling in one of the sitting rooms. Follow your nose and find a cosy bar, fresh flowers everywhere and books galore. The restaurant has garden views, though your eyes are more likely to be fixed on Barbara's delicious old-school food, perhaps potted shrimp terrine, haunch of local venison, meringues with chocolate mousse and toasted almonds. Homely bedrooms fit the bill: comfortable, delightfully priced, a couple with claw-foot baths. Magical Dorset will fill your days with splendour. Don't miss it.

Rooms	4 doubles, 1 twin/double, 1 twin, 1 four-poster, 1 family room for 4: £95–£110. Singles from £70.
Meals	Sunday lunch £25. Dinner, 3 courses, about £27.
Closed	February.
Directions	A354 north from Blandford Forum. 3rd left (about 4 miles up) and on left in village.

Barbara Garnsworthy
Castleman Hotel & Restaurant
Chettle,
Blanford Forum, DT11 8DB

Tel	+44 (0)1258 830096
Email	enquiry@castlemanhotel.co.uk
Web	www.castlemanhotel.co.uk

Entry 84 Map 3

Plumber Manor

A grand old country house that sits in a couple of acres of green and pleasant land with the river Divelish running through. It dates from 1650, with mullioned windows, huge stone flags and a fine terrace for afternoon tea. An avenue of horse chestnuts takes you to the front door. Inside, a pair of labradors rule the roost. Expect no designer trends – Plumber is old-school, defiantly so. Take the first-floor landing with its enormous sofa, gallery of family oils and grand piano thrown in for good measure. Bedrooms are split between the main house and converted barns. The latter tend to be bigger and are good for those with dogs. Décor is dated – 1980s florals – as are most bathrooms, though a couple now sparkle in travertine splendour. The family triumvirate of Brian (in the kitchen), Richard (behind the bar) and Alison (simply everywhere) excel in the art of old-fashioned hospitality. Delicious country food waits in the restaurant, try seared scallops with pea purée, rack of lamb with rosemary and garlic, lemon meringue pie. Bulbarrow Hill is close.

Rooms	2 doubles, 14 twin/doubles; 1 twin/double with separate bath: £150-£230. Singles £120-£140. Dinner, B&B £80-£120 p.p. Extra bed/sofabed available £20 p.p.p.n.
Meals	Sunday lunch £29.50. Dinner 2-3 courses, £29-£36.
Closed	February.
Directions	West from Sturminster Newton on A357. Across traffic lights, up hill & left for Hazelbury Bryan. Follow brown tourism signs. Hotel signed left after 2 miles.

Richard, Alison & Brian Prideaux-Brune
Plumber Manor
Plumber,
Sturminster Newton, DT10 2AF

Tel	+44 (0)1258 472507
Email	book@plumbermanor.com
Web	www.plumbermanor.com

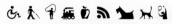

Stapleton Arms

A perfect village inn: loads of style, lovely staff, super food, excellent prices. The Stapleton started life as a Georgian home, becoming an inn after the war. These days, warm, hip interiors carry a streak of country glamour. Downstairs, you'll find sofas in front of the fire, a piano for live music, a restaurant with shuttered windows and candles in the fireplace. You can eat whatever you want, wherever you want; delicious pork pies wait at the bar, but it's hard to resist a three-course feast, perhaps woodland mushrooms on toast, pan-fried sea bass with chilli and fennel, chocolate and Baileys soufflé with spiced orange ice cream. You'll find a beer menu to beat all others (ale matters here) and there's always a separate menu for kids – this is a very child-friendly place. Super rooms are soundproofed to ensure a good night's sleep. All have beautiful linen, fresh flowers, happy colours, excellent showers. You'll find maps and wellies if you want to walk and there's a playground in the garden. Wincanton is close for the races if you want to lose your shirt. One of the best.

Rooms	4 doubles: £90–£120. Singles from £72.
Meals	Lunch & bar meals from £7. Dinner, 3 courses, about £30.
Closed	Rarely.
Directions	A303 to Wincanton. Into town right after fire station, signed Buckhorn Weston. Left at T-junction after 3 miles. In village, pub on right.

Richard Smith
Stapleton Arms
Church Hill, Buckhorn Weston,
Gillingham, SP8 5HS

Tel	+44 (0)1963 370396
Email	relax@thestapletonarms.com
Web	www.thestapletonarms.com

Houndgate Townhouse

Houndgate is a handsome townhouse hotel, the sort of place the term 'boutique' was coined to define. It has a chic contemporary style – airy interiors, cool colours, smart fabrics, the full works. But there's more to it than that. It's subtle, cleverly conceived, a design hotel with a level of craftsmanship you don't expect. At its heart, it's a cool little café/bar, where you can order a coffee, a bowl of soup, afternoon tea or cocktails before dinner. It sits on a smart Georgian street – Darlington itself is a beautiful surprise. Inside you find a mirrored ceiling in the elegant bar, a stylish restaurant with green leather booths, a terraced courtyard for lunch in the sun. Rooms are just as good: beautiful linen, excellent beds, robes in sparkling bathrooms. Two have a free-standing bath in the room, another a panel of original wallpaper that was discovered when refurbishing. Bistro-style food waits downstairs, perhaps moules with white wine, boeuf bourguignon, peanut butter parfait. Don't miss the Bowes Museum in Barnard Castle, a jewel of the North. Durham is close. *Complimentary access to the local swimming pool and gym available.*

Rooms	4 doubles, 2 twin/doubles, 2 four-posters: £72–£145. Singles £72–£135. Extra bed/sofabed available at no charge.
Meals	Lunch from £5. Dinner, 3 courses, £20. Afternoon tea £16.
Closed	Never.
Directions	A1(M), then A167 into Darlington. Take the ring road to its southeastern roundabout and exit into Beaumont Street for its car park. Houndgate runs above, a 2-minute walk.

Natalie Cooper
Houndgate Townhouse
11 Houndgate,
Darlington, DL1 5RF

Tel	+44 (0)1325 486011
Email	info@houndgatetownhouse.co.uk
Web	www.houndgatetownhouse.co.uk

Rose & Crown

Romaldkirk is one of those lovely villages where little has changed in 200 years. It sits peacefully in the north Pennines, lost to the world and without great need of it. As for the Rose & Crown, it dates to 1733 and stands on the village green next to a Saxon Church. Roses ramble across stone walls at the front, so grab a pint of local ale, then sit in the sun and watch life pass by. Inside, you can roast away in front of a fire in the wonderfully old-school bar while reading the *Teesdale Mercury*. There's a peaceful sitting room for afternoon tea, then a panelled restaurant for excellent food, perhaps honey-glazed goats cheese with apple and hazelnut, shoulder of pork wrapped in Parma ham, banana Bakewell tart. Thomas and Cheryl bought the place in 2012 and have been spending money on it ever since: it has never looked better. Stylish rooms – some in the main house, others out back, a couple in a cottage next door – have warm colours, comfy beds, Bose sound systems and super bathrooms. Don't miss High Force waterfall, the magnificent Bowes Museum or the sausage sandwich at lunch. Dogs are very welcome.

Rooms	8 doubles, 3 twins: £115–£160. 3 suites for 2: £180–£200. Singles £95. Dinner, B&B from £79 p.p.
Meals	Lunch from £10.50. Dinner, 3 courses, from £27. Sunday lunch £19.50.
Closed	23-27 December & 1 week in January.
Directions	From Barnard Castle B6277 north for 6 miles. Right in village towards green. Inn on left.

Thomas & Cheryl Robinson
Rose & Crown
Romaldkirk,
Barnard Castle, DL12 9EB
Tel   +44 (0)1833 650213
Email   hotel@rose-and-crown.co.uk
Web   www.rose-and-crown.co.uk

National Treasure

Seaham Hall

Seaham is a grand old pile reborn for the 21st-century. It was home to Lord Byron, the spa is one of the loveliest in the land and the suites are huge and crammed with style. It sits in 37 acres of cliff-top grounds, giving scope to explore if you can pull yourself away (unlikely). The main house dates to 1791 and comes with original fixtures and fittings: a galleried staircase that rises to a glass dome; a vast, stately terrace for afternoon tea. Interiors are dramatic: a chic bar for cocktails, a mirrored sitting room with velvet banquettes, a pool table in the games room, then high-ceilings in the stunning restaurant, where sparkling chandeliers hang. As for the spa, the entrance sweeps you off to the far east, a 30-metre walk across water. You'll find a 20-metre pool, 17 Japanese-style treatment rooms, then hot tubs, a sauna, a steam room and sun loungers on a balcony. There's delicious Asian food in Ozone, too, the spa's circular restaurant. As for the suites, expect huge beds, oodles of style and robes in fine bathrooms. Coastal walks, Seaham beach and the Angel of the North wait. *Minimum stay: 2 nights at weekends in July & August.*

Rooms	21 suites for 2, 1 suite for 4: £195–£750. Extra beds £50.
Meals	Lunch from £6. Dinner, 3 courses in Ozone about £25; in Byron's about £50. Sunday lunch from £23.50. Afternoon tea from £22.
Closed	Never.
Directions	A1(M) past Durham, then A690 north and B1404 east. Hotel signed on right after 5 miles.

Ross Grieve
Seaham Hall
Lord Byron's Walk,
Seaham, SR7 7AG

Tel	+44 (0)191 516 1400
Email	hotel@seaham-hall.com
Web	www.seaham-hall.com

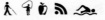

Maison Talbooth

The outdoor swimming pool is heated to 29°C every day, a chauffeur is on hand to whisk you down to the hotel's riverside restaurant, a grand piano waits in the sitting room, where guests gather for a legendary afternoon tea. They don't do things by halves at Maison Talbooth, a small-scale pleasure dome with long views across Constable country. The house, an old rectory, stands in three acres of manicured grounds; the pool house is a big draw with its open fire, honesty bar, beautiful art and treatment rooms. Interiors are equally impressive. There are no rooms, only suites, each divine. Some on the ground floor have doors onto terraces where hot tubs wait, but all pamper you rotten with flawless bathrooms, fabulous beds, cool colours and hi-tech excess. At dinner you're chauffeured to the family's restaurants (both within half a mile): Milsoms for bistro food served informally; Le Talbooth on the river Stour for more serious fare, perhaps poached lobster with orange and fennel, saddle of venison with plums and bitter chocolate, pineapple and coconut soufflé with piña colada ice cream. A great escape.

Rooms	12 suites for 4: £210–£420. Singles from £170.
Meals	Dinner at Milsoms £25; at Le Talbooth £35–£50.
Closed	Never.
Directions	North on A12 past Colchester. Left to Dedham, right after S bend. Maison Talbooth is on right; follow brown signs.

Paul & Geraldine Milsom
Maison Talbooth
Stratford Road, Dedham,
Colchester, CO7 6HN

Tel	+44 (0)1206 322367
Email	maison@milsomhotels.com
Web	www.milsomhotels.com

The Sun Inn

This perennial favourite sits in an idyllic village made rich by mills in the 16th century. You're also in Constable country – the artist attended school in the village and often returned to paint the church. Best of all is the river – you can hire boats, grab a picnic from the inn, float down the sleepy Stour, then tie up on the bank for lunch al fresco. As for The Sun, you couldn't hope to wash up in a better spot. Inside, you find open fires, boarded floors, timber frames and an easy elegance. A panelled lounge comes with sofas and armchairs, the bar is made from a slab of local elm and the airy, beamed dining room offers fabulous food inspired by Italy, perhaps crab ravioli, squid with chilli and garlic, monkfish with truffle mash, chocolate mousse with Morello cherries. Rooms are gorgeous: creaking floorboards, timber-framed walls, a panelled four-poster. Those at the back are bigger and come in grand style, but all are lovely with crisp linen, local art and power showers in excellent bathrooms. There's afternoon tea on arrival if you book in advance and a garden for a pint in summer.

Rooms	5 doubles, 1 twin/double, 1 four-poster: £90–£145. Singles £90–£130. Dinner, B&B £97 p.p.
Meals	Lunch from £10.95, not Monday. Dinner from £16.95.
Closed	Christmas.
Directions	A12 north past Colchester. 2nd exit, signed Dedham. In village opposite church.

Piers Baker
The Sun Inn
High Street, Dedham,
Colchester, CO7 6DF

Tel	+44 (0)1206 323351
Email	office@thesuninndedham.com
Web	www.thesuninndedham.com

The Mistley Thorn

This welcoming inn fits the Sawday bill perfectly – lovely owners with fingers dipped into delicious local pies. Their kitchen shop and cooking school stand four doors down the street; Lucca, their popular wood-fired pizzeria, waits in Manningtree. As for their inn, it stands on the high street and dates to 1746. Interiors have an airy feel, the mood is laid-back with a great little bar, the food is local and utterly delicious. Expect tongue-and-groove panelling, a roaring wood-burner, padded benches and a happy vibe. Nicely-priced rooms (two above the kitchen shop) have a similar feel: pretty fabrics, warm colours, crisp linen on comfy beds, REN lotions for power showers and double-ended baths. There's good art, homemade shortbread and fresh fruit, too, while those at the front have views of the Stour estuary. As for the food, it's delicious stuff, perhaps smoked haddock chowder, mussels with garlic and herbs, sticky toffee pudding. The Witchfinder General lived here, you can walk along the river to Dedham, the Beth Chatto Gardens are close. Sunday nights are a steal: £120 for two with dinner.

Rooms	5 doubles, 3 twin/doubles: £110–£125. Singles from £90. Dinner, B&B from £75 per person.
Meals	Lunch from £4.95. Set lunch, 2–3 courses £12.50–£15. Dinner, 3 courses, about £30.
Closed	Rarely.
Directions	From A12 Hadleigh/East Bergholt exit north of Colchester. Thro' East Bergholt to A137; signed Manningtree; continue to Mistley High St. 50 yds from station.

David McKay & Sherri Singleton
The Mistley Thorn
High Street, Mistley,
Manningtree, CO11 1HE

Tel   +44 (0)1206 392821
Email   info@mistleythorn.co.uk
Web   www.mistleythorn.co.uk

The Pier at Harwich

They don't do things by halves at the Pier – a cool £1.5 million has recently been spent on a 21st-century makeover for this iconic coastal hotel. It sits on the harbourside with views of town and water, its front terrace a big draw in good weather. Inside, a cool new look captivates. A chic warehouse feel waits in the bar – stripped walls, hanging lamps, leather bar stools, big windows to frame the view. You get craft beers and cask ales, a gin library and Prosecco cocktails, then small plates of Nordic design if you fancy a light bite. Hungry souls fly upstairs to the famous first-floor brasserie, where mirrored booths and leather banquettes now come as standard, and doors open onto a balcony, where you can tuck into your lobster Thermidor while gazing out onto the estuary. Bedrooms – some above, others next door in a former inn – have fancy bedheads, seaside colours, crisp white linen and super bathrooms; the suite, with its vast window, has a telescope with which to scan the high seas. Coastal walks and blue flag beaches wait, as does the Electric Palace, the second oldest cinema in Britain.

Rooms	10 doubles, 3 twins: £120-£170.
	1 suite for 2: £200-£230.
	Singles from £95.
	Dinner, B&B from £100 p.p.
Meals	Lunch from £6.50.
	Dinner à la carte £25-£40.
	Sunday lunch from £19.50.
Closed	Never.
Directions	M25 junc. 28, A12 to Colchester bypass, then A120 to Harwich. Head for quay. Hotel opposite pier.

Paul & Geraldine Milsom
The Pier at Harwich
The Quay,
Harwich, CO12 3HH

Tel	+44 (0)1255 241212
Email	pier@milsomhotels.com
Web	www.milsomhotels.com

Horse & Groom

A lovely pub, informally run, with excellent food, stylish interiors and wines and beers for all. It stands at the top of the hill with big views stretching over the Cotswolds. Outside, you can sit in the shade of damson trees and watch chefs gather eggs from the coop or carrots from the kitchen garden. Inside, stripped floors, open fires and the odd stone wall give a smart rustic feel. This is a hive of youthful endeavour with two brothers at the helm. Will cooks, Tom pours the ales (or Cotswold Vodka), and a cheery conviviality flows. Locals love it. They come for the craic, a pint of Butcombe and some deliciously local food, perhaps wild mushroom soup, Fulready lamb with salsa verde, Granny G's unmissable toffee meringue. Uncluttered bedrooms have a contemporary country-house style: crisp linen, good art, smart fabrics, sparkling bathrooms. None are small, three are big, the garden room opens onto the terrace, those at the front are soundproofed to minimise noise from the road. Breakfast is your final feast: homemade croissants, small bottles of local milk, blocks of patted butter. *Minimum stay: 2 nights at weekends.*

Rooms	5 doubles: £120–£170.
	Singles from £80.
Meals	Lunch from £4.75.
	Dinner, 3 courses, £25–£30.
Closed	Christmas Day & New Year's Eve.
Directions	West from Moreton-in-Marsh on A44. Climb hill in Bourton-on-the-Hill; pub at top on left. Moreton-in-Marsh railway station 2 miles away.

Tom & Will Greenstock
Horse & Groom
Bourton-on-the-Hill,
Moreton-in-Marsh, GL56 9AQ

Tel	+44 (0)1386 700413
Email	greenstocks@horseandgroom.info
Web	www.horseandgroom.info

The Old Stocks Inn

Stow, a pretty market town, is nicely positioned for exploring the Cotswolds, with Stratford to the North, Cheltenham to the west, Oxford and Blenheim Palace to the east and the early stretches of the Thames to the south. As for this 17th-century inn, it's just been refurbished from top to toe. It sits on the market square with golden stone walls inside and out. Interiors mix original beams and timber frames with a big dollop of contemporary style – leather banquettes and hanging lamps in the stylish restaurant; panelled walls and an open fire in the cool little bar; a pretty coffee shop that overlooks the square. In summer, you spin onto a beautiful terrace for wood-fired pizzas in the sun. Super-comfy beds in beautiful rooms are wrapped in the crispest linen. You get coffee machines, iPod docks, Bakelite telephones, old Penguin books. All have chic bathrooms, some with claw-foot baths (a couple in the room). Three are dog-friendly, the family suite has bunk beds and an Xbox. Good food waits downstairs, perhaps cured salmon, a chargrilled steak, then lemon and lime mousse. *Minimum stay: 2 nights at weekends in high season.*

Rooms	6 doubles, 9 twin/doubles: £119–£279. 1 family suite: £159–£209. Extra bed/sofabed £10–£20 p.p.p.n.
Meals	Lunch & dinner £5–£35.
Closed	Never.
Directions	A429 to Stow-on-the-Wold. Inn on northeast corner of square in town.

Charlotte Knowles
The Old Stocks Inn
The Square,
Stow-on-the-Wold, GL54 1AF

Tel	+44 (0)1451 830666
Email	info@oldstocksinn.com
Web	www.oldstocksinn.com

No. 131

This funky new addition to Cheltenham's buzzing scene is a bone fide jaw-dropper – impeccable Georgian architecture outside, 21st-century chic within. Interiors mix all the lovely old stuff: stripped floors, chandeliers, ceiling friezes, period colours, with lots of lovely new stuff: enormous sofas, hanging lampshades, a cool collection of contemporary art. You'll find roaring fires, blue leather bar stools, vintage tiles, old wooden fridges piled high with hams and cheese. Downstairs, the bar has a retractable roof, turning itself into a terrace in summer, with a DJ station for the odd weekend. Upstairs, bedrooms have huge style: piles of art books, big beds, the best linen, perhaps a fancy bath in your room; all have robes and walk-in showers in flawless bathrooms. Downstairs, you mingle with happy locals in the bars and restaurants, where great food waits, perhaps grilled sardines with chilli and garlic, half a lobster or a juicy steak, treacle tart with clotted cream. In summer life spills onto the front terrace, overlooking Imperial Gardens. Don't miss the jazz festival in May.

Rooms	11 doubles: £150–£220.
Meals	Lunch from £7.
	Dinner, 3 courses, about £40.
	Sunday lunch from £21.
Closed	Never.
Directions	Pick up one-way system in the middle of town and follow it to its southwestern corner at Imperial Square; left onto the Promenade, signed 'M5, Gloucester, Oxford'. Hotel on right after 400m, before lights.

Stephen Wadcock
No. 131
131 The Promenade,
Cheltenham, GL50 1NW

Tel	+44 (0)1242 822939
Email	reservations@no131.com
Web	www.no131.com

Beaumont House

Fan and Alan have lived all over the world and came back to England to open the sort of hotel they like to stay in themselves. It's a very friendly place, nothing is too much trouble. Throw a few luxuries into the mix – stylish bedrooms, excellent breakfasts, an honesty bar in the airy sitting room – and you have a great base for all things Cheltenham. Spotless bedrooms spread over three floors. Some are simpler, others more extravagant, but all have lovely bathrooms and every budget will be happy. Compact, airy doubles on the lower ground floor are perfect for short stays. Rooms above are bigger, some with striking design. One has an African theme, another has far-eastern wood carvings, there are vast headboards, smart furniture and flat-screen TVs. You breakfast in an elegant dining room, perhaps freshly made porridge, American pancakes, smoked haddock, the full cooked works. Good restaurants wait in town (and there's live jazz at Daffodil's on Monday nights). As for Cheltenham, it has festivals coming out of its ears: folk, jazz, food, science, music, literature and horses. Brilliant.

Rooms	9 doubles, 2 twin/doubles: £90–£249. 2 suites for 4: £235–£300. 1 family room for 4: £235–£270. 2 singles: £75–£85. Extra bed/sofabed £30 p.p.p.n.
Meals	Restaurants within walking distance.
Closed	Rarely.
Directions	Leave one-way system in centre of town for Stroud (south) on A46. Straight ahead, through lights and right at 1st mini-roundabout. On left after 500m.

Alan & Fan Bishop
Beaumont House
56 Shurdington Road,
Cheltenham, GL53 0JE

Tel	+44 (0)1242 223311
Email	reservations@bhhotel.co.uk
Web	www.bhhotel.co.uk

Three Choirs Vineyards

England's answer to the Napa Valley. After 15 years of tilling the soil (very sandy, good drainage), Thomas's 75 acres of Gloucestershire hillside now produce 300,000 bottles a year. There are regular tastings, a shop in which to buy a bottle or two, and paths that weave through the vines – a perfect stroll after a good meal. What's more, three fabulous lodges wait down by the lake, all with decks and walls of glass. You'll find claw-foot baths and comfy beds, so camp out in grand savannah style and listen to the woodpeckers. Rooms up at the restaurant are smart and spacious with terraces that overlook the vineyard. They come with padded bedheads, walls of colour, leather armchairs, flat-screen TVs and good bathrooms. Finally, the restaurant: claret walls, lovely views, sofas in front of an open fire. Excellent food waits, perhaps twice-baked Gloucester soufflé, fillet of bream with rocket and watercress, rhubarb crème brûlée with lemon shortbread. World wines are on the list, but you'll want something from the vines that surround you; there's a microbrewery, too. Perfect. *Minimum stay: 2 nights at weekends*

Rooms	6 doubles, 2 twins, 3 vineyard lodges: £140-£195. Singles from £135.
Meals	Lunch from £7.50. Dinner à la carte about £35.
Closed	Christmas & New Year.
Directions	From Newent north on B4215 for about 1.5 miles. Follow brown signs to vineyard.

Thomas Shaw
Three Choirs Vineyards
Castle Tump,
Newent, GL18 1LS

Tel	+44 (0)1531 890223
Email	info@threechoirs.com
Web	www.three-choirs-vineyards.co.uk

Tudor Farmhouse Hotel

A gorgeous small hotel, one of the best. It sits on the edge of the Forest of Dean, a magical world of woodland walks, medieval castles, meandering rivers and bleating sheep. You're in the middle of a tiny village with country views all around. Step inside to find sparkling interiors – Colin and Hari have spent a small fortune turning their realm into something very special indeed. An airy elegance mixes with golden stone walls and original timber frames, the house bearing testament to its Tudor roots. Big or small, bedrooms are divine – stylishly uncluttered with smart fabrics, robes in fine bathrooms and super-comfy beds. Those in the main house have ancient beamed ceilings, those in the old barns have original stone walls. The bigger rooms are faultless: the best beds, claw-foot baths, enormous showers, the lap of luxury. Lovely local food waits downstairs, perhaps cider-cured salmon, haunch of venison, rhubarb Bakewell tart; there are home-laid eggs for breakfast, too. You can kayak on the Wye, forage in the forest, take to cycle tracks. Don't miss Puzzlewood or Clearwell Caves. *Minimum stay: 2 nights at weekends*

Rooms	10 doubles, 3 twins, 2 four-posters: £100-£230. 5 suites for 2: £180-£230. Singles £90-£220. Extra bed/sofabed £25 p.p.p.n.
Meals	Lunch from £6.95. Dinner, 3 courses, £30-£40. Sunday lunch from £14.50.
Closed	Never.
Directions	South from Monmouth on A466. Clearwell signed left after 3 miles.

Colin & Hari Fell
Tudor Farmhouse Hotel
High Street,
Clearwell, GL16 8JS

Tel	+44 (0)1594 833046
Email	info@tudorfarmhousehotel.co.uk
Web	www.tudorfarmhousehotel.co.uk

Chewton Glen

Chewton Glen is one of England's loveliest country-house hotels. It opened in 1964 with eight bedrooms and even though it now has 70, it remains delightfully intimate. Fifty years of evolution have brought a pillared swimming pool, a hydrotherapy spa, a golf course and a tennis centre. It recently added 12 treehouse suites, which sit peacefully in their own valley with hot tubs on balconies and wood-burners waiting inside. As for the hotel, beauty waits at every turn: stately sitting rooms, roaring fires, busts and oils, a bar that opens onto a sun-trapping terrace. Bedrooms are the best. Some come in country-house style, but most have a contemporary feel. Expect marble bathrooms, private balconies, designer fabrics, faultless housekeeping. Outside, four gardeners tend 130 acres of lawns and woodland, with a kitchen garden that helps the restaurant, so you'll eat well; perhaps Dorset crab, Devon duck, Charantais melon soup. You can atone in style: a walk on the beach, mountain biking in the New Forest, croquet on the lawn in summer. *Minimum stay: 2 nights at weekends.*

Rooms	5 doubles, 30 twin/doubles: £325–£685.
	23 suites for 2: £610–£1,580.
	12 treehouses for 2: £700–£1,450.
Meals	Breakfast £21–£26. Lunch, 3 courses, £25.
	Sunday lunch £39.50.
	Dinner, 3 courses, £55–£65.
	Tasting menu £70.
	Light meals available throughout the day.
Closed	Never.
Directions	A337 west from Lymington. Through
	New Milton for Christchurch. Right at
	r'bout, signed Walkford. Right again;
	hotel on right.

Andrew Stembridge
Chewton Glen
Christchurch Road,
New Milton, BH25 7QT

Tel	+44 (0)1425 275341
Email	reservations@chewtonglen.com
Web	www.chewtonglen.com

The Manor at Sway

A big house in a small village in the middle of the New Forest – lovely gardens run down to woodland, the odd deer comes in to nibble the roses. Inside, country-house interiors have a distinctly contemporary feel – airy and nicely stylish with wood floors, pretty wallpapers and a relaxed feel. You'll find smart sofas in the sitting room, then a chic bar with a wall of glass that opens onto the terrace, perfect for afternoon tea in the sun. Bedrooms are lovely. They come in different shapes and sizes, but all have the same comforts: excellent beds, crisp linen, warm colours, sparkling bathrooms. Three are dog-friendly, those in the eaves are warmly cosy, larger rooms have armchairs, most have garden views. The big surprise is the delicious food, so work up an appetite in the forest by day, then come home for a feast, perhaps scallops with curried cauliflower, local venison in a port sauce, Bakewell tart with blackberry jam. There are simpler dishes, too: posh fish and chips, pork belly with buttered greens, beetroot tarte tatin. Fabulous walking, mountain bike trails and sun loungers in the garden wait. *Minimum stay: 2 nights at weekends.*

Rooms	12 doubles, 3 twin/doubles: £90–£210.
Meals	Lunch from £6.
	Dinner, 3 courses, £30–£40.
	Sunday lunch £19.50–£24.50.
Closed	Rarely.
Directions	South from Brockenhurst on B3055 for 3 miles. In village, right at Skoda garage, then right at x-roads, for station. On left after 500m.

Tim Holloway
The Manor at Sway
Station Road, Sway,
Lymington, SO41 6BA

Tel	+44 (0)1590 682754
Email	info@swaymanor.com
Web	www.themanoratsway.com

Daisybank Cottage Boutique B&B

This cute B&B in the New Forest mixes a warm contemporary style with some fine, old-fashioned hospitality – Ciaran and Cheryl go out of their way to make your stay special. As for their Arts & Crafts house, it sits on the southern fringes of Brockenhurst with a pretty garden at the back, where free-range hens strut their stuff. Inside, spoiling bedrooms come with airy colours, plantation shutters, then Vi-Spring mattresses for beautiful beds and robes in striking bathrooms. One has a small courtyard, another a claw-foot bath, the room at the back opens onto the garden. All have coffee machines, silent fridges in which to chill drinks, iPod docks and flat-screen TVs. Breakfast is a local feast – eggs from the garden, artisan jams and honey, home-baked soda bread and granola, bacon and sausages from a New Forest farm. After which you can walk by the sea, hire bikes and explore the forest or spin across to the Isle of Wight. A shepherd's hut in the garden may soon be available for B&B. Good restaurants wait in town (a ten-minute stroll); posher ones are further afield. *Children over 10 welcome.*

Rooms	5 doubles: £110–£150.
	Extra bed/sofabed £35–£40 pp.p.p.n.
Meals	Local restaurants within half a mile.
Closed	One week over Christmas.
Directions	M27, junc. 1, then A337 south for Lymington. Right onto B3055 as you approach Brockenhurst. Over x-roads and signed left after half a mile.

Cheryl & Ciaran Maher
Daisybank Cottage Boutique B&B
Sway Road,
Brockenhurst, SO42 7SG

Tel	+44 (0)1590 622086
Email	info@bedandbreakfast-newforest.co.uk
Web	www.bedandbreakfast-newforest.co.uk

Entry 102   Map 3

The Master Builder's House Hotel

The position here is hard to beat: lawns run down to the river, yacht masts flutter in the breeze, ancient woodland runs along the water, soundproofing this beautiful landscape. As for the house, it dates to 1729 and was home to the shipwrights who built Nelson's fleet; several ships built here saw action at Trafalgar. These days peace reigns. A chic sitting room opens onto a smart garden, where gravel paths weave past colourful beds to tables for lunch in the sun. There's a lovely old bar and an airy restaurant — both have terraces that drink in the view, and both serve tasty local fare, too, perhaps a pizza or posh fish and chips in the bar, perhaps smoked rabbit chorizo, pot au feu with local veg, salted butterscotch crème brûlée in the restaurant. Bedrooms in the main house have big views, Indian furniture, then colour and character in spades. Those in the annexe, recently refurbished (a few await their turn), come in crisp blues and whites, with a wall of wood, Bose sound systems and excellent walk-in showers. As for the New Forest, walk, cycle or kayak though it. A great forest base. *Minimum stay: 2 nights at weekends*

Rooms	Main House – 8 doubles: £95-£320. Annexe – 9 doubles, 9 twin/doubles: £95-£320. 2 cottages for 4: £205. Singles from £100.
Meals	Lunch from £5. Dinner, in bar from £12; in restaurant, 3 courses, £30-£35. Afternoon tea from £15. Sunday lunch £19.95-£23.95.
Closed	Never.
Directions	From Lyndhurst B3056 south past Beaulieu turn-off. 1st left, signed Buckler's Hard. Signed left after 1 mile.

Clive Watts
The Master Builder's House Hotel
Buckler's Hard, Beaulieu,
Brockenhurst, SO42 7XB

Tel	+44 (0)1590 616253
Email	enquiries@themasterbuilders.co.uk
Web	www.themasterbuilders.co.uk

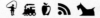

The Montagu Arms Hotel

Beaulieu, an ancient royal hunting ground, was gifted to Cistercian monks by King John in 1204. Their abbey took 40 years to build and you can see its ruins in the nearby grounds of Palace House, seat of the Montagu family since 1538. As for the village, its tiny high street is a hotchpotch of 17th-century timber-framed houses that totter by the tidal estuary drinking in the view. The hotel dates to 1742, but was re-modelled in 1925 and interiors have an Edwardian country-house feel. You'll find roaring fires, parquet flooring, a library bar and a courtyard garden, where you can eat in summer. Traditional bedrooms vary in size, but all come with pretty fabrics, period furniture, good bathrooms, a sofa if there's room. Downstairs, a Michelin star in the dining room brings with it some fabulous food, so try Dover sole with brown shrimps, saddle of roe deer with parsnip purée, praline soufflé with dark chocolate ice-cream. There's a gastro pub if you want something lighter: local fish pie, great steaks, ham and chips with poached eggs from resident hens. Beautiful walks start from the front door. *Minimum stay: 2 nights at weekends.*

Rooms	7 doubles, 3 twin/doubles, 4 four-posters: £157-£317. 5 suites for 2: £257-£377. Singles £129-£189. Dinner, B&B £277-£478 p.p.
Meals	Lunch & dinner, 3 courses, £75. Tasting menu £90. Set lunch menu, 2-3 courses £22.50-£30. Sunday lunch menu, 2-3 courses £32.50-£37.50.
Closed	Never.
Directions	South from M27, junc. 1 to Lyndhurst on A337, then B3056 for Beaulieu. Left into village and hotel on right.

Sunil Kanjanghat
The Montagu Arms Hotel
Palace Lane, Beaulieu,
Brockenhurst, SO42 7ZL

Tel	+44 (0)1590 612324
Email	reservations@montaguarmshotel.co.uk
Web	www.montaguarmshotel.co.uk

The Verzon

This English auberge has a cute rustic style and serves some seriously good food. It sits on the Hereford to Ledbury road and is owned by Will and Kate Chase, farmers who turn their potatoes and apples into Chase vodka and gin. Not that this is the limit of their world. They also rear cattle and pigs and have a vineyard in the Lubéron. The Verzon exists to bring it all together – a gin and tonic on the terrace in summer, then a lovely dinner washed down by French wines. Most of the food is sourced within 30 miles, perhaps a hoppy Hereford rarebit, a perfect Chase steak, an ambrosial pecan tart with espresso mousse. Interiors mix old and new playfully, with timber frames and Union-Jack sofas in the bar, then a white marble fireplace in the theatrical dining room. Bedrooms have warm colours, crisp linen and robes in fine bathrooms. Two have baths in the room, those at the back have views over fields to the Malvern Hills. Local ales and a roaring fire wait in the bar, while the Chase distillery is up the road, with tours easily arranged. Don't miss Hereford cathedral for the Mappa Mundi.

Rooms	4 twin/doubles: £90-£140. 3 suites for 2: £160-£180. 1 single: £80. Extra beds £15.
Meals	Lunch from £12. Dinner, 3 courses, £30-£40. Sunday lunch £22-£27. Afternoon tea from £15.
Closed	Never.
Directions	A438 west from Ledbury for 4 miles. On right, signed.

Will & Kate Chase
The Verzon
Hereford Road, Trumpet,
Ledbury, HR8 2PZ

Tel	+44 (0)1531 670381
Email	info@verzonhouse.com
Web	www.verzonhouse.com

Castle House

Hereford's loveliest hotel stands 200 paces from the city's magnificent 11th-century cathedral, home to the Mappa Mundi. It's English to its core with a beautiful garden that overlooks what remains of the castle moat – in summer you can eat here watching ducks glide by. Inside, the lap of luxury: a fine staircase, painted panelling, a delicious restaurant for the best food in town. Big bedrooms are lavish. Those in the main house are more traditional (the top-floor suite runs all the way along the front of the house); those in the townhouse (a 30-second stroll) are distinctly 21st century. All have a smart country-house feel with beautiful fabrics, super-comfy beds, crisp white linen, excellent bathrooms. Seriously good food, much from the owner's nearby farm, waits in the restaurant, perhaps beetroot panna cotta, roast bream with saffron mash, banana mousse with chocolate brownies. You can walk it off along the river Wye, which runs through the park behind. Hereford has lots to offer: pop-up opera, guided walks, Evensong in the cathedral, the Three Choirs Festival in July.

Rooms	4 doubles: £150–£190.
	16 suites for 2: £195–£250.
	4 singles: £130.
Meals	Lunch from £5.
	Dinner, 3 courses, about £35.
	Sunday lunch from £18.50.
Closed	Never.
Directions	Follow signs to Hereford city centre, then City Centre east. Right off Bath St into Union St, through St Peters Sq to Owen's St, then right into St Ethelbert St. Hotel on left as road veers right.

Michelle Marriott-Lodge
Castle House
Castle Street,
Hereford, HR1 2NW

Tel	+44 (0)1432 356321
Email	info@castlehse.co.uk
Web	www.castlehse.co.uk

Brooks County House

Led Zeppelin used to stay here when recording at studios on a nearby farm, and there's definitely a bit of a rock-star feel to the place. A big house in the country, a swimming pool in the kitchen garden and its own vineyard that produces wine for the restaurant... There's a rather good view, too, a clean sweep over ten miles of rolling country to rising mountains. The house once stood in 1,000 acres and now has a mere 12, but the land beyond is owned by the National Trust and you can walk straight out, skirt a copse and find yourself at a 14th-century church. As for the hotel, it's going to make a small splash – Andrew and Carla are far too down-to-earth for anything bigger. It's a total refurbishment – smart, but relaxed, a place to feel at home. Expect an open fire in the sitting room, wood floors in the restaurant, then cowhide rugs in a bar that opens onto a sun-trapping garden. Nicely priced rooms are scattered about, some grander, others smaller, all with good beds, warm colours and lovely bathrooms. As for the food, it's earthy stuff: homemade soups, a local rib-eye, a sinful chocolate tart. Hard to beat. *Minimum stay: 2 nights at weekends.*

Rooms	14 twin/doubles, 6 four-posters: £69-£169. 2 suites for 2: £99-£169. Singles from £59. Dinner, B&B from £85 p.p. Extra bed/sofabed available £10-£20 p.p.p.n.
Meals	Dinner £18-£24 (not Sundays). Sunday lunch from £19-£23.
Closed	Never.
Directions	West from Ross-on-Wye on A49. Through Peterstow and hotel signed right after 1 mile.

Carla & Andrew Brooks
Brooks County House
Pengethley Park,
Ross-on-Wye, HR9 6LL

Tel   +44 (0)1989 730211
Email   info@brookscountryhouse.com
Web   www.brookscountryhouse.com

The Bridge House

Kevin and Kathryn left high-flying jobs to cook, clean, polish and shine; extraordinarily, they couldn't be happier. Their new home is this attractive 17th-century merchant's house with the best view in town – lawns run down to the river Wye, then views shoot up the other side to St Mary's church. Inside, you find original elm floors and painted beamed ceilings, but the feel is contemporary, with cool colours, beautiful armchairs and antler chandeliers in the sitting room. Bedrooms have an easy elegance: comfy beds, crisp linen, pretty art, the odd timber frame. Four have the view, two have a claw-foot bath, others have power showers; a couple at the front face the road. Delicious breakfasts set you up for the day, so walk in the hills, kayak on the Wye, mountain bike in the Forest of Dean. Come home to an honesty bar in the sitting room, then a decked terrace amid beds of colour in the well-kept garden – a lovely spot for tea in the sun. Wilton Castle, a 12th-century ruin, stands across the field; Hereford is close for the Mappa Mundi; good restaurants are a short stroll. Dogs are welcome. *Minimum stay: 2 nights at weekends.*

Rooms	6 doubles: £95–£125.
	Singles from £70.
Meals	Restaurants within walking distance.
Closed	December – January.
Directions	Leave A40 in Wilton for B4260, signed Ross-on-Wye. On left after 250m.

	Kevin & Kathryn Whyte
	The Bridge House
	Wilton,
	Ross-on-Wye, HR9 6AA
Tel	+44 (0)1989 562655
Email	info@bridgehouserossonwye.co.uk
Web	www.bridgehouserossonwye.co.uk

Wilton Court Restaurant with Rooms

This Grade-II listed house dates to 1510 and looks across the lane to the river Wye: herons dive, otters swim, kingfishers nest. Roses ramble outside, happy guests potter within. This is a small hotel with pretty rooms, good food and owners that care. Bedrooms upstairs come in different shapes and sizes, but all have style. Those at the front have watery views, William Morris wallpaper, lots of space, perhaps a four-poster. A couple of rooms are small (as is their price), but, along with several others, have recently been refurbished. Expect lots of colour, a wall of paper, white bathrooms and sofas in the bigger rooms. Back downstairs there's a bar for pre-dinner drinks, a wood-burner in the panelled library, then a conservatory restaurant for tasty food, perhaps Shropshire blue cheese soufflé, Herefordshire beef with savoy cabbage, caramel panna cotta with vanilla ice cream. Berries from a Grade-I listed mulberry tree in the garden are turned into sorbets and pies. You can cross the lane to a second garden for drinks by the river in summer. Ross is a five-minute stroll. *Minimum stay: 2 nights at weekends.*

Rooms	4 doubles, 5 twin/doubles, 1 four-poster: £135-£185. 1 family room for 4: £165-£205. Singles from £100.
Meals	Lunch snacks from £6.95. Lunch, 2-3 courses, £16.95-£19.95. Dinner: 2-3 courses, £27.50-£32.50; 3 course à la carte £35-£40.
Closed	Rarely.
Directions	South into Ross at A40/A49 Wilton roundabout. 1st right into Wilton Lane. Hotel on right.

Roger & Helen Wynn
Wilton Court Restaurant with Rooms
Wilton Lane, Wilton,
Ross-on-Wye, HR9 6AQ

Tel	+44 (0)1989 562569
Email	info@wiltoncourthotel.com
Web	www.wiltoncourthotel.com

The George Hotel

You get the best of two worlds here – the loveliest hotel on the island and the prettiest town, too. Yarmouth has the feel of a seaside village from the 1960s. As for the George, it's been around for over 400 years and has never looked better. Dianne bought the place recently and has poured in love and money, restoring former glories; Charles II stayed in 1671, but he didn't have it this good. Step off the street and find yourself in a grand hall, where flowers scent the air. Outside, a beautiful garden and terrace roll down to the Solent; it's flanked on one side by the east wall of Yarmouth Castle, a perfect spot for lunch in the sun. Inside, panelled walls wait in an elegant sitting room, then a roaring fire in the beautiful bar with pop art on the walls. Two restaurants keep you happy: a brasserie that opens onto the terrace; then Isla's for some serious food, perhaps hand-dived scallops, roasted brill, caramelised banana bavarois. Bedrooms are gorgeous. Four have been refurbished, others will follow soon. Expect smart beds, fabulous bathrooms, perhaps a balcony for sea views.

Rooms	17 twin/doubles: £195–£375. Singles £180. Extra bed/sofabed available £25 p.p.p.n.
Meals	Lunch from £6. Dinner, in the brasserie from £14.50; 3 courses in the restaurant £65. The Conservatory serves an à la carte menu, lunch & dinner, £6–£35.
Closed	Rarely.
Directions	Lymington ferry to Yarmouth, then follow signs to town centre.

The George Hotel
The George Hotel
Quay Street,
Yarmouth, PO41 0PE

Tel	+44 (0)1983 760331
Email	info@thegeorge.co.uk
Web	www.thegeorge.co.uk

Hillside

A lovely small hotel with a cool Scandinavian feel that stands at the foot of forested hills with fine views over Ventnor and out to sea. Outside, five and a half acres of lawn, field and woodland with beehives, Hebridean sheep, red squirrels and white doves; there's an extensive kitchen garden, too, that provides much for the table. Inside, a pristine wonderland in white. There's a cosy bar with books, newspapers and a wood-burner, a sitting room/gallery with Danish leather sofas, a conservatory that opens onto a manicured terrace, and an airy restaurant with great art on the walls. Spotless bedrooms upstairs have a smart, uncluttered feel with comfy beds, vintage throws, more good art and lovely bathrooms. Those at the front look out to sea. Back downstairs, tasty food flies from the kitchen. The hotel has a share in a local fishing boat and lands its own fish, rears its own cattle in nearby fields and harvests fresh vegetables from the kitchen garden. It also has a bistro with an open-kitchen in town, so you can make the most of two culinary worlds. Beaches, gardens and the coastal path wait. *Minimum stay: 2 nights at weekends.*

Rooms	6 doubles, 2 twin/doubles, 1 twin: £156–£196. 3 singles: £78–£143. 2 apartments for 4: £206–£292. Dinner, B&B from £108 p.p.
Meals	Dinner £21–£25. Bistro from £12 (in town).
Closed	Never.
Directions	South to Ventnor on A3055, then right (on approach to town) onto B3277. Past tennis courts, up hill, on right.

Gert Bach
Hillside
151 Mitchell Avenue,
Ventnor, PO38 1DR

Tel	+44 (0)1983 852271
Email	mail@hillsideventnor.co.uk
Web	www.hillsideventnor.co.uk

Entry 112   Map 3

Hever Castle Luxury Bed & Breakfast

Hever is out of this world, a 13th-century moated castle that was home to Anne Boleyn, second wife to Henry VIII, mother of Elizabeth I. It is one of those places that thrills at every turn. It has all the regal trimmings: 625 acres of green and pleasant land with formal gardens and a 38-acre lake. You either stay in the Astor Wing or the Anne Boleyn wing, both built in Tudor style in 1903. Bedrooms are fit for a queen. Expect period colours, panelled walls, perhaps a golden chaise longue or a glimpse of the castle through leaded windows. Lots have pretty wallpaper, one has a vaulted ceiling, several have four-poster beds, while bigger rooms have sofas. Bathrooms are faultless, some with claw-foot baths, others with walk-in power showers; a few have both. There's a panelled sitting room, a timber-framed billiard room, and a small courtyard for summer sun, but don't linger too long – entrance to the castle and gardens is included in your room price. You can boat on the lake, have picnic dinners, they even host the odd spot of jousting. The village pub for a good dinner is a short stroll. Unbeatable.

Rooms	22 doubles, 3 twins: £155-£205.
	2 singles: £105-£120.
	Extra bed/sofabed available £50 p.p.p.n.
Meals	Picnic lunches by arrangement.
	Restaurants within 0.25 miles.
Closed	Rarely.
Directions	Castle signed west out of Edenbridge.

Roland Smith
Hever Castle Luxury Bed & Breakfast
Hever,
Edenbridge, TN8 7NG

Tel	+44 (0)1732 861800
Email	stay@hevercastle.co.uk
Web	www.hevercastle.co.uk

The Milk House

The gardens at Sissinghurst Castle were designed by Vita Sackville-West. They're some of the loveliest in the land and if you stay at this cute village pub, you can stroll over after breakfast, via apple orchards and bluebell woods. As for The Milk House, its a great base from which to explore this deeply rural area – stylish, welcoming, nicely priced. It's also a place for a very good meal, seasonal and mostly sourced within 20 miles. In summer, you decant onto a smart terrace with an outside bar and wood-fired pizza oven, not a bad spot for a jug of Pimm's and a crispy margherita. There's a duck pond, too, lawns for a pint in the sun, then views over open country. Airy interiors have an easy style: woven willow lampshades hanging above the bar, a timber-framed dining room, where you dig into fabulous food, perhaps home-cured smoked salmon, free-range Park Farm beef, chocolate tart with kirsch-soaked cherries; there are matchless local cheeses, too. Beautiful bedrooms are crisply uncluttered. Expect chic fabrics, relaxing colours, excellent bathrooms and a sofa if there's room.

Rooms	3 doubles, 1 twin: £80–£140. Extra bed/sofabed available £10 p.p.p.n.
Meals	Lunch from £5. Dinner, 3 courses, from £35. Sunday lunch from £15.
Closed	Rarely.
Directions	East into Sissinghurst on A262. In village, on left.

Dane & Sarah Allchorne
The Milk House
The Street, Sissinghurst,
Cranbrook, TN17 2JG

Tel	+44 (0)1580 720200
Email	fresh@themilkhouse.co.uk
Web	www.themilkhouse.co.uk

Cloth Hall Oast

This attractive Kentish oast house dates to 1780 and sits in peace a mile across the fields from Cranbrook. Mrs Morgan, the star of the show, lived in the 15th-century manor next door for 40 years; now she's turned her perfectionist's eye upon these five acres. The garden is beautiful – well-groomed lawns, a carp-filled pond, pergola, summer house, heated swimming pool, flower beds full of colour. You breakfast grandly at a mahogany table with the hall open to the rafters above, a sparkling chandelier hanging gracefully, a grand piano on the minstrels' gallery; in good weather you nip outside and eat on the deck overlooking the pond. Three bedrooms wait: a circular four-poster in the roundel on the ground floor, then a family room and a small double above. Colours are soft, fabrics are frilled, but nothing is busy or overdone. You'll find spotless bathrooms, fine mattresses, crisp linen, flowered chintz. In summer, the pool is yours, with sun loungers to take the strain. There are good local pubs for dinner and a Michelin starred restaurant in the village. Sissinghurst Gardens are close. *No credit cards.*

Rooms	1 double, 1 four-poster: £95-£135. 1 family room for 3: £125-£135.
Meals	Dinner from £25, by arrangement. Pub & restaurant 1 mile.
Closed	Christmas.
Directions	Leave village with windmill on left, taking Golford Road east for Tenterden. After a mile right, before cemetery. Signed right.

Katherine Morgan
Cloth Hall Oast
Course Horn Lane,
Cranbrook, TN17 3NR

Tel	+44 (0)1580 712220
Email	clothhalloast@aol.com
Web	www.clothhalloast.co.uk

The Relish

It's not just the super-comfy interiors that make The Relish such a tempting port of call. There's a sense of generosity here: a drink on the house each night in the sitting room; tea and cakes on tap all day; free internet throughout. This is a grand 1850s merchant's house on the posh side of town – lovely old bricks and mortar, softly contemporary interiors. Laura and Rakesh took over recently and have already pulled out the paintbrushes, so wind up the cast-iron staircase to find bedrooms that make you smile. You get Hypnos beds with padded headboards, crisp white linen and pretty throws. There's a sense of space, a sofa if there's room, big mirrors and lovely bathrooms. All are great value for money. Downstairs candles flicker on the mantelpieces above an open fire, the high-ceilinged dining room comes with stripped floors and padded benches and in summer you can decamp onto the terrace for breakfast, a communal garden stretching out beyond. You're one street back from Folkestone's cliff-top front for big sea views. Steps lead down to smart gardens, the promenade and waterside restaurants. *Minimum stay: 2 nights at weekends in summer.*

Rooms	9 doubles: £98–£150.
	1 single: £75.
Meals	Restaurants nearby.
Closed	22 December to 2 January.
Directions	In centre of town, from Langholm Gardens, head west on Sandgate Road. 1st right into Augusta Gardens/Trinity Gardens. Hotel on right.

Laura & Rakesh Sharma
The Relish
4 Augusta Gardens,
Folkestone, CT20 2RR
Tel   +44 (0)1303 850952
Email   reservations@hotelrelish.co.uk
Web   www.hotelrelish.co.uk

Albion House

This is quite some house, a Regency pile that dates to 1790, with huge rooms, high ceilings and grandeur at every turn. It stands at the top of a hill in the middle of town with fine views over the Royal Harbour. Incredibly, it was left to decay by its last inhabitants, Ramsgate Town Council, whose headquarters this was until 2008. Now, after a long renovation, interiors shine, mixing contemporary design with the feel of a colonial gentleman's club. There's a fire in reception, watery views through big windows in the restaurant, then a fabulous bar with a grand piano, exotic pot plants, a roaring fire, and sofas everywhere. Classical prints are jammed on the wall, the bar itself came from the town hall. The whole place is a work of art, nothing is here by accident. Downstairs, there's a treatment room, a steam room, a meeting room that doubles as a cinema, then a vaulted cavern for wine tastings. Big bedrooms get smaller as you climb the house, but the best views are at the top. Expect good beds, crisp linen, neutral colours, robes in white marble bathrooms. Don't miss afternoon tea. Brilliant. *Minimum stay: 2 nights in high season. Pets by arrangement.*

Rooms	12 twin/doubles, 1 four-poster: £125–£220. 1 suite for 2: £180–£345. Dinner, B&B £80–£170 p.p.
Meals	Lunch from £14. Afternoon tea £14. Dinner, 3 courses, £25–£35. Sunday lunch from £16.
Closed	Rarely.
Directions	M2, A299, then B2054 into Ramsgate. Follow signs for town centre, pick up coast on right, down hill, up the other side, on left at top.

Ben & Emma Irvine
Albion House
Albion Place,
Ramsgate, CT11 8HQ

Tel	+44 (0)1843 606630
Email	enquiries@albionhouseramsgate.co.uk
Web	www.albionhouseramsgate.co.uk

Sands Hotel Margate

Hoteliers don't do things by halves, and Nick is a case in point. He bought a crumbling pile, knocked the place down, then built it back up again. The result is a delicious hotel with huge views of beach and sea, a view framed triumphantly by walls of glass in the enormous restaurant and bar. Coastal light floods the room, there's a balcony for afternoon tea, three chandeliers hanging above the bar, crushed velvet banquettes to salute Victorian roots and, with Turner Contemporary a five-minute stroll along the seafront, big canvases that resemble the great man's work. Bedrooms have bags of style; nine have sea views, six have balconies and all have chic fabrics, padded bedheads, smart TVs and robes in fine bathrooms. There's a roof terrace above for the best views in town and an ice-cream parlour and pizzeria below, but you'll want to stop in the middle for the food as well as the view; perhaps gin and juniper-cured salmon, or confit pork belly with candied apple, finished off with a spiced pineapple tarte tatin. Canterbury, Broadstairs and Ramsgate are close and the train from Victoria takes less than two hours. *Minimum stay: 2 nights at weekends in high season.*

Rooms	10 doubles, 10 twin/doubles: £120–£210. Dinner, B&B £95–£130 p.p. Extra bed/sofabed £20–£40 p.p.p.n.
Meals	Lunch from £11.50. Dinner, 3 courses, £35. Cream tea £6.50. Full afternoon tea £14.95.
Closed	Never.
Directions	A28 into Margate. Keep straight ahead with the coast on your left and hotel on right at end of beach.

Nick Conington
Sands Hotel Margate
16 Marine Drive,
Margate, CT9 1DH

Tel	+44 (0)1843 228228
Email	info@sandshotelmargate.co.uk
Web	www.sandshotelmargate.co.uk

Read's Restaurant with Rooms

A gorgeous country-house restaurant with rooms, Read's stands in five acres of lawned grounds with a half-acre kitchen garden that supplies much for the table. Inside, you find warm elegance at every turn. There's a sitting room bar for pre-dinner drinks, then a couple of beautiful dining rooms where you eat at smartly clothed tables surrounded by ornamental fireplaces and lots of good art. As for the food, it's some of the best in Kent. David and Rona came here 33 years ago, and locals and travellers come for their delicious delights: a hot soufflé of Montgomery's Cheddar on a bed of smoked haddock, local venison with pickled pears and walnut croquettes, a chestnut and whisky parfait with toasted hazelnuts and Seville orange curd meringues. The bedrooms are just as good – country-house splendour in spades. Expect decanters of sherry, Roberts radios, huge beds dressed in crisp white linen, wonderful bathrooms with robes to pad about in. Canterbury, Whitstable and Leeds Castle are close, as is Rochester for all things Dickens.

Rooms	5 doubles, 1 twin/double: £165–£195. Singles from £125. Dinner, B&B from £135 p.p.
Meals	Lunch £28. Dinner £60.
Closed	Sunday & Monday. 1st week in January, 1st 2 weeks in September.
Directions	M2, junc. 7, then A2 west into Faversham. Past petrol station and signed left after 400m.

David & Rona Pitchford
Read's Restaurant with Rooms
Macknade Manor, Canterbury Road,
Faversham, ME13 8XE

Tel	+44 (0)1795 535344
Email	enquiries@reads.com
Web	www.reads.com

The Inn at Whitewell

It is almost impossible to imagine a day when a better inn will grace the English landscape. Everything here is perfect. The inn sits just above the river Hodder, and doors in the bar lead onto a terrace where guests can enjoy five-mile views across parkland to rising fells. Inside, fires roar, newspapers wait, there are beams, sofas, maps and copies of *Wisden*. Bedrooms, some in the Coach House, are exemplary and come with real luxury, perhaps a peat fire, a lavish four-poster, a fabulous Victorian power shower. All have beautiful fabrics, top linen and gadgets galore; many have the marvellous view – you can fall asleep at night to the sound of the river. There are bar meals for those who want to watch their weight (the Whitewell fish pie is rightly famous) or a restaurant for splendid food, so dig into seared scallops, Bowland lamb, a plate of local cheese (the Queen once popped in for lunch). Elsewhere, a wine shop in reception, seven miles of private fishing and countryside as good as any in the land. Dogs and children are very welcome. Magnificent.

Rooms	17 doubles, 5 twin/doubles: £120-£215. 1 suite for 2: £210-£240. Singles £92-204.
Meals	Bar meals from £8. Dinner £25-£35.
Closed	Never.
Directions	M6 junc. 31A, B6243 east through Longridge, then follow signs to Whitewell for 9 miles.

Charles Bowman
The Inn at Whitewell
Dunsop Road, Whitewell,
Clitheroe, BB7 3AT

Tel	+44 (0)1200 448222
Email	reception@innatwhitewell.com
Web	www.innatwhitewell.com

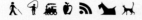

The Cartford Inn

Patrick and Julie know how to run a great little inn: whisk up some fabulous food, throw in a pinch of quirky style, then add lovely bedrooms and serve informally. The inn stands on the banks of the river Wyre – views from the restaurant drift upstream with the Trough of Bowland looming beyond. The front bar, with its cool art, roaring fire and friendly locals, is a great place to stop for a pint of local ale, though a courtyard garden will draw you out in good weather. In typically relaxed style you can eat whatever you want wherever you want, perhaps a smoked black pudding doughnut, oxtail and beef pudding with green beans and mash, a crème caramel with banana crisp. Bedrooms are just as good – gilded sleigh beds, signature wallpapers, crisp white linen and river views. All have lovely bathrooms with REN lotions, two have roll-top baths in the room, the penthouse suite has a shower for two and a rooftop terrace. You can walk by the river – a two-mile circular walk will spin you round – head east into the Yorkshire Dales, or spin off to Blackpool and jump on a rollercoaster.

Rooms	10 doubles, 1 twin: £120–£130.
	1 suite for 2: £200.
	2 family rooms for 3–4: £140.
	Singles from £65.
Meals	Lunch from £8.50, not Mon.
	Dinner, 3 courses, £25–£35.
Closed	Christmas Day.
Directions	M6 junc. 32, M55 junc. 3, then A585 north. Right at T-junction onto A586 for Garstang. Little Eccleston signed left.

Patrick & Julie Beaume
The Cartford Inn
Cartford Lane, Little Eccleston,
Preston, PR3 0YP

Tel	+44 (0)1995 670166
Email	info@thecartfordinn.co.uk
Web	www.thecartfordinn.co.uk

The William Cecil

This attractive townhouse hotel stands yards from the gates of the Burghley estate. Inside, interiors offer a pleasing mix of English quirkiness and splendour. Downstairs, informality reigns. There are armchairs in front of the fire in the bar, smart wicker tables in the conservatory, doors onto a lovely terrace in summer, then hanging lamps and half-panelling in the colourful restaurant. The food is fresh and local with seasonal delights that include game from the estate. You might find lobster mousse with avocado ice-cream, slow-cooked Burghley venison casserole, lemon curd pie with lime sorbet. You can walk it all off with a stroll through historic Stamford or spin over to Burghley for one of the finest Elizabethan houses in the realm. Come back to country-house bedrooms that mix eclectic Rajasthan furniture with a little English decorum. You'll find beautiful art, a wall of paper, perhaps a day bed or a ceiling rose. Some have views onto the estate, all have good bathrooms, the best with roll top tubs and vast walk-in showers. Dogs don't fare badly either with Union Jack beds.

Rooms	20 doubles, 7 twin/doubles: £100–£180.
Meals	Lunch from £6.50. Dinner from £12. Sunday lunch, 3 courses, £24.50.
Closed	Never.
Directions	A1 north past Easton-on-the-Hill, then B1081 for Stamford. On right as you enter town.

Paul Brown
The William Cecil
St Martins,
Stamford, PE9 2LJ

Tel	+44 (0)1780 750070
Email	enquiries@thewilliamcecil.co.uk
Web	www.thewilliamcecil.co.uk

Washingborough Hall

In its day Lincoln was one of the most important cities in England. Its castle holds a copy of the Magna Carta and was built by William the Conqueror in 1068; its cathedral dates to 1090 and remains one of the finest in Europe. All of which makes it a great city to visit, and if you want to beat a peaceful retreat into the country at the end of the day, this is the place to stay. It sits two miles east of town in a small village on the river Witham – footpaths by the water lead back into town. As for this Georgian rectory, you'll find smart lawns to the front, then a big welcome within – Edward and Lucy go out of their way to make your stay special. There's a wood-burner in the hall, a breakfast room with garden views, a sitting-room bar for afternoon tea, then a light-filled orangery restaurant. Stylish bedrooms offer unstinting comforts. Rooms at the front are bigger and have the view, all have good beds, bold wallpapers, excellent bathrooms, a sofa if there's room. As for the food, there's posh fish and chips in the bar or sea bass with spring greens in the orangery.

Rooms	6 doubles, 3 twin/doubles, 2 four-posters: £85-£175. Singles from £75.
Meals	Lunch from £5.50. Dinner, 3 courses, £25-£35. Sunday lunch from £18.50.
Closed	Never.
Directions	East out of Lincoln on B1190. In village, right at mini r'bout onto Church Hill. On left after 500m.

Lucy & Edward Herring
Washingborough Hall
Church Hill,
Washingborough, LN4 1BE

Tel	+44 (0)1522 790340
Email	enquiries@washingboroughhall.com
Web	www.washingboroughhall.com

The Castle Hotel

Lincoln, a medieval powerhouse, has been at the centre of British life for 2,000 years. Romans, Vikings and Normans have ruled it, the cathedral is one of the finest in Europe, an original copy of the Magna Carta sits in its castle. All of which makes the city a great short break and where else to stay than this lovely hotel. It stands in the old town with views to the front of the castle's enormous walls and the cathedral's towers soaring two streets east. Interiors have a soft, contemporary feel, with an airy bar in reception and a stylish restaurant for excellent food, perhaps salt and pepper squid, pork belly with spicy chorizo, caramelised banana tarte tatin. Smart bedrooms are nicely priced. Expect warm colours, chic fabrics, padded bedheads, excellent bathrooms. Lincoln's wonders wait: the castle and its dungeon, the jaw-dropping cathedral, then Steep Hill (for old-world tearooms), which leads down to Brayford Pool, where you can sit on café terraces and watch the world go by. The Christmas market in December is one of the best in Britain. Come by train, it's only two hours from London.

Rooms	17 twin/doubles: £110-£130.
	1 suite for 2: £140.
	2 cottages for 2: £220.
	Dinner, B&B from £90 p.p.
Meals	Lunch from £4.50. Bar meals from £10.
	Dinner £30-£35.
	Sunday lunch from £12.95.
Closed	24-26 December.
Directions	Sent on booking.

Paul Catlow & Saera Ahmad
The Castle Hotel
Westgate,
Lincoln, LN1 3AS

Tel	+44 (0)1522 538801
Email	info@castlehotel.net
Web	www.castlehotel.net

The New Inn

The North Lincolnshire wolds pass most people by – too remote, wrong part of the country. Yet browse Google images and you find an unblemished corner of England: sweeping fields, ancient woodlands, old England trapped in aspic. This attractive Georgian inn sits in a village on the Brocklesby Estate, seat of the Earls of Yarborough; parkland walks past temples and monuments start from the front door. As for the inn, country-house interiors have a smart, contemporary feel with antiques and period art from the big house, then red banquettes and an open fire in the local's bar. You'll find fresh flowers, a library bar, paved terraces for summer sun, then some lovely local food, perhaps Lincoln red beef, organic vegetables from the estate's kitchen garden, rhubarb and cinnamon crumble with vanilla ice cream. Rooms in the main house have period colours, smart fabrics, perhaps a grand armoire or a claw-foot bath. Those in the converted barn are more contemporary, with cool colours, local photography and big power showers. Free-range eggs for breakfast come straight from the estate. Worth a detour.

Rooms	8 doubles, 2 twin/doubles: £80–£135. Dinner, B&B from £70 p.p.
Meals	Lunch from £4. Dinner, 3 courses, £25–£35. Not Sunday eve or Monday lunch. Sunday lunch from £18.95.
Closed	Never.
Directions	North from Lincoln on A15, then east on M180. Exit at junc. 5 and take A18 east for 5 miles. In village, on right.

Chloë Kirkby
The New Inn
2 High Street,
Great Limber, DN37 8JL
Tel   +44 (0)1469 569998
Email   enquiries@thenewinngreatlimber.co.uk
Web   www.thenewinngreatlimber.co.uk

The Levin Hotel

A great London base for shopaholics – Harrods waits at one end of the street, Harvey Nicks at the other. As for the hotel, it sits quietly on Basil Street, a peaceful retreat in the middle of Knightsbridge. There's no sitting room, but a lively café/bar/restaurant, which acts as the social hub. Bedrooms spread over four floors with a lift to carry you up, though you may prefer to walk – a contemporary chandelier with an 18-metre drop fills the stairwell. As for the rooms, some are bigger, others smaller, but all have the same chic style: bold colours, Art Nouveau furnishings, hand-stitched beds, white marble bathrooms. Bigger rooms have sofas, all have Bose radios, flat-screen TVs, white robes and beautiful linen. You can breakfast on croissants from the owner's bakery, nip back early for afternoon tea, or dine on lovely comfort food, perhaps salmon fishcakes, shepherd's pie, Eton mess with mixed berries. If that's not enough, there's a Michelin star next door at the Capital (their sister hotel). All rooms are air conditioned, there's a full concierge service and iPads are available at reception. *Pets by arrangement.*

Rooms	3 doubles, 8 twin/doubles: £245–£479. 1 suite for 2: £395–£619. Extra bed/sofabed available £45 p.p.p.n.
Meals	Lunch from £5.50. Dinner, 3 courses, about £30. Afternoon tea from £22.99.
Closed	Never.
Directions	Tube: Knightsbridge (for Heathrow). Station: Victoria (for Gatwick). Bus: 09, 10, 19, 22, 52, 137, C1. Parking: £45 a day.

	Harald Duttine
	The Levin Hotel
	28 Basil Street,
	Knightsbridge, SW3 1AS
Tel	+44 (0)20 7589 6286
Email	reservations@thelevinhotel.co.uk
Web	www.thelevinhotel.co.uk

Lime Tree Hotel

You'll be hard pressed to find better value in the centre of town. The Lime Tree – two elegant Georgian townhouses – stands less than a mile from Buckingham Palace, with Westminster, Sloane Square and Piccadilly all a short stroll. Add warm interiors, kind owners and a smart gastropub waiting round the corner and you've unearthed a London gem. The airy dining room serves a mean breakfast and is soon to turn into a café, with light meals served throughout the day. Rooms are just the ticket: smart without being lavish, all with mod cons. Expect warm colours, crisp linen, attractive wallpaper and excellent bathrooms (most have big showers). One on the ground floor has doors onto the garden; others on first floor have high ceilings; those at the top (a few stairs!) are cosy in the eaves; rooms at the back are the quietest. Charlotte and Matt are hands-on and will point you in the right direction, while there's a tiny sitting room for guide books and a computer for guests to use. The Thomas Cubitt pub – 50 paces from the front door – serves great food. A very handy base for the Chelsea Flower Show. *Minimum stay: 2 nights at weekends*

Rooms	12 doubles, 4 twins: £180-£210. 6 singles: £120-£160. 3 triples: £230.
Meals	Restaurants nearby.
Closed	Never.
Directions	Train: Victoria (to Gatwick). Tube: Victoria or Sloane Square. Bus: 11, 24, 38, 52, 73, C1. Parking: £34 a day off-street.

Charlotte & Matt Goodsall
Lime Tree Hotel
135 Ebury Street,
Belgravia SW1W 9QU

Tel	+44 (0)20 7730 8191
Email	info@limetreehotel.co.uk
Web	www.limetreehotel.co.uk

The Georgian House

Serena's great-great grandfather was commissioned by Thomas Cubitt to build this row of houses and liked the results so much he kept one for himself. They were built to rival Belgravia and have the same august credentials: pillars at the door, porticos and friezes, then high-ceilinged interiors as befits elegant Georgian architecture. Fast forward 160 years and the house, still in the same family, is now a B&B hotel, with a friendly brigade of international staff and a lovely sitting room in reception, where you can make a coffee and read the papers. As for the bedrooms, they have all been recently refurbished and are simply lovely: big, with white walls, a roll of paper, pretty fabrics, perhaps a sofa. Breakfast hits the spot with free-range eggs and Musk's sausages (also popular with Her Majesty). Why not enjoy it in the remodelled large, light dining room? You're close to Victoria (and the train to Gatwick) and Buckingham Palace. A couple of Harry Potter themed rooms are popular with younger guests.

Rooms	35 doubles, 12 triples: £99-£219. 4 family rooms for 4: £159-£239. 8 singles: £99-£155. Bower House – 7 doubles: £99-£219. Bower House – 3 singles: £99-£155. 2 apartments for 5, 2 apartments for 6: £259-£349.
Meals	Pubs/restaurants within walking distance.
Closed	Never.
Directions	Tube: Victoria, Pimlico, Sloane Square. Train: Victoria (for Gatwick). Bus: 6, 11, 16, 24, 38, 52, 73, 82, 185, 211, 239, C10

Serena von der Heyde
The Georgian House
35-37 St Georges Drive,
Pimlico, SW1V 4DG

Tel	+44 (0)20 7834 1438
Email	reception@georgianhousehotel.co.uk
Web	www.georgianhousehotel.co.uk

Entry 128 Map 3

Artist Residence London

This gorgeous small hotel is a bit of a game changer, a new template of British cool, a space designed wholly to exercise your pleasure receptors. It proves resoundingly that small is more beautiful than big ever can be and while large hotels will try to copy it, they'll fail to pull it off, unable to match the intimacy or the lovely staff who look after you all the way. So what do you get? A small slice of heaven between Pimlico and the King's Road. It's a phoenix from the ashes, a Thomas Cubitt pub recently rescued from neglect. Inside, you find fat sofas in front of a roaring fire in the sitting room; pop art and exposed brick walls in the cellar cocktail bar; then the Cambridge Street Kitchen, a lovely new restaurant serving excellent food – banana pancakes for breakfast, crab burgers for lunch and salt marsh lamb with toasted almonds for dinner. Bedrooms are flawless: cool art, chic fabrics, the best beds, power-showered bathrooms. Smaller rooms are divine, bigger rooms have sofas, the suites have free-standing baths. Buckingham Palace and Battersea Park are both close. Don't miss it.

Rooms	8 doubles: £170–£285.
	2 suites for 2: £295–£520.
Meals	Lunch from £9.50.
	Dinner, 3 courses, about £35.
Closed	Never.
Directions	Tube: Victoria, Pimlico, Sloane Square.
	Train: Victoria (for Gatwick).
	Bus: 6, 11, 16, 24, 38, 52, 73, 82, 185,
	211, 239, C10.

Charlie & Justin Salisbury
Artist Residence London
52 Cambridge Street,
Pimlico, SW1V 4QQ

Tel	+44 (0)20 7828 6684
Email	london@artistresidence.co.uk
Web	www.artistresidencelondon.co.uk

The Tommyfield

The Tommyfield is a cool little find – a lively pub for a good pint, a restaurant serving tasty food, a small hotel with well-priced rooms that deliver in spades. It sits between Vauxhall and Kennington, with two tube lines to whizz you into town and three buses passing outside. Inside, you find wooden floors, high ceilings and the odd ionic pillar. Lamps hang above the bar, where you can order a pint of Wandle, then dig into posh fish and chips. Leather banquettes run along big windows, an open kitchen is on display, a couple of booths are nicely private. Rooms are the big surprise, some with painted panelling, others with planked walls. You get pop art, good beds, coffee machines and flat-screen TVs. Excellent bathrooms have walk-in power showers, two have claw-foot baths. On weekdays a continental breakfast is left in your fridge, on weekends the full English is on tap below. As for the food – half-price for residents – pies, steaks and burgers sit alongside pumpkin ravioli, Chateaubriand and banoffee pie. Tuesday is quiz night, Oval is close for the cricket. *Cots available.*

Rooms	4 doubles, 2 twin/doubles: £99–£139.
Meals	Continental breakfast included, cooked breakfast on weekends £6–£9. Lunch & dinner from £12.50. Sunday lunch from £13.50. Food half-price for residents.
Closed	Never.
Directions	Tube: Vauxhall, Kennington, Oval (all a 5-minute walk). Bus: 3, 59, 159. Train: Vauxhall (for Gatwick/Victoria).

Daniel Glackin
The Tommyfield
185 Kennington Lane,
Kennington, SE11 4EZ

Tel	+44 (0)20 7735 1061
Email	info@thetommyfield.co.uk
Web	www.thetommyfield.com

Temple Lodge Club

Temple Lodge, once home to the painter Sir Frank Brangwyn, is sandwiched between a courtyard and a lushly landscaped garden. The peace is remarkable making it a very restful place – simple yet human and warmly comfortable, a nourishing experience. Michael and his devoted team run it with quiet energy. You breakfast overlooking the garden, there are newspapers to browse, a library instead of TVs. Bedrooms are surprisingly stylish: pretty art, crisp linen, no clutter, a hint of country chic. They're exceptional value for money, too, so book well in advance. Some rooms have garden views, only two have their own bathrooms and loo; if you don't mind that, you'll be happy. The Thames passes by at the end of the road, the Riverside Studios is round the corner for theatre and film, and the Gate Vegetarian Restaurant is across the courtyard, a well-known eatery, its food so good even committed carnivores can't resist. It was also Brangwyn's studio, hence the artist's window. The house is a non-denominational Christian centre with two services a week, which you may take or leave as you choose.

Rooms	1 double, 1 double with separate wc; 1 double with separate bathroom; 1 double sharing bath & shower, 2 twins sharing baths & shower with singles: £76–£120. 5 singles sharing baths & shower: £58–£72. Extra bed/sofabed £12–£14 p.p.p.n.
Meals	Continental breakfast included. Vegetarian restaurant across courtyard.
Closed	Never.
Directions	Tube: Hammersmith (5-minute walk). Bus: 9, 10, 27, 295.

Michael Beaumont
Temple Lodge Club
51 Queen Caroline Street,
Hammersmith, W6 9QL

Tel	+44 (0)20 8748 8388
Email	templelodgeclub@btconnect.com
Web	www.templelodgeclub.com

The Portobello Hotel

In 1969, in the days of Bowie and the Rolling Stones, this small hotel opened its doors, making it London's first boutique hotel. It was a new idea, a hip little place, not dull and formal like other hotels, but relaxed and friendly with lots of colour and a bohemian feel. These days, not much has changed, and it remains a popular base for artists and movie stars, designers and musicians, a star-studded list of regulars who come for its seductive combination of privacy, informality and style. It stands in the middle of Notting Hill, peacefully hidden away on a side street yet close to the tube, with Portobello Road and the shops and cafés of Westbourne Grove a short stroll. Inside, a beautiful sitting room has pine bay windows and carved ceiling roses, then fresh flowers, big art and views onto communal gardens. Bedrooms vary in size, not style. Lots have claw-foot baths in the room, one has a small terrace, another a high four-poster with library steps to help you up. Bigger rooms have sofas, all have cool colours, antique furniture, coffee machines and robes for the bathroom.

Rooms	19 doubles: £195–£395. 2 singles: £155–£175.
Meals	Continental breakfast included, cooked dishes from £5. Light bites from £6. Good restaurants within 500m.
Closed	Never.
Directions	Tube: Notting Hill Gate. Bus: 12, 27, 28, 52, 70, 94. Parking: £25 per 24 hrs.

Douglas Cooper
The Portobello Hotel
22 Stanley Gardens,
Notting Hill Gate, W11 2NG

Tel	+44 (0)20 7727 2777
Email	stay@portobellohotel.com
Web	www.portobellohotel.com

22 York Street

A Regency townhouse on a quiet street, a family home for over 60 years. It defies most attempts to pigeonhole it, but we'd say it's a little like staying with an eccentric aunt, who has lovely staff on hand to help. It's a convivial place. A continental breakfast is taken communally at a curved wooden table in the big kitchen/dining room, with guests chatting over coffee and croissants while they plan their day. There's always something to catch your eye, be it the red-lipped oil painting outside the dining room or old riding boots on the landing. A lovely big sitting room waits on the first floor with sofas, books, backgammon, and a baby grand piano, which, of course, you are welcome to play. Spotless bedrooms are simple: homely, but comfortable, with good beds, rugs on wood floors and the odd antique; if you're looking for oodles of hotel luxury, this probably isn't for you. However, you're in the middle of trendy Marylebone with great bars and restaurants on your doorstep. This is Sherlock Holmes country, too, with Madame Tussaud's and Lord's both close. A very friendly place.

Rooms	5 doubles, 2 twins: £150.
	3 singles: £95-£120.
Meals	Continental breakfast included.
	Pubs/restaurants nearby.
Closed	Never.
Directions	Train: Paddington (to Heathrow).
	Tube: Baker Street (2-minute walk).
	Bus: 2, 13, 30, 74, 82, 113, 139, 274.
	Parking: £25 a day, off-street.

Michael & Liz Callis
22 York Street
Marylebone, W1U 6PX

Tel	+44 (0)20 7224 2990
Email	mc@22yorkstreet.co.uk
Web	www.22yorkstreet.co.uk

The Zetter Townhouse

This is a deliciously quirky hotel, part 19th-century Viennese coffee house, part 20th-century bohemian dive, part 21st-century gentleman's club. It sits peacefully on St John's Square in the epicentre of trendy Clerkenwell, both away from the city and very much a part of it. A formal London exterior gives way to theatrical interiors. Rooms overflow with beautiful things – period furniture, claret wallpaper, glass cabinets filled with curios, a couple of Corinthian columns for good measure. You get rugs on wood floors, cool tunes in the air, then a mirrored cocktail bar where you chat to the barman as he mixes you a Calpis Sour. Rooms have lots of colour, art everywhere and robes in sparkling bathrooms. One has a four-poser with a Union Jack canopy, those in the eaves have painted bedheads; you get Hypnos beds and crisp linen, antique furniture and bluetooth speakers. Downstairs, dig into potted shrimps, shepherd's pie, chocolate and hazelnut brownie or spin across the square to their sister hotel for something more substantial. Farringdon Station is close, with Crossrail coming in 2018.

Rooms	5 doubles, 6 twin/doubles: £200–£315.
	1 suite for 4: £345–£425.
	1 apartment for 4: £475–£500.
Meals	Breakfast £9.50–£10.50.
	Lunch & dinner from £6.
Closed	Never.
Directions	Tube: Barbican.
	Train: Farringdon (2 minutes).
	Also: Kings Cross, Euston & Liverpool
	Street (for Stansted).
	Bus: 19, 38, 56, 63, 243, 341.

	Angela Ellis
	The Zetter Townhouse
	49–50 St John's Square,
	Clerkenwell, EC1V 4JJ
Tel	+44 (0)20 7324 4567
Email	reservations@thezetter.com
Web	www.thezettertownhouse.com/clerkenwell

Chalk & Cheese

Andrew and Bridget's Victorian schoolhouse stands on the village green. If its exterior gives the impression of English decorum, its interiors do the very opposite; the bust of Aristotle draped in a feather boa is a bit of a giveaway. It's all refreshingly original – interior design laced with humour. The big room takes centre stage, its high ceiling and stained glass giving an ecclesiastic feel. You'll find Cambodian lampshades and Vietnamese water puppets, mismatching sofas and a crackling fire, William Morris wallpaper and books by the hundred, then a quirky bar with light descending from on high. Homely bedrooms are warm, simple and nicely priced. One has a four-poster, another a slipper bath, two next door in a cute cottage can be taken together to self-cater. There's even a bunk house and a wheelchair-friendly bolthole in the garden. Pizzas fly from a wood-fired oven, while pea and ham soup, homemade cottage pie and sticky toffee pudding costs under £25. There's a conservatory breakfast room, a terrace for summer and a farm shop selling the odd antique. Good walks and the coast wait.

Rooms	3 doubles, 1 twin, 1 four-poster: £75-£95. 1 bunk room for 4: £35 p.p. Singles from £65. Extra beds from £10. Garden cottage £105-£125.
Meals	Lunch from £4.50. Dinner, 3 courses, £20-£25 (not Sun-Wed). Sunday lunch from £9.95.
Closed	Never.
Directions	North of A1122 between Swaffham and Downham Market. In village, on green.

Andrew & Bridget Archibald
Chalk & Cheese
1 Eastgate Street, Shouldham,
King's Lynn, PE33 0DD

Tel	+44 (0)1366 348039
Email	info@chalkandcheesenorfolk.co.uk
Web	www.bed-and-breakfast-west-norfolk.co.uk

Congham Hall

This is a beautiful Georgian merchant's house set in 30 acres of parkland. It's also a cool little spa hotel with an indoor pool and treatment rooms, a perfect blend of old and new. Outside, three gardeners grow flowers for the house, vegetables for the kitchen and keep the gardens looking serene. Inside, country house interiors have an elegant contemporary feel. There's an open fire in the sitting room, a chic bar with low-hanging lampshades, then an airy dining room for excellent local food, perhaps crayfish salad, slow-cooked chicken, hot chocolate fondant with banana ice cream. After which you'll need to atone, so roast away in the sauna before a dip in the pool; there are sunbeds and a hot tub on the decked terrace, too. Refurbished rooms are gorgeous. House rooms have beautiful fabrics and excellent beds. The suite has a balcony for breakfast, all have robes in striking bathrooms (one is entered through cupboard doors). Courtyard rooms are big and airy and open onto the kitchen garden. Children are welcome and have their own menu. Sandringham is close. There's tennis and croquet, too. *Minimum stay: 2 nights at weekends.*

Rooms	25 twin/doubles: £135–£260. 1 suite for 2: £275. Dinner, B&B from £110 p.p. Extra beds: children under 12 free.
Meals	Breakfast £8–£15. Lunch from £5. Dinner, 3 courses, about £35. Afternoon tea from £8.75. Sunday lunch, 3 courses, £27.50.
Closed	Rarely.
Directions	A10 to King's Lynn, then A149 north. At second r'bout, A148 east for 500m, then right for Grimston. Hotel signed.

Julie Woodhouse
Congham Hall
Grimston,
King's Lynn, PE32 1AH
Tel   +44 (0)1485 600250
Email info@conghamhallhotel.co.uk
Web   www.conghamhallhotel.co.uk

The Hoste

Nelson was a local, now it's farmers, fishermen and film stars who jostle at the bar. In its 300-year history the Hoste has been a court house, a livestock market, a gallery and a brothel. These days it's the social hub of the village and even on a grey February morning it buzzes with life, the locals in for coffee, guests polishing off their breakfasts. The place has a genius of its own with sofas and armchairs scattered about, a panelled bar for a pint of Wherry's, local art hanging on the walls and treatment rooms in the beauty spa. You can eat wherever you want, though the stylish restaurant with a wall of glass that opens onto the garden is a great spot for a good meal, perhaps Brancaster Staithe lobster risotto, seared Norfolk venison, sticky toffee pudding with butterscotch sauce; in summer life spills onto tables at the front and the terrace at the back. Chic rooms are all different. Some have four-posters, chandeliers and wonky floors; others have a contemporary style with cool colours and sparkling bathrooms. Explore the coast by day, come back for afternoon tea. Brilliant.

Rooms	45 twin/doubles: £130–£230. Railway House – 7 twin/doubles: £130–£230. Railway House – 1 train carriage for 2: £170–£230. Singles from £110. 9 self-catering cottages for 6: £160–£200. Dinner, B&B from £85 p.p.
Meals	Lunch from £6. Dinner, 3 courses, from £25. Sunday lunch from £14.
Closed	Never.
Directions	On B1155 for Burnham Market. By green & church in village centre.

Martin De Sousa
The Hoste
The Green, Burnham Market,
King's Lynn, PE31 8HD

Tel	+44 (0)1328 738777
Email	reservations@thehoste.com
Web	www.thehoste.com

The White Horse

A smart little inn on the North Norfolk coast with beautiful views that shoot across tidal marshes to Scolt Head Island. At high tide boats bob, birds swoop and the water laps at the garden edge; at low tide, the marshes appear and fishermen come to harvest the mussels and oysters. In summer you can eat on the terrace and drink it all in, then drop down to the coastal path at the bottom of the garden and follow your nose. But the view here is weatherproofed – a big conservatory restaurant looks out on it all. It's a popular haunt for locals and visitors alike, who come for consistently good food, perhaps oysters from the bay, sea bass with squid risotto, lemon tart with a chocolate macaroon. There's a sunken garden that catches the sun, then an open fire in the locals' bar, where you'll find well-kept ales, the daily papers, bar billiards and sofas for a game of scrabble. Chic, uncluttered bedrooms have seaside colours, robes for spotless bathrooms, good beds and fine linen. Some in the main house have the view, dog-friendly garden rooms have terraces. Sandringham is close. *Minimum stay: 2 nights at weekends*

Rooms	11 doubles, 4 twins: £100–£230. Extra beds £30. Cots £5. Dogs £10.
Meals	Lunch & bar meals from £9.95. Dinner from £13.95.
Closed	Never.
Directions	Midway between Hunstanton & Wells-next-the-Sea on A149.

Cliff & James Nye
The White Horse
Brancaster Staithe, PE31 8BY
Tel   +44 (0)1485 210262
Email   reception@whitehorsebrancaster.co.uk
Web   www.whitehorsebrancaster.co.uk

The Globe Inn at Wells-next-the-Sea

It's as English as England can be – a beautiful inn on a Georgian green, where Nelson used to catch the coach to London. Potter down to the water and find a sandy beach for family fun, then a small harbour, where day boats land their catch on the quay. As for the Globe, it's an inn for all seasons. Outside, there's a sun-trapping terrace at the front, a flower-filled courtyard where you can eat in summer, then a colourful roof terrace for guests. Inside, wood-burners sit at both ends of the bar, there are sofas and armchairs, games for rainy days, then local ales and excellent wines with which to wash down delicious local food. You eat in an airy restaurant with local art of the walls, perhaps clam linguini with chilli and garlic, dressed Wells crab or a rib-eye steak, then chocolate mousse with pistachio ice cream. Rooms above have the comfiest beds in the land. Those at the front have views of the green, all have crisp linen, padded heads and vintage tiles in sparkling bathrooms. Rooms connect for families, dogs are very welcome, boat trips can be arranged. Sandringham is up the road. *Minimum stay: 2 nights at weekends. Pets by arrangement.*

Rooms	4 doubles, 3 twin/doubles: £110–£170. Extra bed/sofabed £30 p.p.p.n.
Meals	Lunch from £6. Dinner, 3 courses, £25–£30.
Closed	Rarely.
Directions	A149 east into Wells. In village, on green.

Antonia & Stephen Bournes
The Globe Inn at Wells-next-the-Sea
The Buttlands,
Wells-Next-The-Sea, NR23 1EU
Tel   +44 (0)1328 710206
Email   hello@theglobeatwells.co.uk
Web   www.theglobeatwells.co.uk

Cley Windmill

The setting here is magical: rushes flutter in the salt marsh, raised paths lead off to the sea, a vast sky hangs overhead. The windmill, now with new sails, dates to 1713. It became a house in the 1920s, the family home of James Blunt no less. Square rooms are bigger, a couple have sofas, while round rooms in the tower are impossibly romantic (one is for mountaineers only). Six rooms are in the mill and you really want to go for these, though the cottage is set up for self-catering and visiting dogs. Inside, you find the loveliest drawing room – low ceiling, open fire, stripped floorboards and a cute little window seat. Bedrooms have a chic feel with Farrow & Ball colours, beautiful fabrics, the odd claw-foot bath. Those in the tower (with compact shower rooms) get smaller as you rise, but the view improves with every step; there's a viewing platform halfway up for all. You eat in a pretty dining room, perhaps crab fishcakes, Norfolk Lamb, pear tarte tatin with cinnamon ice cream. But plans are afoot to build an orangery and when it's ready, you'll eat there surrounded by the walled garden. *Minimum stay: 2 nights.*

Rooms	6 doubles, 2 twin/doubles: £159–£219. 1 self-catering cottage for 4: £390 for 3 days; extra days £50–£130; 7 days £495–£625. Children under 12, £30.
Meals	Dinner, 3 courses, £27.50–£32.50.
Closed	Christmas.
Directions	Head east through Cley on A149. Mill signed on left in village.

Simon Whatling
Cley Windmill
The Quay, Cley,
Holt, NR25 7RP

Tel	+44 (0)1263 740209
Email	info@cleywindmill.co.uk
Web	www.cleywindmill.co.uk

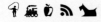

The Fritton Arms

This is a small, chic, country-house inn on the Somerleyton estate – well worth the detour to this far-flung realm. And stately it is: 5,000 acres of green and pleasant land, with parkland behind running down to Fritton Lake. Inside, airy interiors mix original features with contemporary design. You'll find period colours, rugs on stripped floors, 16th-century sand-blasted beams, then beautifully upholstered armchairs in front of a lovely old fireplace. There are sofas in the sitting room, fresh flowers on the piano, a roaring fire in the well-stocked bar. Food is served here and there: at green leather booths in the Fish Room; in the low-ceilinged restaurant with original brick walls; or out on the gravelled terrace in summer. Try wood-fired pizzas, sizzling steaks, perhaps ham hock terrine, sea bass with chorizo, a plate of local cheeses. Attractive bedrooms have warm colours, smart fabrics, comfy beds, white robes for good bathrooms. Some in the eaves are open to the rafters, bigger rooms may have a sofa. Don't miss Somerleyton Hall, one of the finest in the land. The Broads are close.

Rooms	6 doubles, 3 twin/doubles: £110–£140. Singles from £95. Extra beds £25.
Meals	Lunch from £5.50. Dinner, 3 courses, £25–£30. Sunday lunch from £12.50.
Closed	Rarely.
Directions	From Beccles A143 north for Great Yarmouth. In Fritton, right, signed Fritton Lake. Hotel on right before lake.

Stephen David
The Fritton Arms
Church Lane, Fritton,
Great Yarmouth, NR31 9HA

Tel	+44 (0)1493 484008
Email	info@frittonarms.co.uk
Web	www.frittonarms.co.uk

The Blakeney Hotel

The view here is matchless, a clean sweep across the salt marshes up to Blakeney Point. The estuary passes five paces from the front door and guests are prone to fall into graceful inertia and watch the boats slide by. You can do this from a sun-trapping terrace, a convivial bar, a traditional restaurant and the stunning first-floor sitting room that comes with binoculars to follow the wildlife. Most bedrooms have been refurbished in a contemporary country-house style with lovely fabrics, cool colours, an armchair or sofa, then gorgeous bathrooms; those at the front have the view. Six traditional rooms remain – simpler, but still pretty, with yellow and red chintz, good beds and crisp linen. There's a bar for light lunches, a drawing room with an open fire, then a stylish indoor pool with steam room and sauna; a snooker room and children's games' room wait too. Outside, paths lead down to the marshes, there are seals to spot, birds to watch, links golf at Sheringham and Cromer. Lovely food awaits your return, perhaps potted brown shrimps, Gressingham duck, sticky toffee pudding.

Rooms	19 doubles, 36 twin/doubles: £182–£322. 8 singles: £91–£149.
Meals	Lunch from £9.50. Dinner, 3 courses, £29–£43.50.
Closed	Never.
Directions	A148 north from Fakenham, then B1156 north to Blakeney. In village on quay.

Stannard Family
The Blakeney Hotel
The Quay, Blakeney,
Holt, NR25 7NE

Tel	+44 (0)1263 740797
Email	reception@blakeneyhotel.co.uk
Web	www.blakeneyhotel.co.uk

Saracens Head

Lost in the lanes of deepest Norfolk, an English inn that's hard to match. Outside, Georgian red-brick walls stand to attention at the front, but nip round the back and find them at ease in a beautiful courtyard where you can knock back a pint of Wherry in the evening sun before slipping inside to eat. Tim and Janie upped sticks from the Alps, unable to resist the allure of this lovely old inn. A sympathetic refurbishment has worked its magic, but the spirit remains the same: this is a country-house pub with lovely staff who go the extra mile. Downstairs the bar hums with happy locals who come for Norfolk ales and good French wines, while the food in the restaurant is as good as ever: Norfolk pheasant and rabbit terrine, wild duck or Cromer crab, treacle tart and caramel ice-cream. Upstairs, there's a sitting room on the landing, then six pretty rooms. All have have smart carpets, wooden furniture, comfy beds and sparkling bathrooms. There's masses to do: ancient Norwich, the coast at Cromer, golf on the cliffs at Sheringham, Blickling Hall, a Jacobean pile. Don't miss Sunday lunch.

Rooms	5 twin/doubles: £100-£110. 1 family room for 4: £110-£140. Singles from £70.
Meals	Lunch from £6.50. Dinner, 3 courses, £25-£35.
Closed	Christmas.
Directions	From Norwich A140 past Aylsham, then 3rd left for Erpingham. Right into Calthorpe, through village, straight out the other side (not right). On right after about 0.5 miles.

Tim & Janie Elwes
Saracens Head
Wolterton,
Norwich, NR11 7LZ

Tel	+44 (0)1263 768909
Email	info@saracenshead-norfolk.co.uk
Web	www.saracenshead-norfolk.co.uk

Strattons

Strattons isn't a hotel, it's a place that tickles your senses. First there's the house, a beautiful Queen Anne villa that wouldn't look out of place in the French countryside. Then you step inside and you're immediately surrounded by art, not one or two interesting pieces, but a treasure trove of wonderful stuff that spills from every corner, sits on every wall or dangles from the odd ceiling. You'll find august busts, contemporary chandeliers, murals by the dozen. Bedrooms are just as good: a carved four-poster in priestly red, Botticelli's angels hovering on a wall, bedside lights that hang from the ceiling. Some have double-ended baths in the room, others a roof terrace with sun loungers. As for the food, there's a deli across the courtyard for homemade treats: naughty cakes, sweet smelling bacon rolls, local cheeses and oils to take home. The restaurant (turn right at the chaise longue), is another art-filled room where local food follows the seasons, perhaps game pie with honey and fennel, slow-cooked beef with roasted roots, hazelnut tart with crème fraîche. Don't miss the Brecks for magical walking. *Minimum stay: 2 nights at weekends. Pets by arrangement.*

Rooms	6 doubles, 1 twin/double: £109–£185.
	5 suites for 2: £155–£275.
	2 apartments for 2: £172–£275.
	Singles from £92–£175.
Meals	Lunch (deli), Mon-Sat, from £6.
	Sunday lunch (hotel), from £12.
	Dinner, 3 courses, about £30.
Closed	Never.
Directions	Ash Close runs off north end of market place between W H Brown estate agents & fish & chip restaurant.

Vanessa & Les Scott
Strattons
4 Ash Close,
Swaffham, PE37 7NH

Tel	+44 (0)1760 723845
Email	enquiries@strattonshotel.com
Web	www.strattonshotel.com

Eshott Hall

A beautiful Palladian mansion set in 35 acres of medieval woodlands and pasture. Wisteria runs across the front of the house, there's an ancient fernery, paths that weave past rare trees, red squirrels, and an extremely productive kitchen garden. Inside is equally grand. You find Corinthian columns and an ornate ceiling in the drawing room, a roaring fire and leather sofas in the striking library bar, then a panelled dining room from which you might spot the odd deer tucking into garden roses. Nip up the stairs, passing a stained-glass window designed by William Morris, and find a clutch of stylish, airy bedrooms. A couple come with free-standing baths in the room. Others are huge with high ceilings, several have garden views, perhaps a sofa or a four-poster bed, too. Natural stone bathrooms are spotless and come with white robes and posh oils. There's tennis in the garden, peace at every turn, then white beaches, Holy Island and Alnwick Castle. Come back early for afternoon tea or later for a good dinner, perhaps squid and scallop risotto, pan-roasted duck, tangy lemon mousse. Fabulous.

Rooms	6 doubles, 11 twin/doubles: £99-£185. Singles from £69. Dinner, B&B from £95 p.p. Extra beds £28. Cots £15. Dogs in rooms £10.
Meals	Lunch from £5.50. Dinner £22-£42. Sunday lunch from £13. Afternoon tea from £16.
Closed	Sunday nights & Mondays, October-March.
Directions	East off A1 7 miles north of Morpeth, 9 miles south of Alnwick, at Eshott signpost. Hall gates approx. 1 mile down lane.

Mark Rawlings-Lloyd
Eshott Hall
Eshott,
Morpeth, NE65 9EN

Tel	+44 (0)1670 787454
Email	info@eshotthall.co.uk
Web	www.eshotthall.co.uk

The Pheasant Inn

A super little inn lost in beautiful country, the kind you hope to chance upon. The Kershaws run it with great passion and an instinctive understanding of its traditions. The bars are wonderful. Brass beer taps glow, 100-year old photos of the local community hang on stone walls, the clock above the fire keeps perfect time. Fires burn, bowler hats and saddles pop up here and there, varnished ceilings shine. House ales are expertly kept, Timothy Taylor's and Wylam waiting for thirsty souls. Fruit and vegetables come from the garden, while Robin's lovely food hits the spot perfectly, perhaps twice-baked cheese soufflé, slow-roasted Northumberland lamb, brioche and marmalade bread and butter pudding; as for Sunday lunch, *The Observer* voted it 'Best in the North'. Bedrooms in the old hay barn are light and airy, cute and cosy, great value for money. You're in the Northumberland National Park – no traffic jams, not too much hurry. You can sail on the lake, cycle round it or take to the hills and walk. For £10 you can also gaze into the universe at the Kielder Observatory (best in winter). Brilliant. *Minimum stay: 2 nights at weekends.*

Rooms	4 doubles, 3 twins: £95–£100. 1 family room for 4: £95–£140. Singles £65–£70. Dinner, B&B £70–£75 p.p. Extra bed/sofabed available £15 p.p.p.n.
Meals	Bar meals from £9.95. Dinner, 3 courses, £20–£30. Sunday lunch from £11.50.
Closed	Christmas.
Directions	From Bellingham follow signs west to Kielder Water & Falstone for 9 miles. Hotel on left, 1 mile short of Kielder Water.

Walter, Irene & Robin Kershaw
The Pheasant Inn
Stannersburn,
Hexham, NE48 1DD

Tel	+44 (0)1434 240382
Email	stay@thepheasantinn.com
Web	www.thepheasantinn.com

The Collingwood Arms Hotel

The Collingwood is all things to all men, an elegant country house, a distinctly stylish pub, and a favourite of fishermen, who come to try their luck. Step inside and find a sofa in front of the fire in the hall, a beautiful sitting room with books and fresh flowers, then a welcoming bar with rugs on wood floors and the odd fishing rod on the walls. Fires burn, tales get told, the odd dram is taken. Lovely bedrooms have a smart country feel: airy, elegant, understated. Some are big with space for a sofa, a couple are smaller, but fine for a night, all have the same gentle style: warm colours, crisp linen, comfy beds, spotless bathrooms. Three overlook the garden, one has a claw-foot bath amid timber frames. Downstairs, a convivial restaurant has parquet floors, doors onto a well-kept garden and some excellent local food, perhaps wood pigeon with juniper, halibut with saffron and samphire, stem ginger panna cotta. You can fish the river from quirkily named beats: The Slap, Craw Point, Monument. Coast and castles wait, as do gardens, golf and beautiful walking. Hard to beat.

Rooms	10 doubles, 3 twin/doubles: £130-£170. 2 suites for 2: £200. Singles from £120. Extra beds £20.
Meals	Lunch from £4.50. Dinner: bar meals from £11.50; 3 courses in the restaurant £30-£40.
Closed	Never.
Directions	A697 north to Cornhill-on-Tweed. In town, left at roundabout and hotel on right after 150m.

Shona Wedderburn
The Collingwood Arms Hotel
Main Street,
Cornhill-on-Tweed, TD12 4UH

Tel	+44 (0)1890 882424
Email	enquiries@collingwoodarms.com
Web	www.collingwoodarms.com

Hart's Nottingham

A small enclave of good things. You're on the smart side of town at the end of a cul-de-sac, thus remarkably quiet. You're also at the top of the hill and close to the castle with views that sweep south for miles; at night, a carpet of light sparkles beneath you. Inside, cool lines and travertine marble greet you in reception. Smart bedrooms do the trick. They're not huge, but come with all the trimmings: wide-screen TVs, Bose sound systems, super little bathrooms, king-size beds wrapped in crisp white cotton. Those on the ground floor open onto the garden, each with a terrace where you can breakfast in good weather; rooms on higher floors have better views (six overlook the courtyard). There is a cool little bar, the hub of the hotel, but Hart's Restaurant across the courtyard serves breakfast and light bites, and offers excellent food: perhaps wild mushroom arancini, sea bream with lemon and hazelnut, quince soufflé with vanilla ice cream. There's lots to explore: the Lace Market, the city caves, Trent Bridge for the cricket (the England team stay here). There's a private car park for hotel guests, too.

Rooms	29 doubles: £134–£184.
	2 suites for 2: £274.
	1 family room for 4: £144–£202.
Meals	Continental breakfast £9; full English £14.
	Lunch from £14.95.
	Dinner, 3 courses £30–£35.
	Sunday lunch, 3 courses, £25.
Closed	Never.
Directions	M1 junc. 24, then follow signs for city centre and Nottingham Castle. Left into Park Row from Maid Marian Way. Hotel on left at top of hill. Parking £8.50 per night.

Adam Worthington
Hart's Nottingham
Standard Hill, Park Row,
Nottingham, NG1 6GN

Tel   +44 (0)115 988 1900
Email   reception@hartshotel.co.uk
Web   www.hartsnottingham.co.uk

Langar Hall

Langar Hall is one of the loveliest places in this book — reason enough to come to Nottinghamshire. It sits at the top of a hardly noticeable hill in glorious parkland, bang next door to a medieval church. It was Imogen Skirving's family home and she turned it into a hotel in 1983, her exquisite style and natural joie de vivre making it a mecca for those in search of relaxed informality in a grand old house. Inside, you find beautiful things: statues and busts, a pillared dining room, ancient tomes in overflowing bookshelves, an eclectic collection of oil paintings. Smart, homely bedrooms are wonderful, some resplendent with antiques, others with fabrics draped from beams or trompe l'œil panelling. Heavenly food is another treat, perhaps wild garlic soup, local venison, pistachio soufflé with lemon sorbet. There's a conservatory for afternoon tea that opens onto a terrace, then grounds that hold medieval fishponds, an adventure play area and, once a year, Shakespeare on the lawn. Imo died in June 2016 and will be missed by many. Happily, Langar remains in family hands, so don't miss it.

Rooms	7 doubles, 2 twins, 1 four-poster: £100–£199. 1 suite for 2: £199. 1 chalet for 2: £100–£199.
Meals	Lunch from £18.50. Dinner, 3 courses, £25–£35.
Closed	Never.
Directions	From Nottingham A52 towards Grantham. Right, signed Cropwell Bishop, then straight on for 5 miles. House next to church on edge of village, signed.

The Skirving Family
Langar Hall
Church Lane, Langar,
Nottingham, NG13 9HG
Tel   +44 (0)1949 860559
Email   info@langarhall.co.uk
Web   www.langarhall.com

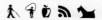

Old Bank Hotel

You're in the heart of old Oxford, with Merton College and Christ Church Meadow to the south, the Radcliffe Camera and the Bodleian Library to the north, and University College and the Botanic Gardens at Magdalen Bridge to the east. As for the Old Bank, its stylish interiors are home to an exceptional collection of modern art and photography. The hub is the old tiller's hall, now a cocktail bar and brasserie, with six arched windows overlooking the high street. Food is on tap all day long, anything from a pizza or a steak to afternoon tea, with meat from the owner's farm and fish from the Channel Islands. Bedrooms are gorgeous: fine beds, piles of cushions, original art, robes in chic bathrooms. Some have padded window seats, others have sofas, all have flat-screen TVs and good WiFi. Staff are lovely, beds are turned down, the daily papers delivered to your door. There's a decked courtyard for breakfast in summer, free off-street parking, then daily walking tours for guests. The University Church of St Mary stands opposite, so climb its tower for the best views of Oxford. *Minimum stay: 2 nights at weekends.*

Rooms	26 doubles, 14 twin/doubles: £215-£485. 2 suites for 3: £395-£560.
Meals	Breakfast £5-£15. Lunch & dinner £5-£30. Afternoon tea from £6.95.
Closed	Never.
Directions	Cross Magdalen Bridge for city centre. Straight through 1st set of lights, then left into Merton St. Follow road right; 1st right into Magpie Lane. Car park 2nd right.

Rebecca Mofford
Old Bank Hotel
92-94 High Street,
Oxford, OX1 4BJ
Tel   +44 (0)1865 799599
Email   info@oldbank-hotel.co.uk
Web   www.oldbank-hotel.co.uk

Turl Street Kitchen & Tower House Rooms

You land in the middle of Oxford at this quirky restaurant with rooms and find yourself surrounded by ancient colleges, with the Ashmolean Museum and the Bodleian Library both close. Interiors come in canteen style, with waitresses buzzing about, an open kitchen on display, a cool, shabby chic feel and happy chatter from people in for breakfast, lunch and dinner – this is a very popular community hub. Local food is sourced ethically and the menu changes twice a day, perhaps spiced carrot soup, steak and kidney pie, blood orange and vanilla cheesecake. There's WiFi throughout, the daily papers, a first-floor sitting room straight out of a student house. It's fun, easy going, a place for all. It's also a social enterprise, with profits going to charity, as they do 50 paces around the corner at Tower House Rooms, a terraced house with a difference: the old city wall runs through it with a 16th-century watch tower attached. Some rooms are small and share a bathroom, others are big, perhaps with a claw-foot bath. Expect good beds, smart colours, white linen, pretty throws. It's a peaceful spot, too.

Rooms	5 doubles; 3 doubles sharing 1 bathroom: £105–£170. Singles from £100. Cots available for children under 5 at no charge.
Meals	Lunch from £6.50. Dinner, 3 courses, £20–£25.
Closed	22 December to 2 January.
Directions	South from Broad Street on Turl Street. Right at Turl Street Kitchen onto Ship Street. On right after 50m.

Charis Sharpe
Turl Street Kitchen & Tower House Rooms
15 Ship Street,
Oxford, OX1 3DA

Tel	+44 (0)1865 246828
Email	info@towerhouseoxford.co.uk
Web	www.towerhouseoxford.co.uk

Old Parsonage Hotel

The Old Parsonage has been at the centre of Oxford life for over 350 years. It stands in the middle of town on land owned by University College and was once home to Oscar Wilde. It is one of the loveliest places to stay in town, not least due to a spectacular refurbishment that has touched every corner. Chief among its virtues are its shaded dining terrace, its exceptional art collection, and its first-floor library (curated by Philip Blackwell), which opens onto a small roof terrace. Inside, logs smoulder in an ancient fireplace, newspapers wait by mullioned windows, fresh flowers scent the air. The restaurant doubles as an art gallery, its charcoal walls crammed with portraits. It's a theatrical setting for a good meal, perhaps Jersey crab, duck with dandelion, rhubarb crumble with rhubarb ice cream. Bedrooms are delicious: pale greys, Oxford art, sublime white marble bathrooms with robes and pots of spoiling oils. Expect the best beds, the crispest linen, pretty throws and padded bedheads. As for Oxford, there are free guided walking tours for guests every day and picnics for lunch by the river. *Minimum stay: 2 nights at weekends.*

Rooms	22 doubles, 7 twins: £215-£485.
	6 suites for 3: £395-£560.
Meals	Breakfast £5-£15. Lunch from £18.50.
	Afternoon tea from £9.
	Dinner, 3 courses, about £35.
Closed	Never.
Directions	From A40 ring road, south onto Banbury Road; thro' Summertown and hotel on right just before St Giles church.

Jeremy Mogford
Old Parsonage Hotel
1 Banbury Road,
Oxford, OX2 6NN

Tel	+44 (0)1865 310210
Email	reservations@oldparsonage-hotel.co.uk
Web	www.oldparsonage-hotel.co.uk

The Feathers Hotel

Woodstock is the estate village to Blenheim Palace, one of Britain's finest houses, seat of the Dukes of Marlborough, birthplace of Winston Churchill. As for the hotel, it was once a draper's, then a butcher's, so it's no surprise it became a stylish hotel serving excellent food. In the morning you breakfast leisurely, then stroll up to the big house and spend the day dropping your jaw before coming home for afternoon tea in the courtyard. Inside, elegant, uncluttered interiors keep things simple: beautiful art, smouldering fires, a wall or two of original panelling, flowers everywhere. Ancient windows flood rooms with light, you find colourful rugs on wooden floors, then more gin than you can shake a stick at in the sitting-room bar (over 300 different bottles). Bedrooms have a contemporary feel with smart fabrics, lovely beds, mohair throws, delicate wallpapers. Some have sofas, all come with robes in fancy bathrooms. Back downstairs, delicious food waits in the restaurant, perhaps crab ravioli, loin of venison, treacle tart with blackberry sorbet. Biscester Village and Oxford are close. *Minimum stay: 2 nights at weekends in summer.*

Rooms	13 doubles, 3 twin/doubles: £169–£229. 5 suites for 2: £259–£319. Singles from £129.
Meals	Lunch from £5. Sunday lunch from £14. Bar meals from £10. Dinner £37.50–£45. 5-course tasting menu £55 (not Sunday eve).
Closed	Never.
Directions	North from Oxford on A44. In Woodstock left after traffic lights & hotel on left.

Dominic Bishop
The Feathers Hotel
Market Street,
Woodstock, OX20 1SX

Tel	+44 (0)1993 812291
Email	enquiries@feathers.co.uk
Web	www.feathers.co.uk

The Swan

Free-range bantams strut in the garden, a pint of Hooky waits at the bar. This lovely old pub sits on the river Windrush with the village cricket pitch waiting beyond. It started life as a water mill and stands on the Devonshire estate, hence the pictures of the Mitford sisters that hang on the walls. Outside, wisteria wanders across golden stone and creepers blush red in the autumn sun. Interiors hit the spot: low ceilings, open fires, beautiful windows, stone walls. Over the years thirsty feet on their way to the bar (including those belonging to prime ministers and presidents) have worn grooves into ancient flagstones. As for the food, seasonal menus brim with local produce, offering delicious delights, perhaps game terrine with pear chutney, roast partridge with a red wine jus, rhubarb and apple crumble. Bedrooms in the old forge have 15th-century walls and 21st-century interior design; those in the cottage across the lane are yards from the river. Expect crisp linen, comfy beds, warm colours and good art. Several have claw-foot baths, one has a pink chaise longue. Burford is close.

Rooms	4 doubles, 1 twin: £125–£150. 1 suite for 2: £180–£195. Cottage rooms: 5 twin/doubles: £125–£150. Singles from £70.
Meals	Lunch from £5. Dinner, 3 courses, about £30. Sunday lunch from £14.95.
Closed	Christmas Day & Boxing Day.
Directions	West from Oxford on A40 for Cheltenham/Burford. Past Witney & village signed right at 1st r'bout.

Archie & Nicola Orr-Ewing
The Swan
Swinbrook,
Burford, OX18 4DY

Tel	+44 (0)1993 823339
Email	info@theswanswinbrook.co.uk
Web	www.theswanswinbrook.co.uk

The Shaven Crown

The Great Hall, with its spectacular roof, dates back to 1368 – quite some sitting room. It was built by monks from Bruern Abbey, reborn as a royal hunting lodge after the Dissolution of the Monasteries, then gifted to the village as an inn. Phil and Evelyn rescued it from neglect, then spent a year restoring long-lost glories – no mean feat. Potter about and find parquet flooring in the airy bar, books and armchairs in the pretty snug, then mullioned windows in the restaurant, where you dig into some lovely local food; rabbit rillettes with pear purée, loin of venison with a port wine sauce, espresso mousse with rum ice cream or a William pear cheesecake. In summer you spill out into a gorgeous courtyard for afternoon tea in the sun. Bedrooms have an elegant simplicity: airy colours, stylish fabrics, beautiful beds, sparkling bathrooms. One has a beamed roof, a couple are smaller, but have courtyard views. You're right in the heart of the Cotswolds, with Stratford for Shakespeare, Cheltenham for the races and Oxford for the spires all within easy reach. There's even jazz in the hall once a month. Dogs are very welcome.

Rooms	3 doubles, 3 twin/doubles: £95-£135.
Meals	Lunch from £6.50.
	Dinner, 3 courses, £25-£35.
	Sunday lunch from £17.95.
Closed	Rarely.
Directions	North from Burford on A361 for 5 miles. In village, on left.

Phil & Evelyn Roberts
The Shaven Crown
High Street,
Shipton under Wychwood, OX7 6BA
Tel   +44 (0)1993 830500
Email   relax@theshavencrown.co.uk
Web   www.theshavencrown.co.uk

The Feathered Nest Country Inn

The village is tiny, the view is fantastic, the bar is lively, the rooms are a treat. This 300-year-old malthouse sits in 55 acres of green and pleasant land and is utterly gorgeous inside and out. The view from the garden is one of the best in the Cotswolds – a five-mile sweep across quilted fields to a distant ridge. Interiors are just as good. A warm rustic style mixes beautifully with original timbers and old stone walls. A fire smoulders in the lovely bar, doors in the restaurant open onto the terrace, the garden room has tartan walls and the white wine cellar on display. Bedrooms delight. One is enormous, two have the view, beds are dressed in crisp linen. Most have power showers, one has a claw-foot bath, all have robes. You get coffee machines and iPod docks, too. Delicious food waits downstairs, perhaps octopus with lemon and garlic, pollock with saffron and fennel, tarte tatin with vanilla ice cream. You eat on the terrace in summer looking out on the lake and distant farms. A couple of luxurious cabins are soon to be sprinkled across the grounds – Amanda and Tony do nothing by halves. Magical. *Minimum stay: 2 nights at weekends.*

Rooms	3 doubles: £190–£250.
	Singles £160–£220.
Meals	Lunch & dinner £6.50–£30.
	Not Sunday eve.
Closed	Rarely.
Directions	North from Burford on A424 for Stow-on-the-Wold. After 4 miles right for Nether Westcote. In village.

Tony & Amanda Timmer
The Feathered Nest Country Inn
Nether Westcote,
Chipping Norton, OX7 6SD

Tel	+44 (0)1993 833030
Email	reservations@thefeatherednestinn.co.uk
Web	www.thefeatherednestinn.co.uk

The Kings Head Inn

The sort of inn that defines this country: a 16th-century cider house made of ancient stone that sits on the green in a Cotswold village with free-range hens strutting their stuff and a family of ducks bathing in the pond. Inside, locals gather to chew the cud, scoff great food and wash it down with a cleansing ale. The fire burns all year, you get low ceilings, painted stone walls, country rugs on flagstone floors. Bedrooms, all different, are scattered about; all are well priced. Those in the main house have more character, those in the courtyard are bigger (and quieter). You'll find painted wood, lots of colour, pretty fabrics, spotless bathrooms; most have great views, too. Breakfast and supper are taken in a pretty dining room (exposed stone walls, pale wood tables), while you can lunch by the fire in the bar on Cornish scallops, steak and ale pie, then a plate of British cheeses. There are lovely unpompous touches like jugs of cow parsley in the loo, and loads to do: antiques in Stow, golf at Burford, walking and riding through gorgeous terrain. The front terrace teems with life in summer. *Minimum stay: 2 nights at weekends.*

Rooms	9 doubles, 3 twin/doubles: £100-£135. Singles £80-£100.
Meals	Lunch from £7.50. Dinner, 3 courses, about £30. Sunday lunch £15.
Closed	25-27 December.
Directions	East out of Stow-on-the-Wold on A436, then right onto B4450 for Bledington. Pub in village on green.

Archie & Nicola Orr-Ewing
The Kings Head Inn
The Green, Bledington,
Chipping Norton, OX7 6XQ
Tel   +44 (0)1608 658365
Email   info@kingsheadinn.net
Web   www.kingsheadinn.net

Hambleton Hall Hotel & Restaurant

Hambleton is matchless, one of the seven wonders of English country-house hotels. It sits on a tiny peninsular that juts into Rutland Water. You can sail on it, cycle round it, or watch terns and osprey commute across it. Back at the house the undisputed wonders of Hambleton wait: sofas by the fire in the panelled hall, a pillared bar in red for cocktails, a Michelin star in the elegant dining room. French windows in the sitting room – beautiful art, fresh flowers, the daily papers – open onto fine gardens. Expect clipped lawns and gravel paths, a formal parterre garden that bursts with summer colour and a walled swimming pool with views over parkland to the water. Bedrooms are flawless: hand-stitched Italian linen, mirrored armoires, Roberts radios and marble bathrooms. Stefa's eye for fabrics, some of which coat the walls, is impeccable; the Pavilion, a two-bedroom suite, has its own terrace. Polish the day off with ambrosial food, perhaps beetroot terrine with horseradish sorbet, fallow venison with Asian pear, passion fruit soufflé with banana sorbet. Barnsdale Gardens are close. *Minimum stay: 2 nights at weekends.*

Rooms	15 twin/doubles: £270–£460. 1 suite for 4: £440–£660. Singles from £195. Dinner, B&B from £195 p.p. Extra bed/sofabed available £35 p.p.p.n. Dogs £10.
Meals	Lunch from £26.50. Dinner, 3 courses, £68. Tasting menu £85. Sunday lunch £55.
Closed	Never.
Directions	From A1, A606 west towards Oakham for about 8 miles, then left, signed Hambleton. In village bear left and hotel signed right.

Tim & Stefa Hart
Hambleton Hall Hotel & Restaurant
Ketton Road, Hambleton,
Oakham, LE15 8TH

Tel	+44 (0)1572 756991
Email	hotel@hambletonhall.com
Web	www.hambletonhall.com

The Olive Branch

A lovely pub in a sleepy Rutland village, where bridle paths lead out across peaceful fields. It dates to the 17th century and is built of Clipsham stone, as is York Minster. Inside, a warm, informal, rustic chic hits the spot perfectly with open fires, old beams, stone walls and choir stalls in the bar. But there's more here than cool design. This is a place to come and eat great food, the lovely, local seasonal stuff that's cooked with passion by Sean and his brigade, perhaps potted pork and stilton with apple jelly, haunch of venison with a juniper fondant, then a boozy rhubarb trifle. Bedrooms in Beech House across the lane are gorgeous. Three have terraces, one has a free-standing bath, all come with crisp linen, pretty beds, Roberts radios and real coffee. Super breakfasts – smoothies, boiled eggs and soldiers, the full cooked works – are served in a stone-walled barn with flames leaping in the wood-burner. The front garden fills in summer, the sloe gin comes from local berries, and Newark is close for the biggest antiques market in Europe. Picnic hampers can be arranged. A total gem.

Rooms	5 doubles, 1 family room for 4: £115–£195 Singles from £97.50. Extra beds £30.
Meals	Lunch from £6.25. Dinner, 3 courses, £25–£35. Sunday lunch from £17.50.
Closed	Rarely.
Directions	A1 5 miles north of Stamford, then exit onto B668. Right & right again for Clipsham. In village (Beech House across the road from The Olive Branch).

Ben Jones & Sean Hope
The Olive Branch
Main Street, Clipsham,
Oakham, LE15 7SH

Tel	+44 (0)1780 410355
Email	info@theolivebranchpub.com
Web	www.theolivebranchpub.com

Pen-y-Dyffryn Country Hotel

In a blissful valley lost to the world, a small country house that sparkles on the side of a peaceful hill. This is one of those lovely places where guests return again and again, mostly due to Audrey and Miles, who run a very happy ship. Outside, fields tumble down to a stream that marks the border with Wales. Daffodils erupt in spring, the lawns are scattered with deckchairs in summer, paths lead into the hills for fine walking. Lovely interiors are just the ticket: Laura Ashley wallpaper and an open fire in the quirky bar; colourful art and super food in the pretty restaurant; the daily papers and the odd chaise longue in the sitting room. Bedrooms hit the spot. Most have the view, one has a French sleigh bed, a couple have jacuzzi baths for two. Four lovely rooms outside are dog-friendly and have their own patios. You get warm colours, crisp linen, pretty fabrics and sparkling bathrooms. After a day in the hills come back for a good dinner, perhaps wild mushroom risotto, pan-fried wood pigeon, hot chocolate fondant with vanilla ice-cream. Offa's Dyke and Powis Castle are close. *Minimum stay: 2 nights at weekends.*

Rooms	8 doubles, 4 twins: £120–£190. Singles from £86.
Meals	Light lunch (for residents) by arrangement. Dinner £30–£37.
Closed	Rarely.
Directions	From A5 head to Oswestry. Leave town on B4580, signed Llansilin. Hotel 3 miles up. Approach Rhydycroesau, left at town sign, first right.

Miles & Audrey Hunter
Pen-y-Dyffryn Country Hotel
Rhydycroesau,
Oswestry, SY10 7JD

Tel   +44 (0)1691 653700
Email   stay@peny.co.uk
Web   www.peny.co.uk

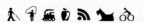

Sebastian's

This cute little restaurant with rooms occupies an old merchant's house that dates from 1640. Michelle and Mark have been at the helm for some 25 years cooking up a fine reputation – not only for their delicious food, but for the quirky, old-world interiors in which they serve it. Inside you find huge beams, timber frames, half panelling and stripped floors. Big warm colours sit on the walls, smartly clothed tables are lit by candles, deco posters of the Orient Express hang in every room (Mark supplies the train with canapés and desserts). Back in the restaurant, sofas wait in front of a fire that smoulders from morning to night in winter. Here you drool over the menu before digging into delicious food, perhaps scallop ravioli with lemon grass and ginger, short rib of beef in a red wine sauce, dark chocolate mousse with honey ice cream. Six nicely-priced rooms wait, two in the main house (timber frames, lots of colour), four off the attractive courtyard (comfy sofas, lovely bathrooms). Plans are afoot for a couple of suites. Welsh hills wait to the west, so bring your walking boots.

Rooms	4 doubles, 2 twin/doubles: £75. Singles £65.
Meals	Breakfast £6.95-£11.95. Dinner, 5 courses, £44.50. Reduced menu for residents Tue-Thurs. Not Sun or Mon.
Closed	Rarely.
Directions	In middle of Oswestry on B4580.

Michelle & Mark Sebastian Fisher
Sebastian's
45 Willow Street,
Oswestry, SY11 1AQ

Tel	+44 (0)1691 655444
Email	info@sebastians-hotel.com
Web	www.sebastians-hotel.co.uk

Meeson Hall

Sitting in eight acres of lawns and woodland with open country all around, this lovely country house dates back to 1640 and is a treasure trove of beautiful things – the Jacobean chimney piece in the dining room is one of the finest in the land. Guests have the run of the ground floor: a grandly panelled hall with a crackling fire, an airy drawing room for afternoon tea and a library filled with original art. You eat communally in the splendid dining room, merrily digging into Mark's lovely home cooking – perhaps pâté with redcurrant jelly, a Barnsley chop with a red wine jus, followed by bread and butter pudding. Bedrooms come in smart country-house style: warm colours, smartly dressed beds, antique furniture, fresh flowers. There are sofas, silver teapots, perhaps a chandelier, then robes and the odd claw-foot bath in wallpapered bathrooms. Outside, chickens provide eggs for breakfast and bluebells run riot in spring. All of which would be blossom in the wind without Adrian and Mark, who go out of their way to make your stay here special. Ironbridge, birthplace of the Industrial Revolution, is close.

Rooms	4 doubles: £165–£215.
	1 suite for 4: £180–£320.
	Singles from £145.
Meals	Lunch from £10. Dinner, 3 courses, £30.
	Sunday lunch £25.
	Afternoon tea from £10.
Closed	Rarely.
Directions	North from Telford on A41. Cross
	B5062, then right in Waters Upton.
	Through village and right at bridge
	after 1 mile for Meeson. Ignore 1st
	left, through village, left at house with
	red-brick wall. On left after 500m.

Adrian Jones & Mark Scarrott
Meeson Hall
Meeson, TF6 6PG

Tel	+44 (0)1952 541262
Email	enquiries@meesonhall.co.uk
Web	www.meesonhall.co.uk

The Castle Hotel

This thriving medieval market town sits amid some of the loveliest country in the land, a launch pad for walkers and cyclists alike, with Offa's Dyke, Long Mynd and the Kerry Ridgeway all close. After a day in the hills, roll back to this quirky hotel for a night of gentle carousing. You'll find heaps of country comforts: hearty food, impeccable ales, super rooms with honest prices. Downstairs, there's a coal fire in the pretty snug, oak panelling in the breakfast room, and Millie the short-haired dachshund who patrols the corridors with aplomb. Stylish bedrooms upstairs have all been refurbished. Expect good beds, warm colours, flat-screen TVs, an armchair if there's room. Some are up in the eaves, several have views of the Shropshire hills, two have baths in the room. Back downstairs you find the sort of food you'd want after a day in the hills, perhaps hot garlic prawns, beef and ale pie, sticky toffee pudding. Don't miss the hugely popular real ale festival in July, the beer drinker's equivalent of Glastonbury. The garden terrace, with long country views, is a fine spot for a sundowner.

Rooms	9 doubles, 1 twin: £95-£150.
	2 family rooms for 4: £130-£155.
	Singles from £75.
	Dinner, B&B from £82.50 p.p.
	Extra beds for children £20.
Meals	Lunch from £4.50.
	Dinner, 3 courses, about £25.
Closed	Christmas Day & 10 days in January.
Directions	At top of hill in town, off A488.

Henry & Rebecca Hunter
The Castle Hotel
Bishops Castle, SY9 5BN

Tel   +44 (0)1588 638403
Email   stay@thecastlehotelbishopscastle.co.uk
Web   www.thecastlehotelbishopscastle.co.uk

Old Downton Lodge

The last time anything really happened here was in 1067 when Edric the Wild got a bit shirty with invading Normans. Fast forward five hundred years and Old Downton is taking shape. It's a fine old building, a little like walking onto the set of Wolf Hall, with original timbers, mighty crossbeams and beautiful stone walls. It sits in pristine country: pheasants strut, hills roll, woodlands sprawl along distant ridges; a stunning walk across it all takes you over to Ludlow. Back at the house Pippa and Willem look after you in great style. There's a lovely sitting room in the old dairy with a roaring fire and an honesty bar, then a dining room in an 11th-century barn that resembles a medieval banqueting hall. In summer, life moves into the courtyard (once used for cattle auctions), where you can eat, drink and make merry in good weather. Big bedrooms mix timber frames, stone walls, flagged floors and oak furniture, while bathrooms have robes and lashings of hot water. Back outside, follow the river Teme up to Downton Gorge for ferns, otters, Roman baths and bluebells in spring. Blissful.

Rooms	5 doubles, 2 twins, 2 four-posters: £125–£175. Extra beds £30.
Meals	Dinner, 5-7 courses, £40–£50 (not Sun or Mon).
Closed	February.
Directions	North from Ludlow on A49, then west after 2 miles on A4113. 1st left (after 2 miles). Straight on for 4 miles; hotel on right.

Willem & Pippa Vlok
Old Downton Lodge
Downton-on-the-Rock,
Ludlow, SY8 2HU

Tel	+44 (0)1568 771826
Email	bookings@olddowntonlodge.com
Web	www.olddowntonlodge.com

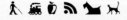

The Oaks Hotel

Where else can you hire an MGB convertible in which to explore beautiful Exmoor? It's no surprise to discover that this hotel is an old school charmer. Tim and Anne do it all themselves, practising the art of old-fashioned hospitality with great flair: they stop to chat, carry bags, ply you with tea and cake on arrival. Their Edwardian house sits above the village, wrapped up in a beautiful garden, with views of hill and sea. Inside, logs smoulder on the hall fire while hot coals glow in the sitting room. There's a snug bar, parquet flooring, floral fabrics, masses of books. Spotless bedrooms, all with sea views, are deeply comfy. Most are big, all are colourful, the price with dinner is a steal. You get bowls of fruit, crisp white linen, fluffy bathrobes and Roberts radios; most have sofas, while beds are turned down every evening. As for dinner, Anne whisks up four-course feasts, perhaps cheese soufflé, smoked haddock mousse, guinea fowl with prunes and brandy, rhubarb and apple crumble. Exmoor, the coast and Dunster Castle all wait – don't miss the tiny villages marooned in the hills.

Rooms	1 double, 6 twin/doubles: £155–£175. Dinner, B&B from £115 p.p.
Meals	Dinner, 4 courses, £37.50.
Closed	November – April.
Directions	A39 west to Porlock. Keep left down hill into village and hotel on left after 200m.

Anne & Tim Riley
The Oaks Hotel
Porlock, TA24 8ES

Tel	+44 (0)1643 862265
Email	info@oakshotel.co.uk
Web	www.oakshotel.co.uk

Cross Lane House

A medieval farmhouse in a National Trust village, where a 500-year-old bridge sweeps you across to ancient woodland. Outside, a cobbled courtyard leads up to a hay barn that's open on one side – not a bad spot for breakfast in good weather. Inside, original panelling survives, while Max and Andrew's flawless design gives a delicious country-house feel, making this an intimate bolthole in which to linger. You'll find a sitting room packed with beautiful things – books galore, original flagstones, sofas in front of a roaring fire. There's a spy hole in the panelling, some ancient graffiti, too, then a gorgeous dining room in period colours with wood floors, beautiful art and wonderful food, perhaps Devon crab cakes, boeuf Bourguignon, chocolate brownies with toffee popcorn and salted caramel ice cream. Bedrooms upstairs are deeply satisfying: lovely beds, bowls of fruit, timber frames, super bathrooms. One is smaller, two are bigger, the family suite has two bedrooms. You get binoculars, Roberts radios, Cowshed oils, even mini bars 'on the house'. Exmoor waits. The road passes quietly at night. *Minimum stay: 2 nights at weekends.*

Rooms	3 doubles: £155–£200.
	1 suite for 3: £185–£215.
	Dinner, B&B from £112 p.p.
Meals	Lunch from £6 (Wed–Sat, Easter–Sept).
	Dinner £27–£34. Sunday lunch £18–£24.
	Afternoon tea £19.95.
Closed	Rarely.
Directions	A39 west from Minehead. On right
	after 5 miles, 1 mile before Porlock.

Max Lawrence & Andrew Stinson
Cross Lane House
Allerford, Minehead, TA24 8HW
Tel   +44 (0)1643 863276
Email   max@crosslanehouse.com
Web   www.crosslanehouse.com

Luttrell Arms

You get a triple whammy here: spectacular Dunster Castle, its beautiful estate village and this medieval coaching inn on the high street – the view from the terrace across to the castle is candy for your eyes. Inside, a recent refurbishment has brought in a warm style. You'll find a beautiful restaurant with papered walls, an attractive sitting room for afternoon tea, an open fire in the high-ceilinged bar, then a boot bar for sleeping dogs and a game of cribbage. There are a couple of terraces for lunch in the sun, sofas on a veranda that overlooks a tiny courtyard. Bedrooms are scattered about, some with village views, others overlooking the estate. Four are huge with grand four-posters, two sitting under a 500-year-old hammer beam roof. Others have period furniture, pretty wallpapers, perhaps a small private terrace; simpler rooms are smaller, but have good beds. Tasty food spans the spectrum, perhaps a posh burger in the bar to smoked haddock chowder, braised shin of beef and chocolate and raspberry tart in the restaurant. Cliff tops and wild moors wait for fabulous walking. *Minimum stay: 2 nights at weekends.*

Rooms	4 doubles, 20 twin/doubles, 4 four-posters: £140-£195. Singles from £100.
Meals	Lunch from £4.95. Bar meals from £10.95. Dinner, 3 courses, about £30. Sunday lunch from £15.95. Afternoon tea £12.95.
Closed	Rarely.
Directions	A39 to Dunster, then south for Dunster on A396. Hotel on High Street on left.

Becca Way
Luttrell Arms
36 High Street,
Dunster, TA24 6SG
Tel   +44 (0)1643 821555
Email   enquiry@luttrellarms.co.uk
Web   www.luttrellarms.co.uk

Swain House

Watchet is a sleepy town on the West Somerset coast, and while its day may have passed, its medieval harbour that once made it rich inspired Coleridge to write his famous poem *The Rime of The Ancient Mariner*. As for this stylish B&B, it makes a great little base for gentle explorations – you'll find excellent hill walking, beaches, the coastal path, even a music festival in August. Once an antiques shop, it sits on the colourful, main street in town with a big window looking out onto the world. Downstairs, there's a stylish dining room that doubles as a sitting room, with a sofa in front of a fire and hanging lamps at the breakfast table. Upstairs, lovely rooms wait, the sort you expect to find in a boutique inn. You get a huge noble portrait covering one wall, then pretty armchairs, smart fabrics, padded bedheads and old-style radiators. Excellent bathrooms have walk-in showers, free-standing baths, robes and REN oils – exactly what you want after a day in the hills. Pub grub waits in town, posher nosh is a little further afield. The nearby car park is nicely priced, too.

Rooms	4 doubles: £135. Singles from £115.
Meals	Restaurants in village.
Closed	Rarely.
Directions	M5, junc. 23, then A39 for Minehead. Right in Williton, then immediately left for Watchet. Approaching town, left over railway, then follow road into town. On right after 200m. Car park right 50m on.

Jason & Annie Robinson
Swain House
48 Swain Street,
Watchet, TA23 0AG

Tel	+44 (0)1984 631038
Email	stay@swain-house.com
Web	www.swain-house.com

Farmers Arms

A lovely inn lost in peaceful hills on the Somerset Levels – a great base for a night or two of affordable luxury. Outside, free-range hens potter about, cows graze neighbouring fields and glorious views from the beer garden drift downhill for a couple of miles – a perfect spot for a pint in summer. Inside, you'll find friendly natives, sofas in front of an open fire and a timber-framed bar, where one airy room rolls into another giving a sense of space and light. There are beamed ceilings, boarded floors, tongue-and-groove panelling and logs piled high in alcoves. Bedrooms – some big, some huge – are just the ticket. They come with whitewashed walls, pretty beds, the odd chaise longue, then power showers or double-ended baths. One has a daybed, others have sofas, another has a private courtyard. Good food flies from the kitchen, perhaps ham hock terrine, crab and crayfish linguini, white chocolate and blackberry brûlée; in summer you can eat in the courtyard garden. There are local stables if you want to ride and great walking, so bring your boots. Taunton is close for cricket in summer.

Rooms	4 doubles, 1 twin/double: £105–£125. Singles £75. Extra beds/sofabeds from £10. Dogs £10.
Meals	Lunch & dinner £5–£35.
Closed	Never.
Directions	M5 junc. 25, then south on A358. On dual carriageway, right, signed West Hatch. Follow signs to RSPCA centre up hill for two miles. Signed on left.

Dionne McEvans
Farmers Arms
West Hatch,
Taunton, TA3 5RS

Tel	+44 (0)1823 480980
Email	farmersarmswh@gmail.com
Web	www.farmersarmssomerset.co.uk

Lord Poulett Arms

An idyllic inn that's hard to beat. It's like stepping onto the pages of a Jane Austen novel. A clipped country elegance runs throughout – old stone walls and period colours, then noble portraits on the walls and beautiful old settles to take the strain. There are drawbacks – sooner or later you will have to leave, probably with a touch of envy for the locals. Smart rusticity abounds. A fire burns on both sides in the dining room, where you eat under beams at antique tables. You'll find the daily papers, sofas in the locals' bar, a pile of logs at the back door, then an informal French garden with a piste for boules. Bedrooms upstairs have a lovely style with fancy flock wallpaper, pretty fabrics and fresh flowers, perhaps a small chandelier or a carved wooden bed. Two rooms have slipper baths in the room; two have claw-foot baths in bathrooms one step across the landing; the suite is enormous and has an open fire. The food is just as lovely, perhaps pea and ham soup, confit pork belly, praline fondant with coffee ice cream. Don't miss Sunday lunch or summer barbecues. An affordable treat.

Rooms	2 doubles; 2 doubles with separate bath: £85-£95. 1 suite for 3: £100-£150. Singles from £60.
Meals	Lunch from £5. Dinner, 3 courses, £20-£35. Sunday lunch £18-£21.
Closed	Never.
Directions	A303, then A356 south for Crewkerne. Right for West Chinnock. Through village, 1st left for Hinton St George. Pub on right in village.

Steve & Michelle Hill
Lord Poulett Arms
High Street,
Hinton St George, TA17 8SE
Tel   +44 (0)1460 73149
Email   reservations@lordpoulettarms.com
Web   www.lordpoulettarms.com

Little Barwick House

A beautiful restaurant with rooms lost in peaceful lanes south of Yeovil. Tim and Emma rolled west 14 years ago and now have a legion of fans who come to feast on their ambrosial food. Their small Georgian country house stands privately in three acres of peace. Horses graze in the paddock below, afternoon tea is served in the garden to the sound of birdsong in summer. Inside, chic interiors flood with light thanks to fine windows that run along the front. There's an open fire in the bar, eclectic reading in the sitting room, then contemporary art in the high-ceilinged dining room. Gorgeous bedrooms have a country-house feel and come with warm colours, pretty fabrics, Roberts radios, a sofa if there's room. You'll find fresh garden flowers, antique furniture, and White Company oils in compact bathrooms. Dinner is the main event, heaven in three courses. Everything is homemade and cooked by Tim and Emma, an equal partnership in the kitchen – perhaps Lyme Bay scallops, saddle of wild venison, dark chocolate tort with armagnac ice-cream. Posh wines by the glass come courtesy of clever technology. *Children over 5 welcome.*

Rooms	4 doubles, 2 twins: £100–£170. Singles £75–£140. Dinner, B&B £105–£130 p.p. Extra bed/sofabed available £25 p.p.p.n.
Meals	Lunch, 2-3 courses, £25.95–£29.95. Dinner, 2-3 courses, £41.95–£47.95. Not Tue lunch.
Closed	Sunday nights & Mondays.
Directions	From Yeovil A37 south for Dorchester; left at 1st r'bout. Down hill, past church, left in village and house on left after 200 yds.

Emma & Tim Ford
Little Barwick House
Rexes Hollow Lane,
Barwick, Yeovil, BA22 9TD

Tel	+44 (0)1935 423902
Email	reservations@barwick7.fsnet.co.uk
Web	www.littlebarwickhouse.co.uk

The Devonshire Arms

What makes a great little inn these days? The Devonshire Arms has all the ingredients: lots of style, good prices, a community feel, some lovely rooms. It's in the right place, too, bang on the village green, with a terrace at the front, a garden at the back and a courtyard in between. Inside, is just as good. This isn't one of those places where every table is laid up for food; on the contrary, the best seats in the house are in the bar – a couple of armchairs in front of the fire. Step inside and find stylish interiors throughout. You get painted panelling in the restaurant – a sort of contemporary take on an 18th-century gentleman's club – then cool colours in the bar, where you can grab a pint of Butcombe, then spin outside to watch village life pass by. Lovely rooms have terrific prices. You'll find good beds, white linen, pretty furniture and excellent bathrooms; one has a free-standing bath. Elsewhere, red leather banquettes, fresh flowers, kind staff, the daily papers. As for the food, it's just the ticket: local partridge, fillet of bream, treacle tart with buttermilk ice cream.

Rooms	8 doubles, 1 twin/double: £95–£140. Singles from £85. Extra bed/sofabed £20 p.p.p.n.
Meals	Lunch from £5.95. Dinner, 3 courses, about £30. Sunday lunch from £12.95.
Closed	Christmas Day & Boxing Day.
Directions	A303, then north on B3165, through Martock to Long Sutton. On village green.

Philip & Sheila Mepham
The Devonshire Arms
Long Sutton,
Langport, TA10 9LP

Tel	+44 (0)1458 241271
Email	mail@thedevonshirearms.com
Web	www.thedevonshirearms.com

The White Hart

Cool inns with lovely rooms in interesting parts of the land are a big hit with lots of us – we like the easy style, the local food, the good prices and the happy staff. The White Hart is a case in point, a beautifully refurbished inn. It sits on Somerton's ancient market square, 16th-century bricks and mortar, 21st-century lipstick and pearls. Inside, old and new mix beautifully: stone walls and parquet flooring, lovely sofas in front of the fire, funky lamps hanging above the bar. You'll find soft colours, padded window seats, country rugs, antler chandeliers. There's a cute booth in a stone turret, then lovely food waits, perhaps a chargrilled steak, Cornish crab cakes or wood-roasted pork loin. In summer, you spill onto a smart courtyard or into the garden for views of open country. Upstairs, fabulous bedrooms await. You might find timber frames, a claw-foot bath, a wall of paper or stripped boards. All have super beds, flat-screen TVs, lovely bathrooms and a nice price. Beautiful Somerset is all around, don't miss it.

Rooms	8 doubles: £85–£130.
Meals	Lunch from £6.
	Dinner, 3 courses, £25–£30.
	Sunday lunch from £15.
Closed	Open all day.
Directions	South from Glastonbury on B3151. Right for Somerton, left into village and on left in square.

Kirsty Schmidt
The White Hart
Market Place,
Somerton, TA11 7LX

Tel	+44 (0)1458 272273
Email	info@whitehartsomerton.com
Web	www.whitehartsomerton.com

The Pilgrims Restaurant with Rooms

Medieval pilgrims in search of King Arthur's tomb would stop here for sustenance before heading out across the marshes on their way to Glastonbury Abbey. These days, the food, the welcome and the rooms are all so lovely you're more likely to suffer a crisis of faith and stay put. Jools is to blame – his food is far too good to miss, good enough to alter the DNA of these walls – the Pilgrims is not an inn these days, but a restaurant with rooms. All the lovely old stuff survives – stone walls, timber frames, panelled walls and a couple of sofas in front of the fire. Tables in the restaurant are nicely spaced apart with subtle lighting and service that hits the spot. As for the food, expect local ingredients cooked to perfection, perhaps Lyme Bay scallops, rack of lamb, smooth dark chocolate pot with a hint of stem ginger. Five lovely bedrooms wait in the old skittle alley. Three have cathedral ceilings, all come with exposed stone walls, flat-screen TVs and crisp linen on good beds. As for the bathrooms, expect double-ended baths, separate power showers, fluffy robes. Wells and Glastonbury are close.

Rooms	4 doubles, 1 twin/double: £70-£110. Singles from £60.
Meals	Lunch from £8. Dinner, 3 courses, about £30. Not Monday. Sunday lunch £19.
Closed	Rarely.
Directions	On B3153 between Castle Cary & Somerton. In village by traffic lights.

Julian & Sally Mitchison
The Pilgrims Restaurant with Rooms
Lovington,
Castle Cary, BA7 7PT

Tel   +44 (0)1963 240597
Email   jools@thepilgrimsatlovington.co.uk
Web   www.thepilgrimsatlovington.co.uk

The Talbot Inn at Mells

The Talbot is an absolute stunner, one of the loveliest inns in the land. It sits in a timeless village lost in a tangle of country lanes, a 15th-century coaching inn reborn for the 21st-century. Sweep under the carriage arch and you enter a cobbled courtyard, where life gathers in good weather. There's a tithe-barn sitting room with big sofas and a Sunday cinema, then the Coach House Grill, where you eat at weekends under hanging beams. As for the main house, weave along ancient passageways and find stone walls, rugs on wood floors, crackling log fires and a low-ceilinged bar for a pint of Butcombe. The restaurant has colonised several cosy rooms and delicious food flies from the kitchen, perhaps white onion and cider soup, monkfish and mussel stew, chocolate and salted caramel sundae. Bedrooms are the best, some smaller, others huge with claw-foot baths, walk-in showers and modern four-posters. Add lovely staff to the mix and you have a slice of heaven. There's a colourful garden and great local walking, so bring your boots. The First World War poet, Siegfried Sassoon, is buried in the churchyard.

Rooms	8 doubles: £95–£150.
Meals	Lunch & dinner £5–£30.
	Sunday lunch from £15.
Closed	Rarely.
Directions	From Frome A362 for Radstock; left for Mells. At mini-roundabout right to Mells. After 1 mile right to Mells.

Matt Greenlees
The Talbot Inn at Mells
Selwood Street, Mells,
Frome, BA11 3PN

Tel	+44 (0)1373 812254
Email	info@talbotinn.com
Web	www.talbotinn.com

The Swan

The Swan is gorgeous, a contemporary take on a village local. It's part of a new wave of pubs that open all day and do so much more than serve a good pint. The locals love it. They come for breakfast, pop in to buy a loaf of bread, then return for afternoon tea and raid the cake stands. It's right on the bustling street, with a sprinkling of tables and chairs on the pavement in French-café style. Interiors mix old and new brilliantly. You get Farrow & Ball colours and cool lamps hanging above the bar, then lovely old rugs on boarded floors and a wood-burner to keep things toasty. Push inland to find an airy restaurant open to the rafters that overlooks the garden. Here you dig into Tom Blake's fabulous food (he's ex-River Cottage), anything from grilled Cornish herring to a three-course feast, maybe crispy Lyme Bay cuttlefish, slow cooked Quantock venison, chocolate and salted caramel tart. Bedrooms are lovely. Two have fancy baths in the room, you get vintage French furniture, iPod docks, colourful throws and walk-in power showers. Glastonbury is close, as are the Mendips.

Rooms	5 doubles, 2 twin/doubles: £85–£125. Extra bed £20. Cots available.
Meals	Lunch from £5. Dinner, 3 courses, about £25. Sunday lunch from £14. Bar meals only Sun night.
Closed	Rarely.
Directions	M5, junc. 22, then B3139 to Wedmore. In village.

Natalie Zvonek-Little
The Swan
Cheddar Road,
Wedmore, BS28 4EQ
Tel   +44 (0)1934 710337
Email   info@theswanwedmore.com
Web   www.theswanwedmore.com

Netherstowe House

Netherstowe is to hotels what Björk is to music – very different, utterly charming, a true original. It's quirky, too – part Ritz hotel, part curiosity shop – and it's full of surprises, not least its peculiar location on the edge of a 1970s housing estate. If that puts you off, don't let it – the house is hidden by beech hedging and once up the drive, you forget the outside world. Staff come to meet you and usher you inside, where gently eccentric interiors mix country-house style with 19th-century colonial overtones. You'll find varnished wood floors, roaring fires, tropical plants erupting from urns, the odd cabinet full of curios. Bedrooms are every bit as flamboyant with beautiful beds, cool colours, old armoires and chic bathrooms; several have free-standing baths. In contrast, contemporary courtyard apartments are utterly uncluttered. They have sofabeds for children and proper kitchens, but breakfast is included and the hotel is yours to roam. As for the food, choose from steaks in the cellar bistro or posh food above, perhaps cured salmon, roast guinea fowl, white chocolate panna cotta.

Rooms	7 doubles, 1 twin: £105–£159. 1 suite for 2: £195. 8 apartments for 4: £130.
Meals	Lunch from £19.95. Dinner, 3 courses, about £30.
Closed	26 December to 2 January.
Directions	A38 northeast from Birmingham towards Burton on Trent. Left for Lichfield at A5192. Over two r'bouts, past Lidl, down hill, right at traffic lights into Netherstowe Lane. 1st left and drive on right.

Ben Heathcote
Netherstowe House
Netherstowe Lane,
Lichfield, WS13 6AY

Tel	+44 (0)1543 254270
Email	info@netherstowehouse.com
Web	www.netherstowehouse.com

The Anchor

The Anchor is one of those lovely places that has resisted the urge to be precious. This is a cool little seaside inn where relaxed informality reigns; kids are welcome, staff are friendly, dogs fall asleep in the bar. You're 500 yards from the sea with a terrace that fills with locals in summer and lawns that run off towards the water. Inside, beautiful simplicity abounds – Cape Cod meets English country local. You get books everywhere, beautiful art, roaring fires, a happy vibe. The big draw is Sophie's lovely food. Game and venison come from local estates, fish and seafood from nearby waters, samphire and sea kale are foraged along the coast. Bedrooms fit the mood perfectly. Those in the house are warm and homely; the suites in the garden are big and airy with sofas inside and terraces that overlook nearby dunes. Don't miss dinner, perhaps fish soup, game ravioli, chocolate fondant with caramel ice cream. You wash it all down with Mark's legendary collection of bottled beers and fancy wines. There are festivals by the score – don't miss Latitude or Folk East. Starry skies amaze. Unmissable.

Rooms	9 doubles, 1 single/double: £95–£150. Singles £85–£110. Extra bed/sofabed available £15–£25 p.p.p.n.
Meals	Lunch from £5.25. Dinner, 3 courses, about £30. Sunday lunch, 2 courses, £20.
Closed	Rarely.
Directions	From A12 south of Southwold, B1387 to Walberswick.

Mark & Sophie Dorber
The Anchor
Main Street, Walberswick,
Southwold, IP18 6UA

Tel	+44 (0)1502 722112
Email	info@anchoratwalberswick.com
Web	www.anchoratwalberswick.com

The Westleton Crown

This is one of England's oldest coaching inns, with 800 years of continuous service under its belt. It stands in a village two miles inland from the sea at Dunwich, with Westleton Heath running east towards Minsmere RSPB Nature Reserve. Inside, stripped floors, smouldering fires, exposed brickwork and ancient beams sweep you back two hundred years. Weave about and find nooks and crannies in which to hide, flames flickering in open fires, a huge map on the wall for walkers. You can eat wherever you want, there's a conservatory breakfast room with fine local photography, then a colourful terraced garden for barbecues in summer. Fish comes straight off the boats at Lowestoft, local butchers provide local meat so you eat well; perhaps wild rabbit and ham hock, spiced sea bass with curried cockles, coconut panna cotta with roasted pineapple. Bedrooms are scattered about (Will and Kate loved theirs!), some in the main house, others in converted stables. Expect lime whites, comfy beds, crisp linen, flat-screen TVs. Pretty bathrooms come courtesy of Fired Earth, some with claw-foot baths. Aldeburgh and Southwold are close. *Min. stay: 2 nights at weekends.*

Rooms	26 doubles, 2 twins: £95–£180. 3 suites for 2: £185–£215. 2 family rooms for 4: £160–£180. 1 single: £90–£100.
Meals	Lunch & bar meals from £5.50. Dinner from £11.95. Sunday lunch from £14.95.
Closed	Never.
Directions	A12 north from Ipswich. Right at Yoxford onto B1122, then left for Westleton on B1125. On right in village.

Gareth Clarke
The Westleton Crown
The Street, Westleton,
Saxmundham, IP17 3AD

Tel	+44 (0)1728 648777
Email	info@westletoncrown.co.uk
Web	www.westletoncrown.co.uk

The Brudenell Hotel

The Brudenell stands bang on the beach in one of England's loveliest seaside towns. It makes the most of its view: a dining terrace at the front runs the length of the building; a glass-fronted restaurant swims in light; an elegant sitting room looks out to sea. The hotel mixes a contemporary style with an informal feel. You get coastal art, sunny colours and driftwood sculptures on display. Smart bedrooms come in different shapes and sizes. Those at the back look onto open country, those at the front have views of sea and sky. A chic style runs throughout: sparkling bathrooms, seaside colours, chic fabrics, blond wood furniture, sofas if there's room. Back downstairs the open-plan brasserie is the hub of the hotel with tasty bistro food on tap, perhaps moules marinière, beef braised in ale with mashed potato and red cabbage, white chocolate panna cotta with pistachio profiteroles. There are beach towels, deckchairs or golf up the road at Thorpeness; on clear nights the starry sky will amaze you, as will coastal walks. Don't miss the music festival in June or the food festival in September. *Minimum stay: 2 nights at weekends.*

Rooms	12 doubles, 30 twin/doubles: £150–£325. 2 singles: £80.
Meals	Lunch from £5. Dinner, 3 courses, about £30.
Closed	Never.
Directions	A1094 into Aldeburgh. Right at T-junction, down high street, last left in village before car park & yacht club.

Peter Osborne
The Brudenell Hotel
The Parade,
Aldeburgh, IP15 5BU

Tel	+44 (0)1728 452071
Email	info@brudenellhotel.co.uk
Web	www.brudenellhotel.co.uk

Wentworth Hotel

The Wentworth has the loveliest position in town, the beach literally a pebble's throw from the garden, the sea rolling east under a vast sky. Inside, fires smoulder, clocks chime and seaside elegance abounds. It's all terrifically English, with vintage wallpapers, kind local staff and an elegant bar that opens onto a terrace garden. The restaurant looks out to sea, spilling onto a sunken terrace in summer for views of passing boats. Delicious English fare is the order of the day: stilton soup, breast of guinea fowl, lemon posset with raspberries and shortbread. The hotel has been in the same family since 1920 and old-fashioned values mix harmoniously with interiors that are refreshed often to keep things sparkling. Spotless bedrooms are deeply comfy, those at the front have huge sea views (and binoculars). Expect warm colours, wicker armchairs, padded headboards and comfortable beds. Bathrooms, all refurbished, are excellent. Sofas galore in the sitting room, but you may want to spurn them to walk by the sea. Joyce Grenfell was a regular. The Snape Maltings are close. *Minimum stay: 2 nights at weekends.*

Rooms	24 twin/doubles: £140-£220.
	4 singles: £85-£119.
	Darfield House – 7 doubles: £140-£220.
	Dinner, B&B from £79 p.p.
Meals	Bar meals from £5. Lunch from £12.
	Dinner, 2-3 courses, £21-£26.50.
Closed	Never.
Directions	A12 north from Ipswich, then A1094 for Aldeburgh. Past church, down hill, left at x-roads; hotel on right.

Michael Pritt
Wentworth Hotel
Wentworth Road,
Aldeburgh, IP15 5BD

Tel	+44 (0)1728 452312
Email	stay@wentworth-aldeburgh.com
Web	www.wentworth-aldeburgh.com

The Crown & Castle

A great place to wash up for a few lazy days. Orford is hard to beat, a sleepy Suffolk village blissfully marooned at the end of the road. River, beach and forest wait, as does the Crown & Castle, a welcoming English hostelry where the art of hospitality is practised with unstinting flair. The inn stands in the shadow of Orford's 12th-century castle. Uncluttered interiors have a warm, airy feel with stripped floorboards, open fires, wonderful art and flickering candles at night. Chic bedrooms have Vi-Spring beds, fancy bathrooms, lovely fabrics, the odd armchair. Four in the main house have watery views, the suite is huge, the garden rooms big and light, the courtyard rooms a real delight. All have crisp white linen, TVs, DVDs and digital radios. Wellington boots wait at the back door, so pull on a pair and explore Rendlesham Forest or hop on a boat and chug over to Orfordness. Ambrosial food awaits your return, perhaps potted brown shrimps, a faultless steak and kidney pie, crushed pistachio meringue with a chocolate ice-cream sundae. Sutton Hoo is close. Dogs are very welcome. *Minimum stay: 2 nights at weekends. Children over 8 welcome.*

Rooms	18 doubles, 2 twins: £130–£260.
	1 suite for 2: £265–£335.
	Dinner, B&B from £95 p.p.
Meals	Lunch from £8.50.
	À la carte dinner around £35.
Closed	Rarely.
Directions	A12 north from Ipswich, A1152 east to Woodbridge, then B1084 into Orford. Right in square for castle. On left.

David & Ruth Watson
The Crown & Castle
Orford,
Woodbridge, IP12 2LJ
Tel   +44 (0)1394 450205
Email   info@crownandcastle.co.uk
Web   www.crownandcastle.co.uk

Fabulous food

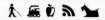

The Crown at Woodbridge

This cool little hotel in the middle of Woodbridge slopes downhill to the river, its rainbow of pastel colours making it a landmark in town. Inside, open-plan interiors flood with light courtesy of a glass ceiling. A Windermere skiff hangs above the bar, you find painted panelling, comfy sofas, slate floors and a wood-burner to keep things cosy. An airy restaurant comes in pale olive with leather banquettes, wooden floors and contemporary art, a fine spot for Daniel Perjesi's fabulous local food, perhaps soy braised ox cheeks with rice noodles, haunch of venison with a juniper crust, toffee apples with salted caramel ice cream. Breakfast is just as good; expect poached fruits, flagons of juice, smoked kippers, the best sausages in Suffolk. Stylish bedrooms above vary in size, but all have the same feel: off-white colours, duck-down duvets, padded headboards, Hypnos beds. You'll find panels of entwined willow, pitchforks hanging on the wall, sparkling bathrooms with power showers. Don't miss Sutton Hoo, the Aldeburgh food festival or Rendlesham Forest, the UK's equivalent of Area 51.

Rooms	8 twin/doubles: £100–£160. 2 family rooms for 4: £120–£160. Singles from £95.
Meals	Lunch & dinner £6–£30. Sunday lunch from £12.50.
Closed	Never.
Directions	A12 north from Ipswich, then B1438 into town. Pass station & left into Quay St. On right.

Garth Wray
The Crown at Woodbridge
Thoroughfare,
Woodbridge, IP12 1AD

Tel	+44 (0)1394 384242
Email	info@thecrownatwoodbridge.co.uk
Web	www.thecrownatwoodbridge.co.uk

Kesgrave Hall

This Georgian mansion sits in 38 acres of woodland and gardens, sound-proofing it from the outside world. It was home to US airmen during WWII, but the locals have reclaimed it as their own now and they come for the easy style, the excellent service, the delicious food and the informal vibe. The emphasis here is firmly on the food, so it's almost a restaurant with rooms, albeit quite a grand one. Inside, you find wellington boots in the entrance hall, high ceilings in the big sitting room, stripped boards in the humming bistro and doors that open onto a terrace in summer. Colourful bedrooms have lots of style. One of the suites is huge and comes with a free-standing bath and a faux leopard-skin sofa. The others might not be quite as wild, but they're lovely nonetheless, some cosy in the eaves, others in beautifully refurbished outbuildings. Expect warm colours, crisp linen, good lighting and fancy bathrooms. Back downstairs, tasty food flies from the kitchen, perhaps smoked haddock fishcakes, a char-grilled steak, a delicious coffee cheesecake with Tia Maria ice cream. Suffolk's magical coast waits.

Rooms	10 doubles, 7 twin/doubles: £130–£230.
	6 suites for 2: £275–£300.
Meals	Breakfast £10–£16.
	Lunch & dinner, 3 courses, £25–£30.
Closed	Never.
Directions	Skirt Ipswich to the south on A14, then north on A12. Left at 4th r'bout; signed right after 0.25 miles.

Oliver Richards
Kesgrave Hall
Hall Road,
Kesgrave, Ipswich, IP5 2PU
Tel   +44 (0)1473 333741
Email   reception@kesgravehall.com
Web   www.milsomhotels.com

The Crown

The Crown is all things to all men, a lovely country pub, a popular local restaurant, a small boutique hotel, a cool little bolthole in Constable country. It sits in a pretty village with long views from its colourful terrace over the Box Valley, not a bad spot for a glass of Pimm's after a day exploring the area. It dates to 1560 and has old beams and timber frames, though interiors have youthful good looks: warm colours, tongue-and-groove panelling, terracotta-tiled floors, a fancy wine cellar behind a wall of glass. You'll find rugs and settles, the daily papers, leather armchairs in front of a wood-burner. Four ales wait at the bar, 30 wines come by the glass and there's seasonal food that will make you smile, perhaps mussel chowder, steak and kidney pie, steamed orange pudding with marmalade ice-cream. Airy bedrooms are hidden away at the bottom of the garden, all exemplary with super bathrooms, excellent beds, lovely linen and a dash of colour. All have armchairs or sofas, three have French windows that open onto private terraces with fine views. A great place to eat, sleep and potter.

Rooms	10 doubles: £135–£225. 1 suite for 2: £195–£245. Singles £95–£150. Extra bed/sofabed available £10–£30 p.p.p.n.
Meals	Lunch & dinner £5–£30.
Closed	Rarely.
Directions	North from Colchester on A134, then B1087 east into Stoke-by-Nayland. Right at T-junction; pub on left.

Richard Sunderland
The Crown
Park Street, Stoke-by-Nayland,
Colchester, CO6 4SE

Tel	+44 (0)1206 262001
Email	info@crowninn.net
Web	www.crowninn.net

The Bildeston Crown

Chris and Haley ran the Crown for ten years, upped sticks to head a few miles north, then got an offer they couldn't refuse and now the place is theirs. Their home is this beautifully preserved 15th-century inn. All the lovely old bits survive – timber frames, sagging beams, an ancient inglenook with a roaring fire – but interiors have an elegant, contemporary style with bold colours, stripped floorboards, comfy sofas and big art on the walls. Farmers drop in to chew the cud, walkers come to defrost in front of the fire while knocking back a pint of local ale, and the world and his wife come from near and far for Chris' delicious local food, perhaps truffled arancini with English asparagus, pheasant and fois gras Wellington, then an After Eight soufflé with chocolate ice cream. Stylish rooms have comfy beds, wonky floors, lots of colour and art. One has a fake Canaletto hanging above a claw-foot bath, another has a four-poster bed, all have robes in good bathrooms and flat-screen TVs. Don't miss Bury St Edmunds, a market town steeped in history. Medieval Lavenham is close, too. *Minimum stay: 2 nights at weekends.*

Rooms	11 doubles, 1 twin: £100–£175. Dinner, B&B from £87.50 p.p. Singles from £70.
Meals	Lunch from £6.50. Bar meals from £14. Dinner, 3 course, £30–£40. Sunday lunch from £17. Afternoon tea £15.
Closed	Never.
Directions	A12 junc. 31, then B1070 to Hadleigh. A1141 north, then B1115 into village & on right.

Hayley & Chris Lee
The Bildeston Crown
104 High Street,
Bildeston, IP7 7EB

Tel	+44 (0)1449 740510
Email	reception@thebildestoncrown.com
Web	www.thebildestoncrown.com

The Great House

Lavenham is a Suffolk gem, a medieval wool town trapped in aspic. The Great House stands across the market place from the Guildhall, its Georgian façade giving way to airy 15th-century interiors, where timber frames and old beams mix with contemporary colours and varnished wood floors. The poet Stephen Spender and his brother Humphrey – famous artist and photographer – once lived here and the house became a meeting place for artists, but these days it's the ambrosial food that draws the crowd. French to its core – the cheese board must qualify as one of the best in Britain – so dig into something delicious, perhaps venison, pistachio and sultana terrine, sea bass served with olives and white wine, then tarte tatin with cinnamon ice-cream. Fabulous bedrooms – all recently refurbished in lavish style – come with delicious bed linen, suede sofas, coffee machines, and robes in magnificent bathrooms. Four are huge, but even the tiniest is a dream. One has a regal four-poster, another has a 14th-century fireplace in its bathroom. All come with an array of gadgets: hi-fi, surround-sound, flat-screen TV... *Minimum stay: 2 nights at weekends.*

Rooms	4 doubles, 1 twin/double: £105-£239. Singles £105-£215. Dinner, B&B £119-£170 p.p. Extra bed/sofabed available £15-£20 p.p.p.n.
Meals	Breakfast £12-£17. Lunch from £24.95 (not Mon/Tue). Dinner £36.50 (not Sun/Mon). À la carte only Sat night.
Closed	January; 2 weeks in summer.
Directions	A1141 to Lavenham. At High Street 1st right after The Swan or up Lady Street into Market Place. On-site parking.

Régis & Martine Crépy
The Great House
Market Place,
Lavenham, CO10 9QZ

Tel	+44 (0)1787 247431
Email	info@greathouse.co.uk
Web	www.greathouse.co.uk

The Swan at Lavenham Hotel & Spa

This medieval inn has never looked better. It's a spectacular tangle of ancient timbers and sagging beams, with roaring fires, soaring ceilings and lovely staff, who weave through the throng, delivering sinful plates of afternoon tea or cocktails before supper. Potter about and find a minstrel's gallery in the vaulted dining room, a fabulous old bar that was a favourite haunt of WWII airmen, then a courtyard garden, where you can stop for a glass of Pimm's in summer. As if that wasn't enough, a beautiful new spa has recently appeared: you'll find six treatment rooms, a sauna and steam room, then sunbeds encircling a vitality pool on the terrace; sheer bliss. As for the stylish bedrooms, some are vast with four-posters and timber-frames, others more contemporary with cool colours and sofas. All have comfy beds, crisp white linen, robes in fancy bathrooms, while beds are turned down during dinner. There's an open-plan brasserie for lighter bites, then a 14th-century hall for weddings. As for Lavenham, it's one of the best preserved medieval towns in the land. Bury St Edmunds is close, too. *On-site parking available. Ask about special offers.*

Rooms	32 twin/doubles, 2 four-posters: £185–£360. 10 suites for 2: £290–£360. 1 single: £105. Dinner, B&B £245–£420 for 2.
Meals	Lunch, 2 courses, from £16.95. Dinner, 3 courses £39.95. Brasserie, 2 courses, from £16.
Closed	Never.
Directions	In village.

Ingo Wiangke
The Swan at Lavenham Hotel & Spa
High Street,
Lavenham, CO10 9QA

Tel	+44 (0)1787 247477
Email	info@theswanatlavenham.co.uk
Web	www.theswanatlavenham.co.uk

The Packhorse Inn

The rise of the cool country inn continues apace and the most recent member to join the club is the Packhorse, a beautifully renovated country pub that was rescued from abject neglect. These days it's a small-scale pleasure dome – striking interiors, ambrosial food, bedrooms and bathrooms that elate – yet it remains a village local with a lovely bar that welcomes all. The downstairs is open plan with a fire that burns on two sides and the odd armchair to take the strain. You'll find varnished floorboards, beautiful art, low-hanging lamps at the cool little bar. Chic bedrooms have beautiful beds, cashmere throws, walk-in showers, perhaps a double-ended bath in the room. Back downstairs irresistible food waits, maybe truffled goat's cheese with quince and figs, Suffolk venison and kidney pudding, plum tarte tatin with fruit-cake ice-cream. There's a terrace for good weather and a private dining room turns into a very cool meeting room. This is prime horse-racing country three miles east of Newmarket (the peerless Frankel is at stud nearby). Cambridge and Bury St Edmunds are also close.

Rooms	6 doubles, 2 twin/doubles: £100–£175. Singles from £85. Extra beds for children £10.
Meals	Lunch from £6. Dinner, 3 courses, about £35.
Closed	Rarely.
Directions	A14, junc. 38, then north onto A11. Take 1st exit east on B1085. Through Kentford and into Moulton. Left at green and on left.

Philip Turner
The Packhorse Inn
Bridge Street, Moulton,
Newmarket CB8 8SP

Tel	+44 (0)1638 751818
Email	info@thepackhorseinn.com
Web	www.thepackhorseinn.com

Hurtwood Hotel

The Surrey Hills are stunning – forest walks, rolling pasture, spectacular views, mountain bike trails. It's an area that remains inexplicably undiscovered, yet it's only an hour from London. As for the Hurtwood, it sits in a pretty village surrounded by wooded hills. It was built by Forte in anticipation of a railway line that never appeared. Caroline recently came home after 20 years in Australia, bought the place, refurbished in style, now it shines. Downstairs, the breakfast room opens onto a terrace, where you can eat in good weather accompanied by bird song. Upstairs, nicely priced rooms have comfort and style with good beds, crisp linen, spotless bathrooms, the odd sofabed. Those at the front flood with light and have views over the village to peaceful hills. Back downstairs, Robi and Lorenzo's fantastic Italian food waits in the restaurant. There's a bar and terrace for pre-dinner drinks, then irresistible food, perhaps tagiolini with fresh Devon crab, ravioli with scallops and prawns, guinea fowl with grapes and Vin Santo. The tasting menu is a steal, you'll think you're in the Tuscan hills. A treat.

Rooms	10 doubles, 3 twin/doubles: £85–£115. Extra beds: children £10; adults £15.
Meals	Lunch from £5.50. Bar meals from £9.50. Dinner, 3 courses, £25–£35. Tasting menu £31.50.
Closed	Never.
Directions	A25 east from Guildford, then south in Shere for Ewhurst. Over railway bridge, after 500m, then left into Hook Lane for Peaslake. On right at end of village.

Caroline Darbishire
Hurtwood Hotel
Walking Bottom, Peaslake,
Guildford, GU5 9RR

Tel	+44 (0)1306 730514
Email	hurtwoodhotel@mail.com
Web	www.hurtwoodhotel.co.uk

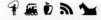

The Barn at Roundhurst

A 17th-century threshing barn on a small farm lost in deep country. Inside, you find a spectacular space, one huge room that's open to its rafters, with equally beautiful timber frames on display. Other than that, it's all deliciously contemporary, with a cool little fire that throws out the heat, leather sofas, beautiful sculpture, soft lighting and cow hide rugs. Upstairs, there's an honesty bar, then a library for books and maps, playing cards and poker chips! Chic rooms spiral around a pretty courtyard to one side of the barn, most with private terraces. You get boarded floors, blond wood furniture, smart fabrics, the odd exposed beam. Gorgeous bathrooms have white robes, walk-in showers and underfloor heating; most have baths, too. Food is on tap with cold platters – cheese, ham, salads and bread – available every day, then a table d'hôte menu from Thursday to Saturday, perhaps fig and goat's cheese tart, rack of local lamb, Cointreau panna cotta. Good dining pubs are a short drive, great local walking starts from the front door. Petworth and Goodwood are both close.

Rooms	6 twin/doubles: £130–£200. Extra beds £20–£30.
Meals	Dinner: cold platters £10.50; 4-course set menu (Thur-Sat) £40. Picnics by arrangement.
Closed	Rarely.
Directions	A3, A283 south for Petworth, then right for Haslemere on B2131. Left into Jobson's Lane, then 1st right. Keep left and on left after 1 mile.

The Bookings Team
The Barn at Roundhurst
Lower Roundhurst Farm,
Jobson's Lane, Lurgashall, GU27 3BN
Tel   +44 (0)1428 642535
Email   bookings@thebarnatroundhurst.com
Web   www.thebarnatroundhurst.com

Halfway Bridge Inn

Sam's gorgeous inn wasn't quite as lovely when he took over the reins a few years ago, but after pouring in love and money in equally large amounts, the place now shines. It sits back from the A272, with Goodwood to the south for the races, Petworth to the east for antiques and the South Downs all around for exhilarating walking. Step inside to find a smart, cosy world of original wood floors, whitewashed walls, smouldering fires, the odd mind-your-head beam. It's a deeply pretty place, small but certainly sweet, with snug rooms giving a Dickensian feel, albeit with a 21st-century makeover. Spin round to the bar and find three local ales, 25 wines by the glass, the daily papers and beautifully upholstered bar stools; there's a door onto the terrace for lunch in summer. Big stylish bedrooms wait across the lane in an old stone barn, where old and new mix beautifully – smart bathrooms and lovely furniture amid beams and panelled walls. As for the food, it's a big draw with the locals, perhaps Cornish scallops with tiger prawns, cannon of lamb with a mead-scented jus, a prune and armagnac tart. *Minimum stay: 2 nights at weekends.*

Rooms	6 doubles: £140–£180. 1 suite for 2: £210–£230. Extra bed/sofabed available £30 p.p.p.n.
Meals	Lunch & dinner £14.50–£28. Bar meals £6.50–£12.50.
Closed	Never.
Directions	On A272 halfway between Midhurst & Petworth.

Sam Bakose
Halfway Bridge Inn
Halfway Bridge,
Petworth, GU28 9BP

Tel	+44 (0)1798 861281
Email	enquiries@halfwaybridge.co.uk
Web	www.halfwaybridge.co.uk

Park House Hotel & Spa

A blissful pocket of rural Sussex. Park House sits in 12 acres of glorious English gardens with quilted fields circling the grounds and the South Downs rising beyond. Potter about outside and find a croquet lawn, a grass tennis court and a six-hole golf course that slips into the country. Fine shrubberies burst with colour while wellington boots wait at the front door for long country walks. You may prefer to stay put; the newest addition is a fabulous spa. It comes with a very swanky indoor pool to go with its outside partner, four treatment rooms, a sauna and steam room, then a proper gym and a terraced bar for lazy afternoons. As for the house, it's just as good. Beautiful interiors abound mixing country-house style with contemporary colours. The pavilion bar overlooks the gardens, you breakfast in the conservatory or out on the terrace, there are flagstones in reception, the daily papers in the sitting room, great food in the dining room. Gorgeous bedrooms are the final luxury: heavenly beds, big country views, fancy bathrooms, iMac TVs. Exceptional. *Minimum stay: 2 nights at weekends. Pets by arrangement.*

Rooms	6 doubles, 10 twin/doubles: £108-£192. 4 family rooms for 4: £222-£318. 1 cottage for 2-4: £250-£315.
Meals	Lunch from £23.95. Dinner from £30. Afternoon tea £19.95.
Closed	Rarely.
Directions	South from Midhurst on A286. At sharp left bend, right (straight ahead), signed Bepton. Hotel on left after 2 miles.

	Rebecca Coonan
	Park House Hotel & Spa
	Bepton,
	Midhurst, GU29 0JB
Tel	+44 (0)1730 819020
Email	reservations@parkhousehotel.com
Web	www.parkhousehotel.com

The Royal Oak Inn

This pretty inn sits in a sleepy village with the South Downs rising above and the south coast waiting below. Inside, attractive, rustic interiors hit the spot with stripped floors, low ceilings and the odd racing print (the inn was once part of the Goodwood estate). There's a small bar for a pint in front of an open fire, but these days it's a mostly dining pub, the restaurant spreading itself far and wide, then bursting onto a couple of terraces in summer. Delicious food flies from the kitchen, perhaps wild mushroom risotto, guinea fowl with apricots and hazelnuts, banana bread and butter pudding. Bedrooms are scattered about, some in courtyard cottages, others upstairs. All have a warm, contemporary style with smart fabrics, leather armchairs, comfy beds and good bathrooms. CD players, smart TVs and DVD libraries keep you amused. Staff stop to chat, complimentary newspapers arrive with breakfast. There's lots do: Goodwood, the South Downs, Chichester and its excellent theatre, and the Witterings for miles of sandy beach. Don't miss Bosham, where King Canute tried to turn back the waves. *Minimum stay: 2 nights at weekends.*

Rooms	2 doubles, 3 twin/doubles: £110–£190. 3 suites for 2-4: £180–£295. Singles from £85.
Meals	Lunch from £7.95. Dinner, 3 courses, about £35. Sunday lunch from £25–£29.
Closed	Never.
Directions	From Chichester A286 for Midhurst. First right at first mini roundabout into E. Lavant. Down hill, past village green, over bridge, pub 200 yds on left. Car park opposite.

Charles Ullmann
The Royal Oak Inn
Pook Lane, East Lavant,
Chichester, PO18 0AX

Tel	+44 (0)1243 527434
Email	rooms@royaloakeastlavant.co.uk
Web	www.royaloakeastlavant.co.uk

The Crab & Lobster

This tiny arrowhead of land south of Chichester is something of a time warp, more 1940s than 21st century. The Crab & Lobster is older still – 350 years at the last count. It sits on Pagham Harbour, a tidal marsh that teems with preening birds. Outside, you find a smart whitewashed exterior and a small garden for views across fields of sheep to the water. Inside, flagged floors, whitewashed walls, a fire at one end, a wood-burner at the other. There's a lovely alcove with banquette seating, candles flicker in the evening, in summer you decant onto the back terrace for lunch in the sun. Upstairs, four super rooms come in duck-egg blue with crisp white linen, flat-screen TVs and gorgeous little bathrooms. Three have views of the water, one is up in the eaves and has a telescope to scan the high seas. There's much to explore: Bosham, where King Canute tried to turn back the waves; Fishbourne, for its Roman palace; the Witterings, for miles of beach and dunes. Don't forget dinner, perhaps Selsey crab cakes with chilli jam, fillet of pork with a calvados cream, caramelised plum tart. *Minimum stay: 2 nights at weekends.*

Rooms	4 doubles: £165-£195. 1 cottage for 4: £280-£300. Singles £90. Extra bed/sofabed available £30 p.p.p.n.
Meals	Bar meals from £6.50. Lunch from £11.95. Dinner, 3 courses, £35. Sunday lunch, 2 courses, £26.
Closed	Never.
Directions	Mill Lane is off B2145 Chichester to Selsey road, just south of Sidlesham.

Sam Bakose
The Crab & Lobster
Mill Lane, Sidlesham,
Chichester, PO20 7NB

Tel	+44 (0)1243 641233
Email	enquiries@crab-lobster.co.uk
Web	www.crab-lobster.co.uk

The Bull

This 16th-century inn on the South Downs has lots to offer – a cracking bar, four fancy bedrooms, tasty local food and an excellent array of ales and craft beers from across the globe. Step inside and it's like travelling back to Dickensian England. Light is rationed on aesthetic grounds, beams sag, fires roar and happy locals gather for a pint of Bedlam, the pub's own brew. You can eat wherever you want – meat from Sussex farms, game from local estates, fish from short-range boats – perhaps scallops with black pudding, roasted sausages with onion gravy, chocolate bread and butter pudding. Upstairs, four stylish bedrooms have recently been refurbished (two larger, two above the bar), with four more coming soon. Expect Farrow & Ball colours, chic fabrics, old-style radiators and comfy beds. Bigger rooms have sofas, you might find timber frames, a cow-hide rug or a low beamed ceiling. All have digital radios, flat-screen TVs and smart little bathrooms. Bring walking boots and mountain bikes and scale the Ditchling Beacon for big views. Brighton and Gatwick are close, don't miss Sunday lunch. *Minimum stay: 2 nights at weekends.*

Rooms	3 doubles, 1 twin/double: £100–£160.
Meals	Lunch from £5. Dinner, 3 courses, £25–£35. Sunday lunch from £14.
Closed	Never.
Directions	Leave A23 just north of Brighton for Pyecombe. North on A273, then west for Ditchling on B2112. In centre of village at crossroads.

Dominic Worrall
The Bull
2 High Street, Ditchling,
Hassocks, BN6 8TA

Tel   +44 (0)1273 843147
Email   info@thebullditchling.com
Web   www.thebullditchling.com

The Griffin Inn

A proper inn, posh with a hint of scruffiness, a community local that draws a devoted crowd. You get open fires, 400-year-old beams, oak panelling and prints on the walls. There's a lively bar, an attractive restaurant and a club room for racing on Saturdays. In summer, life spills onto a pretty terrace for local meat cooked in a wood-fired oven. There are weekend barbecues, too, and deckchairs scattered across the lawns for ten-mile views over Pooh Bear's Ashdown forest to Sheffield Park. Bedrooms are nicely-priced and full of country-inn elegance: uneven floors, the odd four-poster, lovely old furniture and free-standing baths. Rooms in the coach house are quieter, those in Griffin House quieter still. Some in the main house have timber frames, all have robes and colourful art. Back downstairs, seasonal menus do the trick, perhaps rabbit gnocchi, local pheasant, dark chocolate tort with honey ice cream; breakfast sausages are divine. The pub has three cricket teams that travel the world in pursuit of glory – you may find them in the bar on a summer evening after a hot day in the field. *Minimum stay: 2 nights at Bank Holiday weekends.*

Rooms	6 doubles, 7 four-posters: £85-£145. Singles £70-£80 (Sun-Thur).
Meals	Bar meals from £6.50. Dinner, 3 courses, £30-£40.
Closed	Christmas Day.
Directions	From East Grinstead A22 south, right at Nutley for Fletching. On for 2 miles into village.

Nigel & James Pullan
The Griffin Inn
Fletching,
Uckfield, TN22 3SS

Tel	+44 (0)1825 722890
Email	info@thegriffininn.co.uk
Web	www.thegriffininn.co.uk

Wingrove House

This beautiful hotel is proof positive that small hotels are infinitely lovelier than their big brothers. It stands at the end of a pretty village with an ancient church on one side and the South Downs Way passing on the other. You enter through a walled garden that leads up to a stone terrace, a lovely spot to linger in good weather, with wisteria hanging off the balcony and bamboo swaying in the breeze. In winter you retreat to the sitting room, where wood floors and painted panelling give a chic, contemporary feel. Upstairs, gorgeous bedrooms have cool colours, smart fabrics and robes in fabulous bathrooms. Two open onto the veranda, the biggest at the back overlooks the churchyard, some have double-ended baths, others walk-in showers. As for the restaurant, it's just been refurbished in cool greys. An open fire keeps things cosy in winter, a wall of glass opens onto a dining terrace in summer. Delicious food waits, too, perhaps locally smoked salmon, fillet of Beachy Head beef, spiced banana and rum sponge. Walks start from the front door: Cuckmere Haven, Friston Forest and Beachy Head all wait.

Rooms	7 doubles: £95-£200. Singles from £85.
Meals	Lunch from £10 (Thur-Sun). Dinner £29-£35.
Closed	Rarely.
Directions	M23, A23, then A27 east from Brighton. Past Berwick, then south at r'bout for Alfriston. In village on left.

Ian Graham
Wingrove House
High Street, Alfriston,
Polegate, BN26 5TD

Tel	+44 (0)1323 870276
Email	info@wingrovehousealfriston.com
Web	www.wingrovehousealfriston.com

The Tiger Inn

The Tiger sits on a village green that has hardly changed in 50 years and in summer life spills onto the terrace to soak up an English sun. It's all part of a large estate that hugs the coast from Beachy Head to Cuckmere Haven with Birling Gap in between; some of the best coastal walking in the south lies on your doorstep. Back at the inn a fabulous renovation has breathed new life into old bones. Downstairs has bags of character with low beams, wooden floors, pale coloured walls and a roaring fire. Beer brewed on the estate pours from the tap, so try a pint of Legless Rambler before digging into hearty food – Beachy Head beer-battered catch of the day, the famous Tiger burger, sausage and mash with a sweet onion gravy, treacle tart with vanilla ice-cream. Five country-house bedrooms are the big surprise. Find beautiful fabrics, padded bedheads, funky bathrooms, the odd beam. Beds are dressed with lambswool throws, warm colours hang on the walls. Back outside, white cliffs wait, as do the South Downs. Finally, Arthur Conan Doyle knew the village and a blue plaque on one of the cottages suggests Sherlock Holmes retired here.

Rooms	4 doubles, 1 twin: £110–£150.
Meals	Starters from £5.50.
	Lunch & dinner from £9.95.
	Desserts from £5.50.
Closed	Rarely.
Directions	West from Eastbourne on A259.
	Left in village. Parking on right near
	village hall.

Charlie Davies–Gilbert
The Tiger Inn
The Green, East Dean,
Eastbourne, BN20 0DA

Tel	+44 (0)1323 423209
Email	tiger@beachyhead.org.uk
Web	www.beachyhead.org.uk

Belle Tout Lighthouse

A fine old lighthouse atop a white cliff with stunning views in every direction. To your left, Beachy Head, to your right, Birling Gap – it's a magical position with the South Downs rolling down into the English Channel. As for the lighthouse, it dates to 1832. It was once moved 57 feet back to stop it crumbling into the sea and it featured prominently in the BBC's production of *The Life and Loves of a She-Devil*. It re-opened in 2010 after a splendid renovation as a lovely little B&B hotel. Bedrooms are rather wonderful: not huge, but all have windows that bring the outside in. You get white walls to soak up the light, fantastic views of rolling hills, pretty fabrics, lovely linen, the odd exposed brick wall; shower rooms are small but sweet, one room has a bath. Ian's legendary breakfasts are served on high with views of sea and cliff. There's a wood-burner in the sitting room, where guests gather each night before climbing up to explore the lantern. Good food waits in the village: a lovely pub and an excellent Thai restaurant. Magnificent walking waits. *Minimum stay: 2 nights. Over 15s welcome.*

Rooms	6 doubles: £145–£220. Singles from £101.50.
Meals	Pub/restaurant within 1 mile.
Closed	Christmas & New Year.
Directions	A259 to East Dean, then south for Beachy Head. Keep left at Birling Gap and on right above sea.

	Ian Noall Belle Tout Lighthouse Beachy Head Road, Beachy Head, Eastbourne, BN20 0AE
Tel	+44 (0)1323 423185
Email	info@belletout.co.uk
Web	www.belletout.co.uk

Strand House

As you follow the Royal Military Canal down to miles of sandy beach, bear in mind that 600 years ago, you'd have been swimming in the sea. This is reclaimed land and Strand House, built in 1425, originally stood on Winchelsea Harbour. Outside, you find wandering wisteria, colourful flowerbeds and a woodland walk that leads up to the village. Inside, medieval interiors have low ceilings, timber frames and mind-your-head beams. There are reds and yellows, sofas galore, a wood-burner in the sitting room, an honesty bar from which to help yourself. It's a home-spun affair: Hugh cooks breakfast, Mary conjures up tasty meals at weekends. Attractive bedrooms are warm and colourful. One has an ancient four-poster, some have wonky floors, all have comfy beds and compact shower rooms. Airy rooms in the cottage have more space, and the suite, with its balcony and views across the fields, is a treat. The house, once a work house, was painted by Turner and Millais. Local restaurants wait: Webb's Fish Café, The Globe in Rye, a Michelin star at the Curlew in Odium. Dogs are very welcome. *Min. stay: 2 nights at weekends & in high season.*

Rooms	6 doubles, 1 twin/double, 5 triples: £80–£150.1 suite for 4: £180. Singles from £60. Dogs £7.50.
Meals	Pub 5-minute walk. Restaurants 2 miles.
Closed	Rarely.
Directions	A259 west from Rye for 2 miles. House on the left at foot of hill, opposite Bridge Inn pub.

Mary Sullivan & Hugh Davie
Strand House
Tanyards Lane,
Winchelsea, Rye, TN36 4JT

Tel	+44 (0)1797 226276
Email	info@thestrandhouse.co.uk
Web	www.thestrandhouse.co.uk

The George in Rye

Rye is beautiful, old England trapped in aspic. It was a Cinque Port, Henry James lived here and the oldest church clock in England chimes at the top of the hill. The George stands on its cobbled high street right in the thick of things. Built in 1575 from reclaimed ships' timbers, its exposed beams and panelled walls remain on display. Inside, old and new mix beautifully – expect Jane Austen in the 21st century. There's a roaring fire in the bar, screen prints of the Beatles on the walls in reception, a sun-trapping courtyard for lunch in summer. Beautiful bedrooms come in all shapes and sizes (a couple are small), but chic fabrics, Frette linen and Vi-Spring mattresses are standard, as are good books, fine bathrooms, white robes and cashmere covers on hot water bottles. Some are huge with zinc baths in the room, one has a round bed. You eat in the George Grill, an open kitchen on display, perhaps Provençal fish soup, grilled rib-eye with hand-cut chips, gooseberry soufflé with bay leaf ice cream. Walk it off by following the river down to the sea. *Mapp and Lucia* was filmed in the town.

Rooms	8 doubles, 21 twin/doubles: £135–£195.
	5 suites for 2: £295–£325.
	Singles from £95.
Meals	Lunch from £6.
	Dinner, 3 courses, £30–£40.
	Afternoon tea £12.50.
Closed	Never.
Directions	Follow signs up hill into town centre. Through arch; hotel on left, below church. 24-hour parking 5 minutes down hill.

Alex & Katie Clarke
The George in Rye
98 High Street,
Rye, TN31 7JT

Tel	+44 (0)1797 222114
Email	stay@thegeorgeinrye.com
Web	www.thegeorgeinrye.com

Jeake's House

Rye is utterly gorgeous, one of those lovely English country towns that's been around for centuries, but has never lost its looks. The same is true of Jeake's House. It's spent 300 years on this steep cobbled street in the old town accruing a colourful past as a wool store, a school, and the home of American poet Conrad Potter Aiken. Inside: timber frames, ancient beams and small smartly carpeted corridors that weave along to cosy bedrooms, the latter generously furnished, deeply comfortable and excellent value for money. Some have four-posters, all have rich fabrics, one has a telly concealed in the wood-burner. The galleried dining room – once an old Baptist chapel, now painted deep red – is full of busts, books, clocks and mirrors – a fine setting for a full English breakfast. There's also a lovely cosy honesty bar, where a fire burns in winter. Outside, you'll find art galleries, antiques shops, old churches and river walks. All this would be blossom in the wind without Jenny, whose natural friendliness has created a winning atmosphere. Don't miss it. *Children over 8 welcome.*

Rooms	7 twin/doubles; 1 double with separate bath: £95–£128. 3 four-poster suites for 2: £130–£150. Singles from £79.
Meals	Restaurants within walking distance.
Closed	Never.
Directions	From centre of Rye on A268, left off High St onto West St, then 1st right into Mermaid St. House on left. Private car park, £3 a day for guests.

Jenny Hadfield
Jeake's House
Mermaid Street,
Rye, TN31 7ET

Tel	+44 (0)1797 222828
Email	stay@jeakeshouse.com
Web	www.jeakeshouse.com

The Gallivant

This cool little hotel stands across the road from Camber Sands, where five miles of pristine beach are home to kite surfers, beach cricketers and sun worshipers alike. As for the Gallivant, a recent refurbishment has brought a stunning new look. Bedrooms, small and large, are now things of great beauty (two await their turn). Cabin rooms are clad in wood with brass lamps hanging from the ceiling; beach rooms have daybeds and marble bathrooms; deck rooms at the back come in cool whites with doors onto private terraces. Then come the garden rooms – heaven for hedonists – with double-ended baths in the room (and doors that slide for privacy). They come with decks in the garden, where you'll find a massage hut and hammocks in summer. All have flawless bathrooms, great storage and crisp linen on big Hypnos beds. As for the food, most is sourced within 30 miles and you eat in an airy restaurant that opens onto a terrace in summer, perhaps cod with lime and cucumber, salt marsh lamb with root veg, chocolate torte with Frangelico jelly. There's tea and cake 'on the house' every afternoon. *Minimum stay: 2 nights at weekends.*

Rooms	6 doubles; 14 doubles with terraces: £95–£260.
Meals	Lunch from £16. Dinner, 3 courses, from £35.
Closed	Rarely.
Directions	A259 east from Rye, then B2075 for Camber & Lydd. On left after 2 miles.

Mark O'Reilly
The Gallivant
New Lydd Road, Camber,
Rye, TN31 7RB

Tel	+44 (0)1797 225057
Email	enquiries@thegallivant.co.uk
Web	www.thegallivant.co.uk

The Bell Alderminster

A lively inn on the Alscot estate with gardens that run down to a small river. There's a beautiful terrace, too, a popular spot for lunch in the sun, washed down by a pint of home-brewed ale. Inside, chic interiors mix of old and new to great effect – low beamed ceilings and exposed brick walls, then lots of colour and leather banquettes. You'll find candles everywhere, armchairs in front of the fire, black-and-white screen prints of estate life. Recent additions include an airy new restaurant with a wall of glass that opens onto the terrace, then a balcony above, where you can scoff afternoon tea while gazing out on open country. There's good food, too, with lamb and beef straight from the estate. You'll find sharing plates, soups and salads, perhaps seared tuna with chilli fritters, rump steak with a pepper sauce, banana sponge with toffee ice cream. Stylish bedrooms have smart fabrics, crisp linen, sofas or armchairs if there's room. Two are small, suites are enormous and have gorgeous bathrooms. A road passes to the front, quietly at night. Stratford waits up the road for all things Shakespeare.

Rooms	5 doubles, 2 twins: £95-£140.
	2 suites for 2: £145-£165.
	Singles from £70 (Sun-Thur).
Meals	Bar meals from £7.
	Lunch, 2 courses from £14.50.
	Dinner, 3 courses from £18.
	Sunday lunch, 3 courses, £25.
Closed	Rarely.
Directions	On A3400 in Alderminster.

Tina Craven
The Bell Alderminster
Shipston Road, Alderminster,
Stratford-upon-Avon, CV37 8NY
Tel   +44 (0)1789 450414
Email   info@thebellald.co.uk
Web   www.thebellald.co.uk

The Howard Arms

The Howard stands on Ilmington Green, eight miles south of Stratford-upon-Avon. It was built at roughly the same time as Shakespeare wrote *King Lear* and little has changed since. It's a lovely country inn and comes with original fixtures and fittings: polished flagstones, heavy beams, mellow stone walls, a crackling fire. Outside, roses ramble on golden stone walls, while a pretty garden waits at the back. Good food comes as standard, perhaps ham hock terrine with homemade piccalilli, marinated duck breast with bok choy, apple tart tatin with mascarpone cream; there's fish and chips and a good burger, too. Elsewhere, you find oils on walls, books on shelves, settles in alcoves, beautiful bay windows. A colourful dining room floods with light courtesy of fine arched windows that overlook the green. Bedrooms in the main house have a charming old-world feel, garden rooms are more contemporary with excellent bathrooms. You can walk across fields to Chipping Campden; Simon de Montfort once owned this land. The village church dates to the 11th century and has Thompson mice within.

Rooms	5 doubles, 3 twin/doubles: £110–£130. Singles £72–£104. Extra bed/sofabed available £10 p.p.p.n.
Meals	Lunch from £4.50. Bar meals from £9.50. Dinner, 3 courses, £25–£30.
Closed	Never.
Directions	From south take A429 Fosse Way through Moreton-in-Marsh. After 5 miles left to Ilmington.

Robert Jeal
The Howard Arms
Lower Green,
Ilmington, CV36 4LT

Tel	+44 (0)1608 682226
Email	info@howardarms.com
Web	www.howardarms.com

Methuen Arms Hotel

The Methuen has always changed with the times. It started life as a 14th-century nunnery, turned into a coaching inn and brewery in 1608, had a Georgian facelift in the late 1700s, then became a boutique hotel in 2010. It's a lovely little place – cosy and stylish with some gorgeous food. It sits on the edge of the village, with an avenue of trees around the corner leading up to Corsham Court, an Elizabethan pile. As for the hotel, there's a beautiful courtyard at the back where you can eat in summer, a restaurant that opens onto the garden, a locals' bar where the main currency is gossip, then a sitting-room bar where you can sink into an armchair in front of the wood-burner and enjoy a pint of Otter. Chic bedrooms are scattered about. You'll find warm colours, padded bedheads, good art, Roberts radios. There are robes in fine bathrooms, four of which have claw-foot baths, one of which is in the bedroom. Don't miss the excellent food, perhaps cream of shallot soup, monkfish wrapped in Parma ham, chocolate mousse with caramelised oranges. Sunday lunch draws a crowd. Bath is close.

Rooms	11 doubles, 2 twin/doubles: £140–£175. 1 family room for 4: £150–£220. Singles from £90.
Meals	Lunch from £5.95. Early supper £18.50–£21.50. Dinner, 3 courses, about £30. Sunday lunch from £18.50.
Closed	Never.
Directions	M4 junc. 17, then A350 south & A4 west. B3353 south into Corsham. On left.

Martin & Debbie Still
Methuen Arms Hotel
2 High Street,
Corsham, SN13 0HB

Tel	+44 (0)1249 717060
Email	info@themethuenarms.com
Web	www.themethuenarms.com

The Muddy Duck

In 1125 Cluniac monks founded a monastery in the village; this venerable building was their sleeping quarters. It turned into an alehouse in the 19th-century to satisfy the miners who dug Bath stone from under these hills. These days, it's a gorgeous old inn with an ancient wisteria encircling a courtyard at the front and a smart terraced garden overlooking open farmland behind. Inside, old and new mix gracefully: wooden floors, the odd beam and half-panelled walls, then red leather bar stools, armchairs in front of the fire and low-hanging lamps in the restaurant. The bar plays host to a colourful cast of locals, who come to chew the cud over a pint of Butcombe and some tasty food. Three rooms wait above the shop. One is small; the suite is huge with a sofa in front of an open fire and a claw-foot bath in the room; all have warm colours, comfy beds and robes in good bathrooms. Two suites beyond the car park have smart bathrooms, snug sitting rooms and small terraces. Good food waits, perhaps ham hock terrine, Wiltshire lamb, rhubarb and custard meringue. Bath is close.

Rooms	2 doubles, 3 suites for 2: £120–£250. Dinner, B&B from £75 p.p. Mon–Thurs.
Meals	Lunch from £4.95. Dinner, 3 courses, about £30.
Closed	Never.
Directions	M4 junction 18, then A46/A4 to Bathford. South on A363 for 2 miles, then left for Monkton Farleigh. Left at x-roads and on left.

Tom Lakin
The Muddy Duck
Monkton Farleigh,
Bradford-on-Avon, BA15 2QH

Tel	+44 (0)1225 858705
Email	dishitup@themuddyduckbath.co.uk
Web	www.themuddyduckbath.co.uk

Timbrell's Yard

Those lovely people at the Draco Pub Co. have been doing what they do so well – opening another of their small-scale pleasure domes. Their latest inn stands close to the bridge in Bradford-on-Avon with beautiful views across the river to the churchyard. Outside, a terrace at the front catches the sun, with this 18th-century listed building standing grandly behind. It's a lovely spot, good enough for Samuel Spode to paint; a copy of his work hangs in the restaurant, the real thing waits in the town's museum. Inside, you get that winning combination of stylish rooms, lovely food and well-kept ales, with cakes and coffee available all day. You'll find stripped floors, hanging lamps, exposed stone walls, then sofas in front of an open fire. Helpful staff weave about, delivering food that makes you smile, perhaps Dorset crab on toast, pork belly with sea salt crackling, vanilla panna cotta with rhubarb jelly. Bedrooms are beautiful. Fourteen have river views, two have baths in the room, mezzanine rooms have window seats where you can watch the river pass. Bathrooms are predictably divine.

Rooms	17 doubles: £95–£145.
	Extra beds for children £20.
Meals	Lunch & dinner £5–£35.
Closed	Rarely.
Directions	A363 south into Bradford-on-Avon. Over bridge and 1st right.

Anthony Bado
Timbrell's Yard
49 St Margaret's Street,
Bradford-on-Avon, BA15 1DE

Tel	+44 (0)1225 869492
Email	info@timbrellsyard.com
Web	www.timbrellsyard.com

Littleton Lodge

This chic B&B sits in a village ten miles north of Stonehenge. You're close to Salisbury for its medieval cathedral, which holds a copy of Magna Carta, while the house backs onto the a'Beckett's vineyard, and tours and tastings can be arranged. Inside, contemporary design has been beautifully considered – nothing here is skin deep. Downstairs, there's a library with books and charcoal panelling, then a drawing room, where a wardrobe opens to reveal an honest bar. Fires smoulder, doors onto a conservatory, then out to a gravelled garden. Uncluttered rooms have much to admire: contemporary four-posters, beautiful chandeliers, colourful throws, smart grey armchairs. White marble bathrooms are just the ticket: two have walk-in showers, two have baths as well, all have Bramley lotions. You'll find smart TVs, coffee machines and James's delicious homemade shortbread. Breakfast is a local treat – juice from garden apples, honey from the vineyard, bacon and sausage from the village butcher. There's tasty food at the village pub and good local restaurants within five miles. Bath is close, too.

Rooms	1 double, 3 four-posters: £120–£150.
Meals	Good pub in village; good restaurants within 5 miles.
Closed	Christmas & New Year.
Directions	South from Devizes on A360 for 4 miles. On left in village.

James Bell & Sean Purslow
Littleton Lodge
High Street, Littleton Panell,
Devizes, SN10 4ES

Tel	+44 (0)1380 813494
Email	info@littletonlodge.com
Web	www.littletonlodge.com

The Lamb at Hindon

The Lamb has been serving ale on Hindon's high street for 800 years. It's a yard of England's finest cloth, a place where shooting parties come to eat and farmers meet to chew the cud. Inside you find oak settles, roaring fires and painted panelling. A clipped Georgian elegance lingers; you almost expect Mr Darcy to walk in, give a tormented sigh, then turn on his heels and vanish. You'll find flagstone floors, stripped boards, window seats and gilded mirrors; there's even a pine booth where the Fat Controller sat by the window, collecting tolls from passing travellers. At night, candles come out, as do some excellent wines, and you dig into lovely food: perhaps ham hock with piccalilli, roast quail with parsnips, bread and butter pudding. Refurbished rooms have pretty colours, crisp linen, smart bathrooms and Bakelite phones. Some even have their own private garden! Expect padded headboards, lovely art, a huge lampshade or a claw-foot bath. Three suites in converted outhouses have an elegant contemporary style with vintage luggage, the odd chandelier and lovely bathrooms. Stourhead and Stonehenge are close. *Min. stay: 2 nights at weekends May-September.*

Rooms	9 doubles, 3 twins: £99-£149.
	3 suites for 2: £129-£179.
	Extra bed/sofabed available £20 p.p.p.n.
	Dogs £20.
Meals	Lunch & dinner £5-£35.
Closed	Never.
Directions	M3, A303 & signed left at bottom of steep hill 2 miles east of junction with A350.

Bernice Gallagher
The Lamb at Hindon
High Street, Hindon,
Salisbury, SP3 6DP

Tel	+44 (0)1747 820573
Email	lambhindon@youngs.co.uk
Web	www.lambhindon.co.uk

The Beckford Arms

A country-house inn on the Fonthill estate. You sweep in under the Triumphal Arch, which seems appropriate – this is one of the loveliest inns in the land. Outside, in the garden, you find hammocks in the trees and parasols on the terrace, then a church spire soaring beyond. Georgian interiors are no less lovely, a mix of original features and 21st-century style. There's a drawing room with facing sofas in front of a roaring fire; a restaurant with a wall of glass that opens onto the terrace; a bar with parquet flooring for an excellent local pint. Potter about and chance upon the odd chandelier, roaming wisteria and a rather grand mahogany table in the private dining room. Bedrooms are small but perfectly formed with prices to match: white walls, the best linen, sisal matting, good bathrooms. If you want something bigger try the pavilions on the estate; former guests include Byron and Nelson, though we doubt they had it so good. As for the food, it's lovely stuff, perhaps Brixham clam chowder, whole lemon sole, chocolate and Cointreau delice with blood orange sorbet. One of the best.

Rooms	7 doubles, 1 twin/double: £95–£120. 2 pavilions for 2: £175–£195.
Meals	Dinner about £30.
Closed	Never.
Directions	On the road between Tisbury & Hindon, 3 miles south of A303 (Fonthill exit).

Charlie Luxton
The Beckford Arms
Fonthill Gifford, Tisbury,
Salisbury, SP3 6PX

Tel   +44 (0)1747 870385
Email   info@beckfordarms.com
Web   www.beckfordarms.com

AWARD
WINNER

Nicely priced

Howard's House

In a gorgeous English village, a wormhole back in time, this Grade-II listed house dates from 1623 and comes with fine gardens in front of fields that sweep uphill to a ridge of old oak. You can walk straight out, so bring your boots. Inside, airy country-house interiors come with exquisite arched windows, flagstones in reception and the odd beam. Deep sofas, fresh flowers and the morning papers wait in the sitting room, where a fire crackles on cold days. When the sun shines, doors open onto a very pretty terrace for breakfasting. Elegant bedrooms mix old and new to great effect. They're not overly plush, but deeply comfortable with warm colours, mullioned windows, bowls of fruit and a sofa if there's room. Expect oak headboards, pretty fabrics, robes in good bathrooms. Spin downstairs for dinner – perhaps fillet of sea bass with parsnip purée, Scottish beef with roasted shallots, apple crème caramel with a calvados jelly – then climb back up to find your bed turned down. Salisbury, Stonehenge and the gardens at Stourhead are all close.

Rooms	6 doubles, 1 twin/double, 1 four-poster: £190–£210. 1 family room for 4: £190 for 2; £260 for 4. Singles from £120.
Meals	Lunch from £7.95. Dinner, set menu £27–£32.50; à la carte £36–£45; 6-course tasting menu £65.
Closed	Rarely.
Directions	A30 from Salisbury, B3089 west to Teffont. There, left at sharp right-hand bend following brown hotel sign. Entrance on right after 0.5 miles.

Noele Thompson & Simon Greenwood
Howard's House
Teffont Evias,
Salisbury, SP3 5RJ

Tel	+44 (0)1722 716392
Email	enq@howardshousehotel.co.uk
Web	www.howardshousehotel.co.uk

The Fish Hotel

Come for Scandi-chic on a smart estate with some perfectly well-priced rooms. It's like summer camp, only for adults – a place designed for fun. Expect striking simplicity with airy colours, white linen, padded bedheads, robes in sparkling bathrooms. Rooms are scattered about in pretty buildings on the hill, the suites altogether fancier with claw-foot baths in the room, huge beds, maybe a sofa or a wood-burner, too. They spiral around a central lodge, where you eat, drink and make merry. If the style is coolly contemporary, then the feel is cosy and informal, with lovely staff on hand to help. The big bar is the hub: sofas galore, cool colours, walls of glass that open onto a terrace, a funky wood-burner for winter nights. There's a games room for pool and table football, but much more waits outside: tennis, archery, clay-pigeon shooting, quad biking, even segways. Deer roam the hill, there's a nature trail and maps for joggers. As for the food, you can eat in the bar, the restaurant, or out on the terrace in good weather; try crab on toast or lobster hotdog, and finish off with apple crumble and vanilla ice cream.

Rooms	10 doubles, 33 twin/doubles: £99-£155. 4 suites for 2: £175-£225. Dinner, B&B from £82.50 p.p.
Meals	Lunch from £5. Dinner, 3 courses, £25-£35.
Closed	Never.
Directions	A44 east from Broadway for two miles. Turn left halfway up Fish Hill. Keep left at folk and follow signs to the hotel.

Zena Carter
The Fish Hotel
Farncombe Estate,
Broadway, WR12 7LJ

Tel	+44 (0)1386 858000
Email	reservations@thefishhotel.co.uk
Web	www.thefishhotel.co.uk

Brocco on the Park

Sheffield is a friendly city, an arty hub that's full of surprises, a fact ably demonstrated by this stunning small hotel. It sits amid leafy streets, with a smart park to the front, then hills beyond that ripple over to the Peak District. Picasso stayed here when he attended the World Peace Conference in 1950, though things have changed a little since – a recent refit has turned this into a small-scale pleasure dome. Downstairs, there's a Scandi feel in the café/kitchen, with joggers and dog walkers swapping the park for delicious smoothies or a slice of cake. Bedrooms are divine, as good as they look. Expect the best white linen, smart neutral colours, the coolest bathrooms with robes and organic oils. A vast window in one room opens to frame the view; another has a free-standing bath; all are named after birds, their colours reflected in the fabrics. Back downstairs, tasty food waits at night, perhaps cauliflower and pistachio fritters, rib-eye steak with wild mushrooms, spiced plum crumble with vanilla ice cream. Don't miss the Millennium Gallery, the Winter Garden or the cool streets around you.

Rooms	6 doubles, 2 twin/doubles: £85–£220. Extra bed/sofabed available £35 p.p.p.n.
Meals	Breakfast from £7. Lunch from £7. Dinner from £12. Sunday lunch from £16.
Closed	Rarely.
Directions	Leave ring road to southwest at Waitrose, signed Castleton A625. After 1.5 miles, at 1st r'bout, take last exit. Hotel on left.

	Tiina Carr
	Brocco on the Park
	92 Brocco Bank,
	Sheffield, S11 8RS
Tel	+44 (0)114 266 1233
Email	hello@brocco.co.uk
Web	www.brocco.co.uk

The Angel Inn

The old drovers' inn remains staunchly, reassuringly traditional – but comes with wines that have come, over the years, to rival the hand-pumped Yorkshire ales. There's even a 'cave' for functions and private-party tastings. Expect nooks, crannies, beams and crackling fires, and a stylish restaurant. Thought has gone into every detail, from the antique furniture in the timbered rooms (one with a marvellous oak-panelled bar) to the fabrics and the colours. Menus change with each season and include dishes ranging from filo 'moneybags' of seafood in lobster sauce – the fish comes fresh from Fleetwood – to their own Yorkshire twist on tapas ('Yapas'!). Vegetarians are looked after and the sticky toffee pudding is legendary. Exquisite bedrooms, split between the converted barn and adjacent Sycamore House, are all different; perhaps a French armoire, a brass bed, a claw-foot bath, a private garden. All have top-quality fabrics, pretty colours, cosy bathrooms, and, in the newer rooms, a contemporary feel. The glorious up-hill-and-down-dale drive to get here is part of the charm.

Rooms	9 doubles: £150–£175.
	5 suites for 2: £175–£200.
	Singles from £125. Extra beds £25.
Meals	Lunch from £7.50. Bar meals from £15.95.
	Dinner, 3 courses, £35–£55.
	Sunday lunch £24.50.
Closed	Christmas Day & 1 week in January.
Directions	North from Skipton on B6265. Left at Rylstone for Hetton. In village.

Juliet Watkins
The Angel Inn
Hetton,
Skipton, BD23 6LT

Tel	+44 (0)1756 730263
Email	info@angelhetton.co.uk
Web	www.angelhetton.co.uk

The Traddock

A northern outpost of country-house charm, beautiful inside and out. It's a family affair and those looking for a friendly base from which to explore the Dales will find it here. You enter through the drawing room – crackling fire, pretty art, the daily papers, cavernous sofas. Potter about and find polished wood in the dining room, panelled walls in the breakfast room, then William Morris wallpaper in the sitting room bar, where you can sip a pint of Skipton ale while playing Scrabble. Bedrooms are gorgeous, some coolly contemporary, others warmly traditional. The star of the show is the new suite – sand-blasted timbers, a lovely big sofa, a stunning free-standing bath – but all are charming, with chic fabrics, warm colours, comfy beds and the odd claw-foot bath. Downstairs, a white-washed sitting room opens onto the garden for afternoon tea, while delicious food waits in the restaurant, perhaps seafood chowder, braised lamb shank, apple and calvados mousse. Walks start at the front door, there are cycle tracks, even caves to explore (one is bigger than St Paul's). Unbeatable. *Minimum stay: 2 nights at weekends March-November.*

Rooms	8 doubles, 1 twin/double, 2 family rooms for 4: £95–£165. 1 suite for 2: £180–£220. 1 single: £85–£100. Dinner, B&B from £80 p.p. Extra beds £15 per person per night.
Meals	Lunch from £9.50. Dinner, 3 courses, around £30. Picnics from £7.50. Afternoon tea from £15.95.
Closed	Never.
Directions	0.75 miles off the A65, midway between Kirkby Lonsdale & Skipton, 4 miles north west of Settle.

Paul Reynolds
The Traddock
Austwick,
Settle, LA2 8BY

Tel	+44 (0)15242 51224
Email	info@thetraddock.co.uk
Web	www.thetraddock.co.uk

The White Bear Hotel

At five o'clock on a Friday evening there's only one place to be in Masham: the tap room at the White Bear, home of Theakston's beer. The great and the good gather to mark the end of the week, the odd pint is sunk, the air is thick with gossip. Interior design is 1920s trapped in aspic – red leather, polished brass, a crackling fire. But there's more here – a country-house dining room for lovely food; a handsome bar with stripped boards; a flower-filled terrace for lunch in the sun. Bedrooms are lovely, a touch of 21st-century luxury; they occupy the old Lightfoot brewery and come in contemporary style with good fabrics, warm colours, excellent beds and fancy bathrooms. Some have views across town, the vast penthouse suite is open to the rafters and worth splashing out on. There's a courtyard for guests, a sitting room, too; staff will bring drinks if you want privacy and peace. Delicious food waits in the restaurant, perhaps shellfish soup, steak and ale pie, treacle sponge pudding. Tours of the brewery are easily arranged, with a pint of your choice at the end. The Dales are all around.

Rooms	13 twin/doubles: £120.
	1 suite for 2: £200–£220.
Meals	Lunch from £4.95.
	Dinner, 3 courses, about £30.
Closed	Never.
Directions	North from Ripon on A6108.
	In Masham up hill (for Leyburn).
	Right at crest of hill. Signed.

Sue Thomas
The White Bear Hotel
Wellgarth,
Masham, Ripon, HG4 4EN

Tel	+44 (0)1765 689319
Email	sue@whitebearmasham.co.uk
Web	www.thewhitebearhotel.co.uk

The Burgoyne Hotel

Reeth is one of those English throwbacks, a beautiful village in the Dales that's hardly changed in 200 years. It was mentioned in the Domesday Book, has the finest grouse moors in the land and its sweeping views over Swaledale stretch for miles. The Burgoyne looks out over it all – afternoon tea in the garden on a sunny day is hard to beat. Inside, an elegant past lives on: a smart drawing room with a crackling fire where you gather for drinks before dinner; a restaurant in racing green where you feast on delicious Yorkshire food; country-house bedrooms full of comfort, with warm colours, good beds, white linen, a sofa if there's room. You'll find pine shutters, cushioned window seats, a four-poster in the old snooker room; all but one has the view. The food is old-school, but utterly delicious, perhaps pheasant and venison terrine, Dover sole with brown shrimps, lemon tart with raspberry sorbet. Best of all are Julia and Mo, who run the place with unstinting kindness. There are maps for walkers, fishing can be arranged, a market passes on Fridays. Richmond is close, too. A delight.

Rooms	4 doubles, 1 twin, 1 four-poster; 2 doubles, 1 twin, each with separate bathroom: £130-£190. 1 suite for 2: £210. Singles from £112.50. Extra beds for children under 13 £25. Dogs £10 a night.
Meals	Dinner, 2 courses, £27; 4 courses, £40.
Closed	Midweek in January (Mon-Thur).
Directions	From Richmond A6108, then B6270 to Reeth. Hotel on north side of village green.

Julia & Mo Usman
The Burgoyne Hotel
Reeth,
Richmond, DL11 6SN
Tel   +44 (0)1748 884292
Email enquiries@theburgoyne.co.uk
Web   www.theburgoyne.co.uk

The Coach House at Middleton Lodge

You'll think you've washed up at a beautiful country house in Tuscany or Provence. These gorgeous stone barns were crumbling a few years ago, now they're home to one of the loveliest boutique hotels in the north. In summer, life spills onto the courtyard for lunch in the sun, afternoon tea, or cocktails before dinner. Step through the arched glass doors and find a spectacular restaurant open to the rafters, where contemporary design mixes with rustic bricks and mortar. There's a funky bar, an open fire, the odd leather sofa to take the strain. Rooms are equally lovely: chic fabrics, Roberts radios, bath robes, beds for insomniacs to fall asleep in. Five open onto a terrace, one is huge, most have cross beams, claw-foot baths, then a sofa or chaise longue. The food is exceptional, some grown on the estate, much from Yorkshire, perhaps pigeon with praline and pear, roast hake with a clam chowder, toffee chocolate with honeycomb ice cream. You're on a 200-acre estate with the Dales to the west and the Moors to the east. There's the Lodge, too, one of the best wedding venues in the North.

Rooms	9 doubles: £155–£185. Singles from £135.
Meals	Lunch from £5.50. Dinner, 3 courses, £30–£35. Not Mon or Tue mid-Oct to mid-March. Sunday lunch from £12.50.
Closed	Rarely.
Directions	Leave A1 at Scotch Corner and head east for Middleton Tyas. Left in village onto Kneeton Rd. Right after 1 mile; left after 300 yeards. Hotel signed on right.

James & Rebecca Allison
The Coach House at Middleton Lodge
Middleton Tyas,
Richmond, DL10 6NJ

Tel	+44 (0)1325 377977
Email	info@middletonlodge.co.uk
Web	www.middletonlodge.co.uk/coach-house

Estbek House

A cute little find on the Whitby coast. This is a quietly elegant restaurant with rooms ten paces from the beach at Sandsend. It's small, intimate and very welcoming. Tim cooks brilliantly, David talks you through his exceptional wine list and passes on the local news. Cliffs rise to the north, the beach runs away to the south, East Row Beck river passes directly opposite, ducks waddle across the road. There's a terrace at the front for drinks in summer and a small bar on the lower ground, where you can watch Tim at work in his kitchen. Upstairs, two dining rooms swim in coastal light and come with stripped floors, old radiators and crisp white tablecloths. Grab a window seat for watery views and dig into fresh Whitby crab with avocado and mango salad, local lamb with rhubarb compote, apricot tarte tatin. Bedrooms – smallish on the first floor, tiny on the second! – have painted panelling, crisp white linen, colourful throws and shuttered windows. Breakfast is delicious – David's mum makes the marmalade. There are cliff walks, the moors to discover and you can follow the river upstream to Mulgrave Castle.

Rooms	4 doubles, 1 twin/double: £125–£150. Dinner, B&B from £80 p.p.
Meals	Dinner, 3 courses, about £35.
Closed	Occasionally.
Directions	North from Whitby on A174 to Sandsend. On left in village by bridge.

David Cross & Tim Lawrence
Estbek House
East Row, Sandsend,
Whitby, YO21 3SU

Tel	+44 (0)1947 893424
Email	info@estbekhouse.co.uk
Web	www.estbekhouse.co.uk

Broom House at Egton Bridge

As lovely a place to stay on the moors as you could hope for. You wind your way in – up dale, down hill – with a carpet of purple heather in late summer and a golden fleece of bracken in autumn. As for this attractive house, it sits on the edge of a pretty village, with fine views of Esk Dale from the garden terrace. Inside, airy interiors are stylish and comfortable, the perfect tonic after a day in the hills. Downstairs, there's a sitting room with garden views, then a dining room for Michael's delicious breakfasts – Whitby kippers, Glaisdale bacon, smoothies from garden strawberries. In summer, you decant onto the terrace for birdsong with your bacon and eggs. Stylish rooms have warm colours, comfy beds, white cotton, perhaps a sofa or doors onto the terrace. All have fine bathrooms, one with a free-standing bath. By day you explore the moors, spin over to Whitby or try a leg of the coast-to-coast path, which passes outside. At night you follow the river into the village for dinner at one of its pubs. You couldn't be in better hands – Michael and Georgina look after you in style. Pure bliss. *Minimum stay: 2 nights at weekends.*

Rooms	7 doubles, 1 twin: £92–£160.
Meals	Two good pubs in village.
Closed	December – February.
Directions	Leave A171 for Egton. Through village to Egton Bridge, under bridge, then right into Broom House Lane. Under bridge and on right.

Georgina & Michael Curnow
Broom House at Egton Bridge
Broom House Lane, Egton Bridge,
Whitby, YO21 1XD

Tel	+44 (0)1947 895279
Email	mw@broom-house.co.uk
Web	www.broom-house.co.uk

The White Swan Inn

A dreamy old inn that stands on Market Place, where farmers set up shop on the first Thursday of the month. The exterior is 16th century and flower baskets hang from its mellow stone walls. Inside, you find a seriously pretty world: stripped floors, open fires, a tiny bar, beautiful windows. The restaurant is at the back – the heart and soul of the inn – with delicious food flying from the kitchen, perhaps Whitby fishcakes, rack of spring lamb, glazed lemon tart with blood-orange sorbet. Excellent bedrooms are scattered about. Those in the main house have padded bedheads, delicious linen, Osborne & Little fabrics and flat-screen TV/DVDs; bathrooms have robes and Bath House oils. Rooms in the courtyard tend to be bigger and come in crisp contemporary style with black-and-white screen prints, mohair blankets and York stone bathrooms. You'll also find the Bothy here, a cool little residents' sitting room, with a huge open fire and cathedral ceilings. The moors are all around: fabulous walking, Castle Howard and Whitby all wait. *Minimum stay: 2 nights at weekends.*

Rooms	14 doubles, 4 twin/doubles: £149–£179. 3 suites for 2: £149–£189. Singles £115–£179. Dinner, B&B £105–£125 p.p. Extra bed/sofabed available £20 p.p.p.n.
Meals	Lunch from £5.25. Dinner, 3 courses £25–£35. Sunday lunch from £12.95.
Closed	Never.
Directions	From North A170 to Pickering. Entering town left at traffic lights, then 1st right into Market Place. On left.

Catherine Feather
The White Swan Inn
Market Place,
Pickering, YO18 7AA

Tel	+44 (0)1751 472288
Email	welcome@white-swan.co.uk
Web	www.white-swan.co.uk

The Talbot Hotel

A 17th-century hunting lodge on the Fitzwilliam estate, not far from Castle Howard. It stands on the edge of town with Malton's streets on one side and country views on the other. Outside, there's a croquet lawn, a terrace for lunch, and paths that lead down to the river. Inside, an easy elegance abounds. A fire burns in the drawing room, you find fresh flowers, lovely art, the daily papers and cavernous sofas. Bedrooms have chic fabrics, warm colours and botanical prints on the walls. Several have the view, all have robes in gorgeous bathrooms. Now to the serious stuff – delicious local food. Malton, an ancient market town, is the food capital of Yorkshire, with a festival every May that was started by the estate. No surprise then to discover the hotel has two restaurants serving the best Yorkshire produce. They also run a cookery school and have food trails to follow – to pie shops, vineyards, local farms and breweries. Dinner, predictably, is a treat, perhaps pressing of Yorkshire duck, local lamb with an olive jus, coffee crème brûlée. There's a farmers' market every other Saturday, too. *Minimum stay: 2 nights at weekends*

Rooms	23 doubles: £110–£190.
	1 suite for 2, 2 suites for 4: £270–£320.
	Dinner, B&B from £100 p.p.
Meals	Lunch from £4.95. Bar meals from £10.95.
	Dinner, 3 courses, about £35.
	Sunday lunch from £20.
	Afternoon tea from £19.50.
Closed	Rarely.
Directions	A64 north from York, then B2148 into Malton. Keep right in town and on right after half a mile.

David Macdonald
The Talbot Hotel
45-47 Yorkersgate,
Malton, YO17 7AJ

Tel	+44 (0)1653 639096
Email	reservations@talbotmalton.co.uk
Web	www.talbotmalton.co.uk

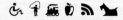

The Black Swan at Oldstead

This is an extraordinary place, a true one-off. At a glance it's a restaurant with a Michelin star and nine stunning bedrooms, but to stop there would be to sell the Black Swan short. It is owned by a family of farmers for whom the journey of food to plate starts in a glasshouse in a two-acre kitchen garden propagating seeds that grow into anything from heritage beetroot to Bolivian cucumbers. The diversity of produce is astounding – they grow eight different types of tomato – and some of it turns into exotic libations – kumquat vodka and rhubarb schnapps to name a couple. As for dinner, cooked by Tommy, it's an eight-course feast, perhaps slow-cooked beetroot, langoustine with kale, Galloway beef with lovage, then a cocktail of local honey and elderflower. After which you retire to beautiful rooms, some behind the restaurant overlooking the kitchen garden, others 50 paces away in a Georgian cottage draped in roses. Expect the best: chic fabrics, perfect beds, walk-in showers, the odd copper bath. You can tour the garden while sipping a cocktail made from produce around you. Unbeatable.

Rooms	7 doubles, 2 four-posters: £200-£400. Price includes dinner for 2.
Meals	Dinner, 8 courses, included in price; non residents £85 per person.
Closed	1-7 January.
Directions	A19 from Thirsk; left to Thirkleby & Coxwold, then left for Byland Abbey; follow signs left for Oldstead.

The Banks Family
The Black Swan at Oldstead
Oldstead, York, YO61 4BL

Tel	+44 (0)1347 868387
Email	enquiries@blackswanoldstead.co.uk
Web	www.blackswanoldstead.co.uk

Channel Islands

The Georgian House

Alderney is pristine – miles of sandy beaches, ancient coastal forts, cliff-top walks and nature trails, wild flowers and migrating birds. It's a slice of heaven and where else to stay than this quirky island bolthole, part village inn, part restaurant with rooms, part friendly chic hotel. After 30 years holidaying here, Holly's family bought one of their favourite places, whipped it into shape and now it's the beating heart of the island, a magnet for locals and visitors alike. It sits on St Anne's cobbled high street, opposite the art-house cinema; filmgoers sneak over for drinks in the interval. Downstairs, the bar comes with wooden floors, an open fire and lots of gossip. An airy restaurant spills onto a sun-trapping courtyard in summer, a fine spot for the freshest seafood, delicious steaks, island ice creams. Bedrooms – some in the hotel, others across the road in Victoria House – are just the ticket: not huge, but deeply comfy, with lovely beds, the odd stone wall and cute bathrooms. Hire bikes, grab a picnic, laze about on the beach. Night skies amaze. A perfect island adventure.

Rooms	2 doubles, 2 twin/doubles: £70-£95. Singles from £45.
Meals	Light lunch from £6. Dinner, 3 courses, £25-£30.
Closed	Mid-January to mid-March.
Directions	Sent on booking. Airport pick-ups.

Holly Fisher
The Georgian House
Victoria Street,
St Anne, GY9 3UF

Tel	+44 (0)1481 822471
Email	info@georgianalderney.com
Web	www.georgianalderney.com

White House Hotel

Herm is unique, a tiny island run benignly by the 40 souls lucky enough to live on it. They keep things blissfully simple: no cars, no TVs, just a magical world of sea and sky, a perfect place to escape the city. A coastal path rings the island; high cliffs rise to the south, sandy beaches laze in the north, cattle graze the hills between. You get fabulous views at every turn – shimmering islands, pristine waters, yachts and ferries zipping about. There's a beach café, succulent gardens, an ancient church, even a tavern for excellent ales. Kids love it, so do parents, and the self-catering cottages are extremely popular. As for the hotel, it's a delightful base from which to explore the island. You'll find open fires, four-course dinners, a tennis court and a pool in the garden to keep you cool. Spotless bedrooms are scattered about, some in the village's colour-washed cottages, others with balconies in the hotel. Most come in contemporary style, a few are warmly traditional, all have sunny colours, watery views, padded headboards and sparkling bathrooms. Hard to beat.

Rooms	28 twin/doubles: £138–£208.
	5 family rooms for 4,
	5 family rooms for 2: £128–£208.
	2 singles: £64–£84.
	20 cottages for 2-6: £273–£1,288 per wk.
Meals	Lunch from £5.
	Dinner, 4 courses, £28.50.
Closed	November – Easter.
Directions	Via Guernsey. Trident ferries leave from the harbour at St Peter Port 8 times a day in summer (£11 return).

Siôn Dobson Jones
White House Hotel
Herm Island, GY1 3HR

Tel   +44 (0)1481 750075
Email   hotel@herm.com
Web   www.herm.com

Hotel Ziggurat

This quirky small hotel has big views of islands and sea and a very pretty terrace from which to drink them in. It sits high on the hill, halfway up Constitution Steps, an ascent that removes all need of membership to a fitness club. But the climb is worth it – you find a warm welcome, a lovely style, some tasty food and excellent cocktails. Interiors have colour in spades. Step inside and you come face to face with Ishtar (well, her statue), the Mesopotamian goddess of love and war. Potter about and find a cute bar with shisha pipes, an airy restaurant where framed Moroccan textiles hang on walls, then doors onto the garden, where three smart, garden huts double as restaurant tables in good weather. Cute bedrooms are scattered about, most with semi-private terraces. You'll find comfy beds (three are cabin-like with one side against a wall), then padded heads, crisp linen and smart, new bathrooms with power showers; a couple have baths, too. Don't miss the food: Persian mezze, lamb shank tagine, Amaretto cheesecake. Ferries for day trips to Herm and Sark are easily arranged. *Minimum stay: 2 nights.*

Rooms	12 doubles, 1 twin: £90–£150. 1 single: £70–£90.
Meals	Dinner, 3 courses, about £25 (not Sunday or Monday). Sunday brunch from £9.95.
Closed	Never.
Directions	Sent on booking.

Paul Hanson
Hotel Ziggurat
No. 5, Constitution Steps,
St Peter Port, GY1 2PN

Tel	+44 (0)1481 723008
Email	stay@hotelziggurat.com
Web	www.hotelziggurat.com

Scotland

The Creggans Inn

If you're looking for a small hotel in a great position with lovely rooms and excellent food, you'll find it here. There's a little history, too – the inn was once owned by the real James Bond. Sir Fitzroy Maclean was one of a cast of characters on whom Ian Fleming based his hero; the fact the Royal Navy send their big ships into Loch Fyne is purely coincidental. These days, life at the inn is decidedly restful. Views from the front stretch for miles, the loch eventually giving way to the distant peaks of the Kintyre peninsular. Inside, an airy elegance abounds. There's a first-floor sitting room with big views; a locals' bar which doubles as the clubhouse for the shinty team; then picture windows in the smart restaurant, where you dig into super food while watching the sun set, perhaps Ramsay haggis with whisky sauce, pot roast chicken with a thyme jus, bread and butter pudding with honey glazed figs. Comfy bedrooms have lots of style: warm colours, pretty fabrics, delicate wallpapers, robes in sparkling bathrooms; most have loch views. Castles and gardens, golf and boat trips wait.

Rooms	4 doubles, 9 twin/doubles: £120–£180. 1 suite for 2: £160–£220. Singles from £85. Dinner, B&B from £80 p.p.
Meals	Lunch from £4.25. Bar meals from £10.95. Dinner, 3 courses, about £30.
Closed	Never.
Directions	From Glasgow, A82 to Tarbert, A83 towards Inverary for 13 miles, then left on A815 to Strachur (10 miles). Hotel on left before village.

Archie & Gillian MacLellan
The Creggans Inn
Loch Fyne, Strachur,
Cairndow, PA27 8BX

Tel	+44 (0)1369 860279
Email	info@creggans-inn.co.uk
Web	www.creggans-inn.co.uk

The Manor House

A 1780 dower house for the Dukes of Argyll – their cottage by the sea. Built of local stone, it sits high on the hill with long views over Oban harbour to the Isle of Mull. It's a smart and proper place, not one to bow to fads of fashions, with sea views from the terrace, a roaring fire in the drawing room, beautiful tiles in the entrance hall, an elegant bay window in the bar, then a half-panelled dining room for excellent food. Some bedrooms are on the small side, but all are pretty with warm colours, fresh flowers, crisp linen, bowls of fruit and piles of towels in good bathrooms; those that look seaward have binoculars with which to scour the horizon. Try Loch Fyne kippers for breakfast, seafood risotto for lunch and, if you've room, roast saddle of lamb with shepherds' pie for dinner; there's excellent home baking, too. Ferries leave for the islands from the bottom of the hill – you can watch them sail from the hotel garden. There's a computer for guests to use, afternoon tea can be arranged, and you can watch the sun set from McCaig's Tower overlooking Oban. *Over 12s welcome.*

Rooms	9 doubles, 2 twins: £120–£235. Dinner, B&B from £87.50 p.p.
Meals	Lunch from £4.25. Dinner, 4 courses, £42.
Closed	Christmas.
Directions	In Oban follow signs to ferry. Hotel on right 0.5 miles after ferry turn-off, signed.

Gregor MacKinnon
The Manor House
Gallanach Road,
Oban, PA34 4LS

Tel	+44 (0)1631 562087
Email	info@manorhouseoban.com
Web	www.manorhouseoban.com

Entry 230   Map 8

The Pierhouse

The position here is unbeatable. You're at the end of the road, on the shores of Loch Linnhe, with views across to Lismore and rising mountains beyond. As for the Pierhouse – well, shipwrecked sailors would refuse rescue. Outside, there's a sun-trapping terrace from which to watch the odd boat chug past while digging into langoustines fresh from the waters around you. Interiors are just as good. Glass walls frame the view, there's a smart bar for a wee dram, a white-washed snug with sofas in front of a wood-burner, then, a restaurant for some of the best seafood on the west coast. Chic rooms have a wing to themselves, so expect deep peace. Those at the front have the view, all have an uncluttered Scandi feel with warm colours, padded bedheads, smart fabrics and robes in sparkling bathrooms. You get bowls of fruit, a sofa if there's room, crisp linen on comfy beds. There's lots to do: the ferry across to Lismore for fine walking, Ben Nevis, magical Ardnamurchan. As for the food, come back for oysters, scallops, lobster Thermidor or a rib-eye steak; the seafood platters are out of this world.

Rooms	4 doubles, 4 twin/doubles: £90-£205. 2 suites for 2: £145-£240. Extra beds: children aged 2-12 £30, 12+ £40.
Meals	Lunch from £4.95. Bar meals from £12.50. Dinner, 3-course à la carte, £30-£50.
Closed	Christmas & Boxing Day.
Directions	A82 north for Fort William, then A828 south for Oban. Right for Port Appin after 12 miles. At end of road.

Nick & Nikki Horne
The Pierhouse
Port Appin,
Appin, PA38 4DE
Tel   +44 (0)1631 730302
Email   reservations@pierhousehotel.co.uk
Web   www.pierhousehotel.co.uk

The Airds Hotel & Restaurant

This chic country-house hotel on the Appin peninsular stands above Loch Linnhe with views across the water to the Morvern Mountains. It came to life in 1750, an inn for passengers taking the paddle steamers up to the Caledonian canal. These days, it's one of the loveliest places to stay on the West Coast. Its whitewashed exterior gives no hint of the wonders within. You enter through a small conservatory, then find yourself in a world of smouldering fires, freshly cut flowers, beautiful wallpapers and sofas by the dozen. Bedrooms are divine: beautiful fabrics, warm colours, Frette linen for Vi-Spring beds, sparkling marble bathrooms with Italian robes; in short, the best of everything. Those at the front have the view, bigger rooms have sofas, some at the back have terraces, all spoil you rotten. Best of all is the exceptional food, perhaps West Coast langoustines with pea purée, sea bass with clams and a lemongrass cream, apple terrine with salted caramel and cinnamon doughnuts. There's a garden for croquet and afternoon tea with views to the water. Worth every penny. *Extra bed / sofabed £25 p.p. per night.*

Rooms	8 twin/doubles: £245–£435.
	3 suites for 4, with sofabed: £360–£480.
	Price includes dinner for 2.
	1 cottage for 5: £625–£940; 3-day
	stays from £210.
Meals	Lunch from £7.
	Dinner, 5 courses, included;
	non-residents £55. Tasting menu £75.
	Sunday lunch £18.95.
Closed	Mon & Tue November to January
Directions	A82 north for Fort William, then A828
	south for Oban. Right for Port Appin
	after 12 miles. On left after 2 miles.

Shaun & Jenny McKivragan
The Airds Hotel & Restaurant
Port Appin,
Appin, PA38 4DF

Tel	+44 (0)1631 730236
Email	airds@airds-hotel.com
Web	www.airds-hotel.com

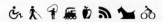

Bealach House

Good food, a lovely welcome and a fine position in Salachan Glen make this an excellent base for those travelling up the west coast. You follow a track through the forest to the only house in the valley. Sheep graze, birds sing, rivers run – other than that you won't hear a thing. Jim and Hilary had a dining pub in the Yorkshire Dales before coming north for a quieter life. Outside, eight acres of gardens have big valley views. Inside, tea and homemade cake is served in front of the wood-burner on colder days or out on the terrace when the sun shines. Bedrooms upstairs aren't huge, but two have room for a sofa and all have warm colours, comfy beds, decanters of sherry and excellent power showers (one has a bath, too). After a hearty breakfast – local eggs, home-made bread – you can climb Ben Nevis, drive up to Loch Ness or take the ferry across to Mull. After which Hilary's food works wonders, perhaps smoked salmon, local venison, chocolate soufflé with a white chocolate sauce (bring your own wine). You can walk from the front door, on clear nights stars fill the sky. *Over 14s welcome.*

Rooms	2 doubles, 1 twin: £90–£110. Singles from £65.
Meals	Dinner £25–£30.
Closed	Mid-October to mid-February.
Directions	A828 south from Fort William for Oban. Signed left, through gate, 2 miles south of Duror. Follow signs up track for 1 mile to house.

Jim & Hilary McFadyen
Bealach House
Salachan Glen, Duror,
Appin, PA38 4BW

Tel	+44 (0)1631 740298
Email	enquiries@bealachhouse.co.uk
Web	www.bealachhouse.co.uk

Glengorm Castle

Few places defy overstatement, but Glengorm does so with ease. It stands in 5,000 acres at the top of Mull with views that stretch across the sea to Coll and the Uists, Barra and Rhum. Directly in front the land falls away, rolls over lush pasture, then tumbles into the sea. Sheep and cattle graze – Tom wins prizes for his cows. Despite the grandeur, this is a family home with children and dogs pottering about. You feel immediately at ease. First you bounce up a four-mile drive, then you step into a vast hall, where sofas wait in front of the fire and big art hangs on the walls. An oak staircase sweeps you up to wonderful country-house rooms; three have the view, all have warm colours, antique furniture and excellent bathrooms. Elsewhere, a panelled library for guests to use with a selection of whiskies 'on the house', then a vast kitchen garden, coastal paths, even a swimming hole. Breakfast is a feast – grab the table by the window. There's a farm shop, a café and a deli, too, even guided wildlife walks and a hide from which to spot otters. Good restaurants wait in Tobermory.

Rooms	3 doubles, 1 four-poster; 1 twin/double with separate bath: £135–£215. Tower Rooms: 1 apartment for 4: £250–£280.
Meals	Restaurants 5 miles.
Closed	Christmas & New Year.
Directions	North to Tobermory on A848. Straight over roundabout (not right for town). Over x-roads after half a mile and straight ahead for four miles to castle.

Tom & Marjorie Nelson
Glengorm Castle
Tobermory,
Isle of Mull, PA75 6QE

Tel	+44 (0)1688 302321
Email	enquiries@glengormcastle.co.uk
Web	www.glengormcastle.co.uk

Tiroran House

The setting is magnificent – 17 acres of gardens rolling down to Loch Scridian. Otters and dolphins pass through, buzzards and eagles glide above, red deer visit the garden. As for this 1850 shooting lodge, you'll be hard pressed to find a more comfortable island base, so it's no surprise to discover it was recently voted 'Best Country House Hotel in Scotland' for the second year in a row. There are fires in the drawing rooms, fresh flowers everywhere, games to be played, books to be read. Airy bedrooms hit the spot: crisp linen, beautiful fabrics, the odd chaise longue; some have watery views, all have silence guaranteed. You eat in a smart dining room with much of the delicious food from the island or waters around it, perhaps mussel and oyster broth, saddle of lamb with carrot purée, chocolate torte with vanilla ice cream. You're bang in the middle of Mull with lots to do: Tobermory, the prettiest town in the Hebrides; Calgary and its magical beach; day trips to Iona and its famous monastery; cruises to Staffa and Fingal's Cave. Come back for afternoon tea – it's as good as the Ritz.

Rooms	5 doubles, 5 twin/doubles: £175–£220.
Meals	Dinner, 4 courses, £48.
Closed	Rarely.
Directions	From Craignure or Fishnish car ferries, A849 for Bunessan & Iona car ferry. Right onto B8035 for Gruline. After 4 miles left at converted church. House 1 mile further.

Laurence & Katie Mackay
Tiroran House
Tiroran,
Isle of Mull, PA69 6ES

Tel	+44 (0)1681 705232
Email	info@tiroran.com
Web	www.tiroran.com

The Colonsay

Another fabulous Hebridean island, a perfect place to escape the world. Wander at will and find wild flowers in the machair, a golf course tended by sheep and huge sandy beaches across which cows roam. Wildlife is ever present, from a small colony of wild goats to a rich migratory bird population; the odd golden eagle soars overhead, too. At low tide the sands of the south give access to Oronsay. The island's 14th-century priory was one of Scotland's finest and amid impressive ruins its ornate stone cross still stands. As for the hotel, it brims with an easy style – airy interiors, stripped floors, fires everywhere, friendly staff. There's a locals' bar for a pint (and a brewery on the island), a pretty sitting room packed with books, a dining room for super food, a decked terrace for drinks in the sun. Bedrooms have local art, warm colours, lovely fabrics and the best beds; some have sea views, all have good bathrooms. Spin around on bikes, search for standing stones, lie in the sun and stare at the sky. There's a festival in May for all things Colonsay. Wonderful.

Rooms	4 doubles, 3 twins: £85–£150. 1 family room for 4: £105–£140. 1 single: £75–£80.
Meals	Lunch from £4.50. Packed lunch £7. Bar meals from £11.50. Dinner, 3 courses, about £25.
Closed	November, January (after New Year) & February.
Directions	Calmac ferries from Oban or Kennacraig (not Tue) or Hebridean Airways (Tue & Thur). Hotel on right, half a mile up road from jetty.

Jane Howard
The Colonsay
Scalasaig,
Isle of Colonsay, PA61 7YP

Tel	+44 (0)1951 200316
Email	hotel@colonsayestate.co.uk
Web	www.colonsayestate.co.uk

Glenisle Hotel

The Glenisle has a great tradition in hospitality – it was once the village jail! These days, it's the best place to stay on Arran – stylish and friendly with views across Lamlash Bay to Holy Island. Outside, there's a pretty terrace for lunch in the sun. Inside, you find stone walls, roaring fires, then books and games in a stylish little sitting room. It's quirky, too – part of the bar was rescued from an old paddle steamer, and the hotel holds a Christmas festival at the end of November. There are two restaurants – one overlooking the garden, the other with mirrors on one wall – and the food hits the spot nicely: perhaps langoustines with lime and chilli, pork belly with a cider jus, dark chocolate brownie with Arran ice cream. Smart, airy rooms have comfy beds, colourful throws and robes in cute bathrooms. Two at the front look out to sea, the suite has a claw-foot bath overlooking the bay. As for Arran, it's a small-scale version of Scotland: mountains to the north, lush farmland to the south, then sandy beaches and the odd castle waiting on the coast. A perfect island base.

Rooms	2 doubles, 9 twin/doubles: £124–£184.
	1 suite for 2: £196–£215.
	2 singles: £90–£94.
Meals	Lunch & dinner £5–£35.
Closed	Never.
Directions	South from Broddick for 3 miles to Lamlash. In village on right.

Geoffrey Dallamore & Timothy Bilings
Glenisle Hotel
Lamlash,
Isle of Arran, KA27 8LY

Tel   +44 (0)1770 600559
Email   enquiries@glenislehotel.com
Web   www.glenislehotel.com

Knockinaam Lodge

Lawns run down to the Irish sea, roe deer come to eat the roses, sunsets turn the sky red. This beautiful hunting lodge is one of the loveliest country-house hotels in the land. There's a Michelin star in the dining room, 150 malts in the panelled bar and a level of service you rarely find in such far-flung corners of the realm. There's history, too. Churchill once stayed and you can sleep in his room, then climb into the deepest of baths and read his books. Immaculate interiors abound: gorgeous bedrooms, faultless bathrooms, a morning room where the scent of fresh flowers mingles with wood smoke. You'll find beautiful art, the daily papers, games and books galore. Outside, cliff walks lead over to Portpatrick, peregrine falcons circle on high, bluebells carpet the hills in spring. When it's stormy, waves crash all around. There's golf on the coast at Portpatrick, then Luce Bay for miles of sand. John Buchan knew the house and described it in *The Thirty-Nine Steps* as the house to which Hannay fled. Remote, beguiling, utterly spoiling – grand old Knockinaam is simply unmissable. *Pets by arrangement.*

Rooms	4 doubles, 5 twin/doubles: £290-£440. 1 family room for 4: £350-£420. Price includes dinner for 2.
Meals	Lunch, by arrangement, £32.50-£40. Dinner, 5 courses, included; non-residents £67.50.
Closed	Never.
Directions	From A77 or A75 pick up signs to Portpatrick. West from Lochans on A77, then left after 2 miles, signed. Follow signs for 3 miles to hotel.

David & Sian Ibbotson
Knockinaam Lodge
Portpatrick,
Stranraer, DG9 9AD

Tel   +44 (0)1776 810471
Email   reservations@knockinaamlodge.com
Web   www.knockinaamlodge.com

Trigony House Hotel

A small, welcoming, family-run hotel with good food, nicely priced rooms and a lovely garden, where you may spot red squirrels. The house dates to 1700, a shooting lodge for the local castle. Inside, you find Japanese oak panelling in the hall, a wood-burner in the pretty sitting room and an open fire in the dining room, where doors open onto the terrace for dinner in summer. Adam cooks lovely rustic fare, perhaps goat's cheese tart, loin of roe venison, chocolate brownie cheesecake with chocolate ice cream; there's a small, organic kitchen garden that provides much for the table in summer. Bedrooms vary in size, but not style – all have pretty fabrics, summer colours and good bathrooms. Some are dog-friendly, one has a conservatory/sitting room that opens onto a private lawn, there's a film library downstairs for your TV. After a full cooked breakfast, head west for the Southern Upland Way or the spectacular country between Moniaive and the Galloway Forest. Don't miss Drumlanrig Castle up the road for its gardens, walking trails and excellent mountain bike tracks.

Rooms	4 doubles, 4 twin/doubles: £85–£130. 1 suite for 2: £155. Dinner, B&B from £82.50 p.p.
Meals	Lunch from £5. Dinner £25–£35.
Closed	24–26 December.
Directions	North from Dumfries on A76; through Closeburn; signed left after 1 mile.

Adam & Jan Moore
Trigony House Hotel
Closeburn, Thornhill, DG3 5EZ
Tel   +44 (0)1848 331211
Email   trigonyhotel@gmail.com
Web   www.trigonyhotel.co.uk

Cavens

The Solway Firth is a magical spot, a patch of heaven most ignore, so you'll mostly have it to yourself. You swoop down from Dumfries through glorious country, then crest a hill and there it is, vast tracts of tidal sands with a huge sky above. It's a magnet for birdlife, the rich pickings of low tide too tempting to refuse. As for this 1752 shooting lodge, it stands in 20 acres of sweeping lawns, native woodlands and sprawling fields. Inside, elegant interiors come as standard. Two lovely sitting rooms are decked out with busts and oils, golden sofas, smouldering fires, a baby grand piano; in summer, you slip onto the terrace for afternoon tea. Country-house bedrooms have garden views, period furniture, bowls of fruit. One is smaller, others big with room for sofas. One has a stunning bathroom, another has an en suite sun-room. Back downstairs, there's an honesty bar for pre-dinner drinks, then Angus's delicious food in the smart restaurant, perhaps scallops with lime and Vermouth, Galloway pork in a mustard sauce, lemon panna cotta. There are gardens aplenty and golf at spectacular Southerness.

Rooms	4 doubles, 1 twin: £100–£190. Extra bed/sofabed available £30 p.p.p.n.
Meals	Dinner: 3-course market menu £25; 3-course à la carte about £35. Packed lunch available.
Closed	Rarely.
Directions	From Dumfries A710 to Kirkbean (12 miles). Signed in village on left.

Jane & Angus Fordyce
Cavens
Kirkbean, Dumfries, DG2 8AA
Tel   +44 (0)1387 880234
Email   enquiries@cavens.com
Web   www.cavens.com

21212

A smart restaurant with rooms in Edinburgh's East End with Holyrood Palace, the Botanic Gardens and lovely Leith all close. Paul left his Michelin star down south, bought this Georgian townhouse, spent a fortune turning it into a 21st-century pleasuredome, then opened for business and won back his star. The house stands at the top of a hill with long views north towards the Firth of Forth. Inside, contemporary splendour waits. High ceilings and vast windows come as standard, but wander at will and find a chic first-floor drawing room, cherubs on the wall, busts and statues all over the place, even a private dining pod made of white leather. Stunning bedrooms have enormous beds, cool colours, fat sofas and iPod docks. Those at the front have the view, all have robes in magnificent bathrooms. As for the restaurant, the kitchen is on display behind a wall of glass and the food it produces is heavenly stuff, perhaps sea bass with cashew nuts, pork with pistachio and onion mustard, lemon curd cheesecake tart with melon juice. Princes Street and its lovely gardens are a short stroll. *Minimum stay: 3 days at New Year.*

Rooms	4 doubles: £95–£295.
Meals	Lunch from £22. Dinner £55–£70. Not Sunday or Monday.
Closed	Rarely.
Directions	A720 ring road, then A702/A7 into town. Right at T-junc. at Balmoral Hotel, then immediately left with flow. Right at second r'bout and 1st right. On right.

Paul Kitching & Katie O'Brien
21212
3 Royal Terrace, Edinburgh, EH7 5AB

Tel	+44 (0)345 222 1212
Email	reservations@21212restaurant.co.uk
Web	www.21212restaurant.co.uk

94DR

Close to Holyrood and Arthur's Seat, this super-friendly designer B&B is not only popular for its contemporary style, but for Paul and John, who treat guests like friends and make sure you see the best of their city. A traditional Victorian exterior gives no hint of the chic interiors that wait within. You'll find original floor tiles and ornate ceilings, but other than that it's a clean sweep of modern splendour: deep charcoal downstairs; pure white above. There's a sitting room with iPads in case you want to book a restaurant, then an honesty bar, an espresso machine and lots of handy guide books. Upstairs, stylish, well-priced bedrooms wait. Some are big with claw-foot baths, others smaller with walk-in power showers. All come with comfy beds, bathrobes, beautiful linen and fine contemporary art. The family suite (two rooms) has bunk beds and a PlayStation for kids. Delicious breakfasts are served in a conservatory overlooking the back garden, a memorable feast orchestrated by Paul, with lively conversation that travels the world. Majestic Edinburgh is yours to explore. *Minimum stay: 2 nights at weekends.*

Rooms	3 doubles: £100–£145.
	2 suites for 2: £125–£200.
	1 family room for 4: £125–£190.
	Singles from £80.
Meals	Restaurants within 0.5 miles.
Closed	2–15 January.
Directions	Leave A720 (ring road) at Sheriff Hall roundabout for A7 north into Edinburgh. Straight ahead for 3 miles and on left.

John MacEwan & Paul Lightfoot
94DR
94 Dalkeith Road, EH16 5AF

Tel	+44 (0)131 662 9265
Email	stay@94dr.com
Web	www.94dr.com

23 Mayfield

A great base for all things Edinburgh. Built in 1868, this Victorian villa was once home to a coffee merchant and stands in the shadow of Arthur's Seat. Outside, much prized, off-street parking waits. Inside, you find original fireplaces, ornate ceilings and a stained-glass window on the landing. Ross has added Victorian colours, newspapers on poles, gilt-framed pictures that hang on chains – but best of all is breakfast, served in winter with candelabra on every table. You'll find chesterfield sofas in the sitting room, then old movies playing on the television. Bedrooms offer modern comforts: excellent beds, travertine bathrooms, bold colours, perhaps a panelled wall. You get iPod docks, Bose CD players, the family room has a Nintendo Wii. There's good art throughout, a hot tub in the garden, you can jump on a bus and whizz into town. Breakfast is the best: porridge with honey, free-range eggs, marshmallow pancakes, Stornoway black pudding with the full cooked works. Ross also has an apartment for six in the centre of town if you need more space. *Minimum stay: 2 nights at weekends.*

Rooms	3 twin/doubles, 3 four-posters: £80–£170. 1 family room for 4: £80–£190. 1 triple: £80–£175. Singles from £70.
Meals	Restaurants within half a mile.
Closed	24–26 December.
Directions	A720 bypass, then north onto A722 for Edinburgh. Right onto A721 at T-junction with traffic lights. Over x-roads with main flow, under railway bridge, on right.

Ross Birnie
23 Mayfield
23 Mayfield Gardens, EH9 2BX

Tel	+44 (0)131 667 5806
Email	info@23mayfield.co.uk
Web	www.23mayfield.co.uk

The Bridge Inn at Ratho

This lovely inn sits in a small village directly above the Union Canal. Footpaths head west into the country, you can hire bikes and follow the tow path into Edinburgh, or jump on the pub's canal boat for a Sunday lunch cruise. If all that sounds too strenuous, then plonk yourself down on the terrace and watch the odd boat chug past while sipping a pint of good ale. Inside, the view is weather-proofed by big windows in the dining room. An easy style runs throughout. You'll find wood-burners, smart colours, a whisky bar, the odd sofa. In summer, there are barbecues on Friday nights, an ice cream shed in the garden, even a small festival in May with live bands and lots of beer. Rooms aren't huge, but hit the spot. They're stylish and comfy with smart beds and crisp linen. All but one has the view, three have walk-in power showers, one has a claw-foot bath. The airport is ten minutes away, but you're not on the flight path, so peace reigns. Finally, don't miss nearby Jupiter Artland in summer, a wonderland of beautiful things. Children and dogs are very welcome.

Rooms	3 doubles, 1 twin/double: £80–£120. Singles from £65.
Meals	Lunch & dinner, £5–£35. Sunday lunch from £12.95.
Closed	Christmas Day.
Directions	West from A720 (ring road) on A71. Right at x-roads after 3 miles, signed Ratho. Right in village and inn on left above canal.

Graham & Rachel Bucknall
The Bridge Inn at Ratho
27 Baird Road, Ratho, EH28 8RA

Tel	+44 (0)131 333 1320
Email	info@bridgeinn.com
Web	www.bridgeinn.com

Entry 244   Map 9

The Ship Inn

There are few inns where you can sit on the terrace and watch a game of cricket on the beach below. But it's not beach cricket as you know it. This is serious stuff, played at low tide, and Mark Waugh, Viv Richards and Wasim Akram have all tried their hand. As for this cute little boutique inn, it's as good as any in the land, and it doubles as the pavilion... and the venue for post-match celebrations, no doubt. On sunny days, you decant onto the terrace for lunch in the sun and gaze across the Firth of Forth to Edinburgh's hills. Inside, contemporary rustic design mixes with roaring fires and the odd stone wall. Sofas and armchairs are scattered about, staff weave through the throng delivering delicious food – fish and seafood from local waters, lamb and beef from nearby farms, sinful puddings you can't resist; there are regular barbecues on the terrace, too. Smart rooms have seaside colours, crisp linen, coffee machines, fancy bathrooms with walk-in showers; those at the front have sea views, too. St Andrews waits for a round of golf, the Fife coastal path for excellent walks. A perfect place.

Rooms	6 twin/doubles: £110–£160. Extra beds £15. Cots free.
Meals	Lunch & dinner £5–£35. Sunday lunch from £12.95.
Closed	Christmas Day & 2 weeks in January.
Directions	A917 east into Elie. In village, right after small green, onto Stenton Row. Straight ahead and on left.

Graham & Rachel Bucknall
The Ship Inn
The Toft,
Elie, KY9 1DT

Tel	+44 (0)1333 330246
Email	info@shipinn.scot
Web	www.shipinn.scot

15 Glasgow

This is a smart Glasgow address – bang in the middle of town, yet beautifully insulated from it. The house, grand Victorian, stands on an attractive square with communal gardens guests can enjoy. Inside, the feel is distinctly contemporary, despite a couple of Corinthian pillars in the entrance hall. It's all been beautifully renovated, and while technically you're in a B&B, the interiors here are a match for any boutique hotel. Downstairs, a vast sitting room has a couple of sofas in front of a fire. Bedrooms upstairs are no less generous. Those at the back are large, the suites at the front are huge. All come with king-size beds, crisp white linen, handmade bedheads and robes in gorgeous bathrooms. Suites have a few added extras: big sofas, beautiful windows, one has a double-ended bath overlooking the square. Breakfast is brought to you whenever you want. As for dinner, you'll find good restaurants nearby: the Finnieston for seafood and gin cocktails; the Gannet for a flat-iron steak; Ben Nevis for a wee dram and live folk music most nights. Don't miss the excellent Burrell Collection. *On-site parking.*

Rooms	3 doubles: £120–£145.
	2 suites for 2: £150–£175.
	Extra beds £20.
Meals	Restaurants on your doorstep.
Closed	Never.
Directions	West into Glasgow on M8. Exit at junc. 18 for Charing X (outside lane), then double back at lights. 1st left, 1st left, 1st left (really). Follow square round to house.

Lorraine Gibson
15 Glasgow
15 Woodside Place,
Glasgow, G3 7QL

Tel	+44 (0)141 332 1263
Email	rooms@15glasgow.com
Web	www.15glasgow.com

Mackay's Rooms

This is the north-west corner of Britain and it's utterly magical: huge skies, sandy beaches, aquamarine seas, cliffs and caves. You drive – or cycle – for mile upon mile with mountains soaring into the heavens and ridges sliding into the sea. If you like big, remote landscapes, you'll love it here; what's more, you'll pretty much have it to yourself. Mackay's – they have the shop, the bunkhouse and the garage, too – is the only place to stay in town, its earthy colours mixing with stone walls, open fires and stripped floors to great effect. Bedrooms (some big, others smaller) are extremely comfy. They come with big wooden beds and crisp white linen, while Fiona, a textiles graduate, has a fine eye for fabrics and upholstery. You also get excellent bathrooms, iPod docks, flat-screen TVs and DVD players. Breakfast sets you up for the day – grilled grapefruit, whisky porridge, venison sausages, local eggs – so head east to the beach, west for great golf or catch the ferry across to Cape Wrath and scan the sea for whales. There's surfing for the brave and the beautiful.

Rooms	6 doubles, 1 twin: £125-£165. 4 cottages for 2-6: £800-£1,600 per wk. Singles from £110.
Meals	Restaurants in village.
Closed	October-May. Cottages open all year.
Directions	A838 north from Rhiconich. After 19 miles enter Durness village. Mackay's is on right-hand side opposite memorial.

Fiona Mackay
Mackay's Rooms
Durine, Durness,
Lairg, IV27 4PN

Tel	+44 (0)1971 511202
Email	stay@visitdurness.com
Web	www.visitdurness.com

Scourie Hotel

This famous old fishing hotel is a treat from top to toe. It's a quirky place run with great panache by the Campbell's, who bought it recently, refurbished in style and now it shines. It's supremely comfy – smart without being swanky, very much a country hotel. You'll find golden wallpapers, antique furniture, beautifully upholstered armchairs, then an open fire in the sitting room. It's an remarkably friendly place. Fishermen tend to come for the same week each year, re-booking when they leave, so everyone knows everyone and they all go out of their way to welcome interlopers into the fold. There's great tradition, too, with a board master allocating fishing beats each morning and a gong to announce dinner. Stylish rooms have comfy beds, pretty fabrics, old-world baths for a good soak and no TVs; bliss. Dinner is a treat, perhaps ham hock terrine, fresh local salmon, profiteroles with chocolate sauce. There's a cocktail bar, a pretty garden, paths that lead down to the sea. This is a wildly beautiful corner of Scotland: spectacular walking, wildlife tours and golf on the north coast wait.

Rooms	6 doubles, 6 twins: £125. 2 family rooms for 3: £135-£150. 6 singles: £75. 1 chalet for 4: £250. Dinner, B&B £90-£99 p.p.
Meals	Lunch from 4.95. Bar meals from £10. Dinner, 3 courses, £32.
Closed	8 October 2016 to 15 March 2017.
Directions	North from Ullapool on A835, then A837. In village on left.

Richard, Fiona & Charlotte Campbell
Scourie Hotel
Scourie,
Lairg, IV27 4SX

Tel	+44 (0)1971 502396
Email	stay@scouriehotel.com
Web	www.scouriehotel.com

The Torridon

It's hard to beat the top of Scotland, the landscapes here feed the soul. Mountains rise, red deer roam, eagles soar, the light changes every minute. This 1887 shooting lodge was built for the Earl of Lovelace and stands in 58 acres that roll down to the shores of Upper Loch Torridon. Inside, sparkling interiors thrill: a huge fire in the panelled hall, a zodiac ceiling in the drawing room, 350 malts in the pitch pine bar. Big windows pull in the view, while canny walkers pour off the hills to recover in style. Bedrooms are hard to fault, some big, others bigger, with a cool, contemporary style running throughout: bold colours, padded headboards, exquisite linen, magnificent bathrooms; one room has a shower in a turret. Outside, a beautiful two-acre kitchen garden provides much for the table, perhaps lovage and courgette soup, then shoulder of lamb with rosemary gnocchi and passion fruit tart with mango mousse. Dan and Rohaise also own the village inn for simpler food and good rooms from £110. Don't miss the free excursions: kayaking, guided walks, abseiling and mountain biking are all on tap. *Pets by arrangement.*

Rooms	10 doubles, 2 twins, 2 four-posters: £230–£465. 4 suites for 2: £465. 1 house for 4: £925–£1,425 per week. Extra bed £40 p.p. per night.
Meals	Lunch from £5.95. Dinner, 5 courses, £60.
Closed	January.
Directions	A9 to Inverness, A835 to Garve, A832 to Kinlochewe, A896 to Annat (not Torridon). Signed on south shore.

Daniel & Rohaise Rose-Bristow
The Torridon
Annat,
By Achnasheen, IV22 2EY

Tel	+44 (0)1445 791242
Email	info@thetorridon.com
Web	www.thetorridon.com

Kilcamb Lodge Hotel & Restaurant

Another beautiful West Coast setting with Loch Sunart at the end of the garden and Glas Bheinn rising beyond. Kilcamb – a barracks during the Jacobite uprising – has a bit of everything: a drawing room with an open fire; an elegant dining room for good food; a cool little brasserie that's recently been refurbished; a handful of lovely bedrooms in warm country-house style. There's a 12-acre garden that rolls down to the sea, where you can spot otters and seals. Ducks and geese fly over, if you're lucky you'll see eagles. Back inside, there's a stained-glass window on the landing, fresh flowers in the drawing room, driftwood lamps and good books. You can eat in the restaurant or the brasserie, either a five-course tasting menu or something simpler, perhaps a plate of seafood, Highland lamb, iced whisky parfait. Bedrooms have warm colours, some with a contemporary feel, others a smart country-house style. All have good bathrooms, crisp linen and comfy beds. Day trips to Mull are easy to arrange. Don't miss Ardnamuchan or Senna Bay at the end of the road.

Rooms	2 doubles, 6 twin/doubles: £190–£335. 2 suites for 2: £290–£415. Price includes dinner for 2.
Meals	Lunch from £7.50. Dinner, 3 courses, included; non-residents about £40. Tasting menu £55. Afternoon tea from £5.50.
Closed	January. Limited opening November & February.
Directions	From Fort William A82 south for 10 miles to Corran for ferry across to Ardgour, then A861 to Strontian. Hotel west of village on left.

David & Sally Ruthven-Fox
Kilcamb Lodge Hotel & Restaurant
Strontian,
Acharacle, PH36 4HY

Tel	+44 (0)1967 402257
Email	enquiries@kilcamblodge.co.uk
Web	www.kilcamblodge.co.uk

Doune Knoydart

There is nowhere quite like Doune. You arrive by boat – there's no road in – a ferry across to Knoydart, the last great wilderness in Britain. You'll find mountain, sea and sky – a thrilling landscape of boundless peace and ever-changing light. It's a haven for wildlife – killer whales, Golden eagles, red grouse, otters and badgers – 120 species live here. As for Doune, it sits on the Sound of Sleat with views across to Skye. It's a tiny community of happily shipwrecked souls and Martin, Jane and Liz look after you with great generosity. The dining room is the hub, pine-clad from top to toe, with a stove to keep you warm and games in case it rains. The food is delicious – crab from the bay, roast lamb from the hill, chocolate tart with homemade ice-cream. Bedrooms along the veranda are delightfully simple; pine-clad cabins with mezzanine bunks for children, hooks for clothes, sparkling showers, armchairs for watching the weather. The walking is magnificent, boat trips can be arranged, the night sky astounds. There's a lodge for groups, too. A very special place, miss it at your peril. *Minimum stay: 3 nights.*

Rooms	2 doubles, 1 twin, each with mezzanine bed for children: £90. 1 single with separate shower: £33. Dinner, B&B £78–£88 p.p. (includes packed lunch).
Meals	Dinner £35.
Closed	October – Easter.
Directions	Park in Mallaig; the boat will collect you at an agreed time.

Martin & Jane Davies
Doune Knoydart
Knoydart, Mallaig, PH41 4PL
Tel   +44 (0)1687 462667
Email   martin@doune-knoydart.co.uk
Web   www.doune-knoydart.co.uk

Hotel Eilean Iarmain

The most beautiful spot on Skye, simple as that. You're at the end of the road, in a whitewashed hamlet, almost paddling in the Sound of Sleat. Mountains rise, the sea sparkles, the odd fishing boat potters by. If you want deep peace in a magical landscape, you'll find it here. Warm Hebridean interiors fit the mood: tartan carpets, panelled walls, a pine-clad hall. There's an open fire in the sitting room, then an airy restaurant for lovely food, perhaps hand-dived local scallops, Highland lamb and venison, cranachan soufflé with fresh raspberries. Bedrooms are split between the main house (warmly traditional), the garden house (nicely uncluttered) and the old stables (pine-clad suites over two floors); the latter two have gardens overlooking the water. You get the odd half-tester, a turret or two, robes in adequate bathrooms. There's an art gallery, a whisky shop and a popular bar, where the odd ceilidh breaks loose and fiddles fly. It was all the work of Sir Iain Noble, who founded Scotland's Gaelic University here to keep the language and culture of the islands alive. He did a fine job.

Rooms	10 doubles, 2 twin/doubles: £120–£190. 4 suites for 2: £170–£250. Singles from £110. Extra beds for children aged 5-13: £20; under 5s: free.
Meals	Bar meals from £11.95. 3-course à la carte dinner, £35–£40.
Closed	Never.
Directions	A87 over Skye Bridge, then left after 7 miles onto A851, signed Armdale. Hotel on left after 8 miles, signed.

Mira Byrne
Hotel Eilean Iarmain
Isle Ornsay, IV43 8QR

Tel	+44 (0)1471 833332
Email	hotel@eileaniarmain.co.uk
Web	www.eileaniarmain.co.uk

Coruisk House

You follow the road for 15 miles through magnificent landscapes – down the glen, around the loch and over the mountain to Elgol. Your reward is this chic little restaurant with rooms waiting at the end of the track. A cool, rustic style has conquered every corner, ambrosial food flies from the kitchen, a glass of prosecco is yours on arrival. The breakfast room runs along the front of the house with a string of windows that frame the view. You'll find hanging lamps, up-cycled furniture, lime-washed walls and a painted settle. Airy rooms have big beds, mohair throws, white linen, robes in quirky bathrooms. New rooms in the cottage next door are coming in 2017; expect the same warm style and the odd claw-foot bath. As for Iain's glorious food, you eat in the restaurant, where a wood-burner keeps things cosy, perhaps crab brûlée with lobster bisque, Highland beef with braised oxtail, ginger steamed pudding with Drambuie ice cream. Drop down to Elgol harbour, where Bonnie Prince Charlie fled for his life, and gaze upon the mighty Cuillins rising from the sea. Boat trips are easily arranged. Heaven.

Rooms	2 doubles: £130–£150.
Meals	Dinner £35–£40.
Closed	November – February (open for New Year).
Directions	West from Broadford on B8083 15 miles over to Algol. Over cattle grid at start of village and on right.

Favourite newcomer

Iain Roden & Clare Winskill
Coruisk House
26 Elgol,
Elgol, IV49 9BL
Tel +44 (0)1471 866330
Email info@coruiskhouse.com
Web www.coruiskhouse.com

Viewfield House Hotel

This old ancestral pile stands high above Portree Bay with fine views tumbling down to the Sound of Rassay below. Twenty acres of mature gardens and woodland wrap around you, with croquet on the lawn and a hill to climb for 360° views of peak and sea. As for this grand Victorian factor's house, expect a few aristocratic fixtures and fittings: hunting trophies in the hall, cases filled with curios, a grand piano and open fire in the drawing room, Sanderson wallpaper in the dining room. Family oils hang on the walls, you'll find wood carvings from distant lands and a flurry of antiques, all of which blend grandeur with touches of humour. Upstairs a warren of bedrooms wait. Most are big, some are vast, all come in country-house style with lovely fabrics, crisply laundered sheets and sea views from those at the front. Dive into Skye — wildlife, mountains, sea lochs and castles all wait, as do a couple of distilleries. Suppers are on tap — tomato and basil soup, lamb noisettes, chocolate and almond cake with vanilla sauce; there's Highland porridge for breakfast, too. Fantastic.

Rooms	3 doubles, 8 twin/doubles: £136–£160. 2 singles: £68–£80. Dinner, B&B £86–£103 p.p.
Meals	Dinner, 3 courses, £25. Packed lunch £7.
Closed	Mid-October to Easter.
Directions	On A87, coming from south, driveway entrance on left just before the Portree filling station.

Hugh Macdonald
Viewfield House Hotel
Viewfield Road,
Portree, IV51 9EU

Tel	+44 (0)1478 612217
Email	info@viewfieldhouse.com
Web	www.viewfieldhouse.com

Culdearn House

Grantown is a great base for Highland flings. You can fish the Spey, jump on the whisky trail, check out a raft of castles, even ski in Aviemore. Loch Ness is close, as is Royal Deeside, there's golf everywhere and the walking is divine; in short, expect to be busy. As for Culdearn, it stands in a row of five identical houses that were built in 1860 by Lord Seafield, one for each of his daughters. These days it's a lovely small hotel where William and Sonia look after guests with unstinting kindness. There's an open fire and facing sofas in the smart sitting room, panelled windows and a marble fireplace in the dining room, then stylish bedrooms that offer the sort of comfort you'd want after a day in the hills. You get the comfiest beds, the crispest linen, then decanters of sherry, pretty furniture and spotless bathrooms. Back downstairs, William looks after a tempting wine list and 60 malts, while Sonia whisks up delicious four-course dinners, perhaps West Coast scallops, bramble sorbet, fillet of beef, a walnut and maple syrup parfait. Don't miss the ospreys at Boat of Garten. *Cildren over 10 welcome.*

Rooms	4 doubles, 1 twin/double, 1 twin: £150-£170. Singles £75-£100. Dinner, B&B £100-£125 p.p.
Meals	Dinner, 4 courses, £45
Closed	Never.
Directions	North into Grantown from A95. Left at 30 mph sign & house directly ahead.

Sonia & William Marshall
Culdearn House
Woodlands Terrace,
Grantown on Spey, PH26 3JU
Tel   +44 (0)1479 872106
Email   enquiries@culdearn.com
Web   www.culdearn.com

Killiecrankie House Hotel

No Highland fling would be complete without a night at Killiecrankie. Henrietta runs the place with great charm and has spent the last five years pouring in love and money; now it shines. Outside, gardens galore: one for roses, another for vegetables, and a fine herbaceous border. Further afield, you'll find much to please: Loch Tummel, Rannoch Moor and magnificent Glenshee, over which you tumble for the Highland Games at Braemar. Return to the indisputable comforts of a smart country hotel: tartan in the dining room, 52 malts at the bar, views at breakfast of red squirrels climbing garden trees. There's a snug sitting room where a fire burns in winter; in summer doors open onto the garden. Delightful bedrooms come in different shapes and sizes. All are smart with pretty linen, warm colours, chic fabrics and lovely views. Dinner is predictably delicious, perhaps pea and mint soup, Highland venison, sticky toffee pudding. There's porridge with cream and brown sugar for breakfast. Castles, hills and distilleries wait. A great wee place with staff who care. *Minimum stay: 2 nights at weekends. Pets by arrangement.*

Rooms	3 doubles, 5 twin/doubles: £250–£320. Singles £140–£150. Price includes dinner. Extra bed/sofabed available £25–£65 p.p.p.n.
Meals	Lunch from £4.50. Dinner included; non-residents £42.
Closed	Christmas, 3 January–18 March.
Directions	A9 north of Pitlochry, then B8079, signed Killiecrankie. Straight ahead for 2 miles. Hotel on right, signed.

Henrietta Fergusson
Killiecrankie House Hotel
Killiecrankie,
Pitlochry, PH16 5LG

Tel	+44 (0)1796 473220
Email	enquiries@killiecrankiehotel.co.uk
Web	www.killiecrankiehotel.co.uk

Craigatin House & Courtyard

Craigatin is one of those lovely places where beautiful rooms have attractive prices and hands-on owners go out of their way to make your stay special. It stands peacefully in two acres of manicured gardens on the northern shores of town; good restaurants are a short stroll. Smart stone exteriors give way to warmly contemporary interiors, where beautiful windows flood rooms with light. There are shutters in the breakfast room, which overflows into an enormous conservatory where sofas wait in front of a wood-burner and walls of glass open onto the garden. Big uncluttered bedrooms – some in the main house, others in converted stables – are super value for money. Expect Farrow & Ball colours, comfy beds, crisp white linen, padded bedheads and pretty shower rooms. Breakfast offers the full cooked works and tempting alternatives, perhaps smoked haddock omelettes or apple pancakes with grilled bacon and maple syrup. As for Pitlochry – gateway to the Highlands – it's a vibrant town with lots to do: castles and mountains, lochs and forests, its famous Festival Theatre. You're on the whisky trail, too. *Minimum stay: 2 nights at weekends.*

Rooms	11 doubles, 2 twins: £95–£105. 1 suite for 2: £122. Singles £85–£112.
Meals	Restaurants within walking distance.
Closed	Christmas.
Directions	A9 north to Pitlochry. Take 1st turn-off for town, up main street, past shops and signed on left.

Martin & Andrea Anderson
Craigatin House & Courtyard
165 Atholl Road,
Pitlochry, PH16 5QL
Tel   +44 (0)1796 472478
Email   enquiries@craigatinhouse.co.uk
Web   www.craigatinhouse.co.uk

Knockendarroch Hotel & Restaurant

This grand old house on a hill was built in 1880, then sold in 1910 for £100! It is also the birthplace of the Pitlochry Festival Theatre, the plays originally performed in the garden. These days it's simply a lovely place to stay with views from the front that shoot across the valley to forested hills. Inside, you find original tiles in the hall, a double sitting room with two fires, a whisky bar for a wee dram, a wallpapered restaurant with views of Ben Vrackie and plenty of original contemporary art. Good paths lead up through forest and moorland for big Highland views, not a bad way to work up an appetite for some very good food, perhaps fillet of hake with chilli and lemongrass, Perthshire lamb with parsnip purée, elderflower panna cotta with pear sorbet. Bedrooms are lovely, it really doesn't matter which you choose, though the big ones at the front do have exceptional views. You'll find comfy beds, smart fabrics, tartan throws and padded headboards, perhaps a cushioned window seat or a sofa if there's room. Two have balconies, most have binoculars to scan the hills. There's a drying room for wet gear, too. *Minimum stay: 2 nights at weekends. Children over 10 welcome.*

Rooms	12 twin/doubles: £140–£195.
	Dinner, B&B from £85 p.p.
Meals	Lunch from £5.
	Dinner, 3 courses, £25;
	£42 non-residents.
Closed	20 December to 6 February.
Directions	A9 north to Pitlochry. Up high street,
	then right into Bonnethill Road. Right
	again into Toberargan Road and on right.

Struan & Louise Lothian
Knockendarroch Hotel & Restaurant
Higher Oakfield,
Pitlochry, PH16 5HT

Tel	+44 (0)1796 473473
Email	info@knockendarroch.co.uk
Web	www.knockendarroch.co.uk

Barley Bree

A few miles north of Gleneagles, a super little restaurant with rooms that delivers what so many people want: stylish interiors, super food, excellent prices, a warm welcome. This is a small family-run affair. Fabrice is French and cooks sublimely, Alison, a Scot, looks after the wine. As for Barley Bree – whisky soup to you and me – it's an 18th-century coaching inn, its name plucked from a Robert Burns poem. Happy locals and travellers from afar come for fabulous Scottish food that's cooked with French flair, perhaps fennel soup with basil pesto, saddle of venison with piquillo purée, tarte tatin with vanilla ice cream. The newly refurbished restaurant, nicely rustic, has a fire that burns on both sides, while in summer you decant onto a terrace for lunch in the sun. The six comfy rooms have neutral colours, crisp linen, good beds and underfloor heating in neat little shower rooms. The big room, with a claw-foot bath, is well worth splashing out on. There's a sitting room for guests with books, a bar, good art, stripped boards and a fire. Don't miss the gardens at Drummond Castle or Innerpeffray Library.

Rooms	6 twin/doubles: £95–£160.
	Singles £75–£85.
Meals	Lunch from £8.
	Dinner, 3 courses, about £40
	(not Sunday evening, Mon or Tue).
	Sunday lunch from £13.50.
Closed	Christmas, 4 July – 19 July.
Directions	A9 north from Dunblane, then
	A822 for Muthill. In village on left
	before church.

Fabrice & Alison Bouteloup
Barley Bree
6 Willoughby Street,
Muthill, PH5 2AB
Tel   +44 (0)1764 681451
Email   info@barleybree.com
Web   www.barleybree.com

The Royal Hotel

An attractive small hotel, intimate and welcoming with stylish interiors – a country house in the middle of town. Queen Victoria once stayed, hence the name. It stands on the river Earn, its eponymous loch glistening five miles up stream. You're well placed to strike out in all directions: Loch Tay, Pitlochry, The Trossachs and Perth are all close. Those who linger fare well. You get a wall of books in a beautiful sitting room where two fires burn. Newspapers hang on poles, logs tumble from wicker baskets, sofas and armchairs are impeccably upholstered. There's a grandfather clock in the hall, rugs on stripped floors in a country-house bar, then walls festooned with beautiful art. You can eat all over the place, in the bar, in the conservatory or at smartly dressed tables in the elegant dining room, perhaps seared pigeon with a whisky sauce, duck breast with a chilli jam, banoffee pancakes with Drambuie ice cream. Smart homely rooms have padded bedheads, crisp linen, mahogany dressers, gilt-framed mirrors. Bathrooms have robes, one four-poster has a log fire. Drummond Castle Gardens are close.

Rooms	5 doubles, 3 twins, 3 four-posters: £150–£190. 1 self-catering house for 4 (minimum stay: 2 nights low season): £320–£890.
Meals	Bar meals from £6.95. Dinner, 3 courses, £25–£30.
Closed	Rarely
Directions	A9 north of Dunblane, A822 thro' Braco, left onto B827. Left for town centre, over bridge, hotel on square.

Teresa Milsom
The Royal Hotel
Melville Square, Comrie,
Crieff, PH6 2DN

Tel	+44 (0)1764 679200
Email	reception@royalhotel.co.uk
Web	www.royalhotel.co.uk

Monachyle Mhor

Monachyle is unique – a designer hotel on a remote hill farm that started life as a B&B. Today it's one of the hippest places to stay in Scotland and it's still run by the same family with the children at the helm. Dick farms, Melanie designs the magical rooms, Tom cooks some of the best food in Scotland. It sits in 2,000 acres of blissful silence at the end of the track with the Trossachs circling around you and Loch Voil shimming below. Sheep graze, buzzards swoop, the odd fisherman tries his luck. Inside, there's a cool little bar, a fire in the sitting room, then a slim restaurant that drinks in the view. Bedrooms ooze 21st-century chic: big beds, cool colours, fabulous design, hi-tech gadgets. Bathrooms are equally good, perhaps a deluge shower in a granite steam room or claw-foot baths with views down the glen. Loft-house suites are enormous, but the smaller rooms are lovely, too. Dinner is a five-course feast with beef, lamb, pork and venison all off the farm. Rob Roy lived in the glen, you can visit his grave. The hotel holds a festival in May – fabulous food and cool Scottish tunes.

Rooms	9 twin/doubles: £195–£215. 5 suites for 2: £265. 1 family room for 4: £195–£265.
Meals	Lunch from £5.50. Dinner, 5 courses, £50. Sunday lunch £32.
Closed	Two weeks in January.
Directions	M9, junc. 11, then B824 and A84 north. Right for Balquhidder 6 miles north of Callander. 5 miles west along road & Loch Voil. Hotel on right, signed.

Tom Lewis
Monachyle Mhor
Balquhidder,
Lochearnhead, FK19 8PQ

Tel	+44 (0)1877 384622
Email	monachyle@mhor.net
Web	mhor.net/monachyle-mhor-hotel/

Mhor 84

The entirely benevolent expansion of the Mhor empire has mastered the Midas touch, turning this old roadside inn into the coolest motel in the land. Outside, the glen shoots down to Loch Voil, with mountains to climb and bike tracks to follow. Inside, chic white minimalism mixes with warm Scottish tradition, a perfect blend of relaxed 21st-century living. There's style and humour in equal measure – boarded floors, tractor seat bar stools, curios hanging on the walls, the odd sofa for afternoon tea. Fires roar, cake stands bulge, happy staff weave through the throng delivering fabulous food that you eat at old school tables – porridge with honey for breakfast, sourdough and hummus for lunch, Scotch rarebit, Tyree lobster and plum crumble for dinner. There's live folk music every Thursday – Ewan MacPherson of Shooglenifty often plays – and a fine selection of malts if you fancy a dram. Simple bedrooms have white walls, contemporary art, small armchairs and honest prices; spotless bathrooms are 1980s originals, all part of the fun. There's a games room, too, with a juke box and pool table.

Rooms	2 doubles, 4 twin/doubles: £70–£80. 1 family room for 4: £80–£110.
Meals	Breakfast from £4.50. Lunch from £3.90. Dinner, 3 courses, £25–£35.
Closed	Christmas Day.
Directions	A84 north from Callander. Through Strathyre, then right after three miles for Kingshouse. In village.

Dugald McGarry
Mhor 84
Balquhidder,
Lochearnhead, FK19 8NY

Tel	+44 (0)1877 384646
Email	motel@mhor.net
Web	mhor.net/mhor-84-motel/

Creagan House at Strathyre

Creagan is a delight – a small, traditional restaurant with rooms run with great passion by Gordon and Cherry. At its heart is Gordon's delicious food, which draws a devoted crowd, perhaps fillet of brill with plum and damson, local venison with a sloe gin and juniper sauce, then an apple, prune and almond flory with clotted cream. Food is local – meat and game from Perthshire, seafood from west-coast boats – and served on Skye pottery; some vegetables come from the garden. A snug sitting room doubles as a bar, where a good wine list and 50 malt whiskies wait; if you like a dram, you'll be happy here. Bedrooms fit the bill: warm and comfy with smart carpets, pretty colours, flat-screen TVs, a sofa if there's room. Breakfast is a treat; where else can you sit in a baronial dining room and read about the iconography of the toast rack while waiting for your bacon and eggs? No airs and graces, just the sort of attention you only get in small owner-run places. Hens, woodpeckers and red squirrels live in the garden. There are hills to climb, boat trips on lochs, secure storage for bikes. Very dog-friendly.

Rooms	3 doubles, 1 twin, 1 four-poster: £135–£155. Singles from £90–£100. Extra bed/sofabed available £30 p.p.p.n.
Meals	Dinner, 3 courses, £37.50.
Closed	28 October to 18 March.
Directions	From Stirling A84 north through Callander to Strathyre. Hotel 0.25 miles north of village on right.

Gordon & Cherry Gunn
Creagan House at Strathyre
Strathyre,
Callander, FK18 8ND

Tel	+44 (0)1877 384638
Email	eatandstay@creaganhouse.co.uk
Web	www.creaganhouse.co.uk

Cringletie House

Cringletie's splendours are hard to miss. You're wrapped up in 65 acres of beautiful grounds with daffodils that erupt in spring, cows that graze in lush fields and a peaceful walled garden for a game of boules. Pheasants strut, buzzards circle, views roll over nearby hills. As for the house, it dates to 1860, its playful turrets giving it a soft grandeur. Inside, you get the full works: an open fire in the hall, then a fine old staircase that sweeps you up to a striking first-floor dining room that has the feel of an 18th-century gentleman's club; expect panelled walls, vintage wallpapers and a spectacular muralled ceiling. There's a sitting room up here, too – equally grand, with fat sofas in front of the fire. Bedrooms are scattered about. Some downstairs open onto the garden, those at the top have the best views. It doesn't matter which you go for, they're all lovely, with warm colours, crisp linen, comfy beds and excellent bathrooms. Friday night barbecues are held in the walled garden in summer. Take to the hills, follow the Tweed or scoot up to Edinburgh; it's less than an hour by car.

Rooms	12 twin/doubles: £135–£245.
	1 suite for 2: £235–£265.
	1 cottage for 6: £235–£465.
Meals	Lunch from £4.50. Dinner, 3 courses, £35.
	Sunday lunch £22.50.
	Afternoon tea £18.50.
Closed	2–22 January.
Directions	North from Peebles on A703. Hotel signed left after 2 miles.

Jeremy Osbourne
Cringletie House
Edinburgh Road,
Peebles, EH45 8PL

Tel	+44 (0)1721 725750
Email	enquiries@cringletie.com
Web	www.cringletie.com

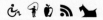

Windlestraw

A small country house with lovely interiors and beautiful views down the Tweed Valley. Hills rise, deer roam, osprey glide through the afternoon sky. John and Sylvia came back from Dubai to do their own thing and have been hard at work presiding over a chic refurbishment. Fires roar, a grand piano waits to be played, there's a sun-trapping terrace for afternoon tea. You find a conservatory sitting room filled with books and curios, a panelled dining room for super food, then binoculars with which to scan the valley – sunsets turn the hills orange. Country-house bedrooms have a warm contemporary style: smart colours, comfy beds, sofas in the bigger rooms, fine views from those at the front. Spotless bathrooms do the trick: one has a claw-foot bath, bigger rooms have robes. Good food waits downstairs, perhaps scallops from Eyemouth, local lamb, an irresistible tarte tatin. There's lots to do: walking, fishing, mountain biking, even kayaking on the Tweed; if you try your hand on Pebbles golf course, the views may well be better than your game! There's a literary festival at Traquair House in August, too.

Rooms	5 doubles, 1 twin: £160–£200. Singles £105–£125. Dinner, B&B £120–£145 p.p. Extra bed/sofabed available £25 p.p.p.n. Extra beds for children £15. Cots free.
Meals	Dinner, 5 courses, £40.
Closed	Christmas, January/February.
Directions	East from Peebles on A72. Into Walkerburn; house signed left on western flank of town.

John & Sylvia Matthews
Windlestraw
Galashiels Road,
Walkerburn, EH43 6AA

Tel	+44 (0)1896 870636
Email	stay@windlestraw.co.uk
Web	www.windlestraw.co.uk

The Allanton Inn

Allanton, population 100. Welcome to the sleepy back of beyond, an untouched corner of the rural idyll that most people skip on their rush north. Well, there's no rush here, just patchwork fields, rolling hills and the river Tweed pottering off to the coast. As for this cute little inn, it's a great base from which to explore. The style is charming, the locals friendly, the prices lovely, the food a treat. It sits on the only street in town with a garden that backs onto open country; in summer you can have lunch in the sun while watching the farmer plough his fields. Inside, home-spun interiors have colour and style. There's an open-plan feel, the airy bar flowing into a half-panelled restaurant. You'll find a smouldering fire, fresh flowers, good art, local ales. Rooms have an easy style: padded bedheads, good bathrooms, Farrow & Ball colours. A couple are big, those at the back have the view. Super local food waits downstairs, perhaps an Eyemouth fish platter, rump of local lamb, lavender and raspberry brûlée. There's local honeycomb at breakfast, too. You can fish, walk, play a bit of golf. Perfect.

Rooms	3 doubles, 2 twin/doubles: £75–£95. 1 family room for 4: £100–£130. Singles from £70.
Meals	Lunch from £6.75. Dinner, 3 courses, £25–£35. Sunday lunch from £12.50.
Closed	Christmas.
Directions	West from Berwick on A6105, then left in Churnside onto B6437. On left in village.

William & Katerina Reynolds
The Allanton Inn
Allanton,
By Duns, TD11 3JZ

Tel	+44 (0)1890 818260
Email	info@allantoninn.co.uk
Web	www.allantoninn.co.uk

Photo: Alec Studerus

Scarista House

All you need to know is this: Harris is one of the most beautiful places in the world. Beaches of white sand that stretch for a mile or two are not uncommon. If you bump into another soul, it will be a delightful coincidence, but you shouldn't count on it. The water is turquoise, coconuts sometimes wash up on the beach. The view from Scarista is simple and magnificent: field, ridge, beach, water, sky. Patricia and Tim are the kindest people. Their home is island heaven: peat fires, rugs on painted floors, books everywhere, a first-floor drawing room that floods with Harris light. Country-house bedrooms have warm colours and stylish bathrooms. There are walking sticks and wellington boots to help you up the odd hill, then a set of golf clubs by the front door in case you wish to play (the view from the first tee is one of the best in the game). Kind staff may speak Gaelic. The food is exceptional, perhaps quail with an armagnac mousse, Harris langoustine with garlic and butter, tarte tatin with cinnamon ice cream. Don't miss Uig Sands or the standing stones at Callanish. A perfect place. *Pets by arrangement.*

Rooms	2 doubles, 1 twin: £207–£245. 2 suites for 2, 1 family room for 4: £233–£245. Singles from £135.
Meals	Dinner, 3 courses, £44. Packed lunch from £7.50.
Closed	Christmas, January–February.
Directions	From Tarbert A859 south, signed Rodel. Scarista 15 miles on left after golf course. W10 bus stops at gate.

Patricia & Tim Martin
Scarista House
Scarista,
Isle of Harris, HS3 3HX

Tel	+44 (0)1859 550238
Email	timandpatricia@scaristahouse.com
Web	www.scaristahouse.com

Wales

The Dolaucothi Arms

Tucked away in the heart of the Carmarthenshire countryside, this gem of a pub shines bright. Lovely Esther and Dave have brought the Dolaucothi back to life – notice little touches like handsome floral reupholstering on the mix-and-match dining chairs, and clutches of blooms in jugs and antique bottles on tables and sills. Dave's gorgeous gardens flank the walk up the little path; as you come in, there's a happy buzz in the air and the tempting scent of fresh home cooking; nearly everything is lovingly cooked from scratch! The dining room and bar are all in warm neutrals, with terracotta tiles and wood-burners. Sink into the velvety green chesterfield in the snug with a bottle of local brew or a glass of wine – Esther and Dave can advise. Food wise, try lamb reared by Dolaucothi farmer Gary, or the homemade pies; both are local and delicious. Hop up the little staircase, and you'll find three quiet bedrooms with garden views in soft tones of olive or wild rose. Snuggle up with wool duvets and pillows topped with colourful Welsh blankets, and enjoy the peace. There's even a little tipple on the chest of drawers for a nightcap.

Rooms	3 doubles: £75–£80. Singles £60. Extra bed/sofabed available £20 p.p.p.n.
Meals	Lunch from £5. Dinner, 3 courses, £20–£25. Sunday lunch from £9.
Closed	26 December–2 January.
Directions	A40 toward Llandovery then right turn onto A482 to Lampeter. After 8 miles, you'll see a Pumpsaint sign as you enter the village. Pub is on your left.

David Joy & Esther Hubert
The Dolaucothi Arms
Pumpsaint, Llanwrda, SA19 8UW

Tel	+44 (0)1558 650237
Email	info@thedolaucothiarms.co.uk
Web	www.thedolaucothiarms.co.uk

Ty Mawr Country Hotel

Pretty rooms, attractive prices and delicious food make this welcoming country house hard to resist. It sits in a very peaceful spot. You drive over hills, drop into the village, then wash up at this 16th-century stone house that comes in soft yellow. Outside, a sun-trapping terrace laps against a trim lawn, which in turn drops into a passing river. Gentle eccentricities abound: croquet hoops take odd diversions, logs are piled high like giant beehives, a seat has been chiselled into a tree trunk. Inside, original stone walls and low beamed ceilings give a warm country feel. There are fires everywhere – one in the attractive sitting room that overlooks the garden, another in the dining room that burns on both sides. Excellent bedrooms are all big. You get big beds, warm colours, crisp linen, good bathrooms. Some have sofas, all are dog-friendly, three overlook the garden. Back downstairs, the bar doubles as reception, while Welsh art on the walls is for sale. Steve's cooking is the final treat, perhaps Cardigan Bay scallops, organic Welsh beef, calvados and cinnamon rice pudding. Top stuff. *Children over 10 welcome.*

Rooms	3 doubles, 3 twin/doubles: £115–£130. Singles £80.
Meals	Dinner £25–£30.
Closed	Rarely.
Directions	M4 west onto A48, then B4310 exit, for National Botanic Gardens. 6 miles north to Brechfa. In village centre.

Annabel & Steve Thomas
Ty Mawr Country Hotel
Brechfa, SA32 7RA

Tel	+44 (0)1267 202332
Email	info@wales-country-hotel.co.uk
Web	www.wales-country-hotel.co.uk

The Cors

A bohemian bolthole, one of the best. Nick is a cook, an artist and a gardener, his two lush acres a beautiful retreat in summer. Gunnera, bamboo and tree ferns flourish while the river Coran potters past – not a bad spot for tea in summer. Inside, a small, personal world of French inspiration: a bar that sweeps you back to 1950s Paris, then doors that open onto a Victorian veranda where roses and clematis ramble. As for the food, you eat accompanied by cool tunes, with busts and paintings all around – perhaps at the front with garden views, or wrapped up behind in claret reds. At weekends the restaurant is open to all with ambrosial delights on the menu, perhaps smoked haddock crème brûlée, roasted rack of salt marsh lamb, a zesty lemon tart. In the week, delicious comfort food is on tap by arrangement: homemade soups, shepherd's pie, a plate of local cheeses. Simple rooms with a chic style wait at the top of a beautiful staircase: rugs on bare boards, vintage William Morris wallpapers, bold colours, the odd armoire – perfect for the price. Don't miss Laugharne for all things Dylan Thomas. *Minimum stay: 2 nights at weekends*

Rooms	3 doubles: £80. Singles from £50.
Meals	Dinner, 3 courses, from £35 (Thur–Sat only). Sunday lunch from £17.
Closed	2 weeks in November.
Directions	A4066 south from St Clears for Laugharne. In village right at pub. Over bridge and on right.

Nick Priestland
The Cors
Newbridge Road,
Laugharne, SA33 4SH
Tel   +44 (0)1994 427219
Email   nick@thecors.co.uk
Web   www.thecors.co.uk

Penbontbren

You're lost in lovely hills, yet only three miles from the sea. Not that you're going to stray far. These gorgeous suites don't just have wonderful prices, they're heaped with comforts, too – this is a great spot to come and do nothing at all. Richard and Huw have thought it all through. You get crockery and cutlery, kettles and fridges, then you're encouraged to bring your own wine or to buy provisions from the farm shop for lunch. As for the suites, expect big beds, super bathrooms, sofas and armchairs in pretty sitting areas, then doors onto semi-private terraces – perfect for lunch in summer. You get iPod docks, flat-screen TVs, robes and White Company lotions, too. The new garden room is a little smaller than the others, but has a big terrace to compensate. Breakfast is served in the main house – the full Welsh works. Beautiful hills, sandy beaches, Cardigan and magical St Davids all wait. Good local restaurants are on hand: lobster from the sea, lamb from the hills. Don't miss The Shed in Porthgain for excellent fish and chips. A great place to unwind with discounts for longer stays. *Minimum stay: 2 nights in high season.*

Rooms	6 suites for 2: £99–£125.
	1 self-catering cottage for 7:
	£700–£1,150 per week.
	Singles £85–£99.
Meals	Restaurants within 3 miles.
Closed	Christmas.
Directions	North from Cardigan on A487. Through Tanygroes, past sign for Tresaith and Penbryn, then 1st right signed Penbontbren. On left after 1 mile.

Richard Morgan-Price & Huw Thomas
Penbontbren
Glynarthen,
Llandysul, SA44 6PE

Tel	+44 (0)1239 810248
Email	contact@penbontbren.com
Web	www.penbontbren.com

Nanteos Mansion

A grand old manor house lost at the end of a one-mile drive, with a small lake, a walled garden and 25 acres of ancient woodland. Views at the front stretch across fields to nearby hills, four pillars stand at the front door, sofas wait by a wood-burner in the hall. The house dates to 1731, but stands on medieval foundations. It is most famous for the Nanteos Cup – the Holy Grail to you and me – which legend says was carried here by monks from Glastonbury Abbey. A grand renovation recently brought the house back to life – electric-shock therapy performed by interior designers. Downstairs, there's a morning room, a sitting-room bar and an elegant restaurant where you dig into Nigel Jones' delicious food, perhaps chilli salt squid, roast partridge stuffed with chorizo, chilled chocolate fondant. Upstairs, big suites are grand and gracious, some panelled, others with fine wallpaper, but all rooms are lovely with lots of colour, original art and robes in chic bathrooms. There's lots to do: rivers to fish, mountains to climb, coastal paths to follow. Don't miss the music room (Wagner visited).

Rooms	4 doubles: £120–£220.
	10 suites for 2: £140–£260.
	Dinner, B&B from £125 p.p.
Meals	Lunch from £7.50. Dinner £33.95–£39.50.
	Sunday lunch from £22.
Closed	Rarely.
Directions	Leaving Aberystwyth to the south, take A4120 Devil's Bridge Road, then immediately right onto B4340. House signed left after 1 mile.

Sarah-Jane Thomas
Nanteos Mansion
Rhydyfelin,
Aberystwyth, SY23 4LU

Tel	+44 (0)1970 600522
Email	info@nanteos.com
Web	www.nanteos.com

Ffin Y Parc

If you love art, if beautiful things tickle you pink, if you like big old houses stylishly refurbished with a streak of contemporary flair, then you should cancel whatever you're doing next week and head for Ffin Y Parc. This is a gorgeous country pad – homespun, quirky, a creative bolthole that sits in 14 peaceful acres. Inside it's an exceptional gallery, not any old gallery showing a little local art, but one that curates some of the best Welsh art, with two artists a month on display – in the conservatory café where you scoff your bacon and eggs, in the airy bar where cool tunes play, and in the big sitting room where you sink into armchairs and watch smouldering logs on the fire. Bedrooms (weekends only) are equally lovely, with beautiful colours, elegant furniture, more fabulous art and some very fancy bathrooms. Two cool stone cottages wait outside if you want to stay a while. Lunch is served in the café: soups, quiche, perhaps a club sandwich, there are light meals in the evening for guests and a restaurant that comes to life at weekends. Snowdonia waits – for bikes and feet.

Rooms	2 doubles, 1 twin/double: £165–£185. 1 suite for 2: £195–£215. 1 self-catering cottage for 2 (short breaks from £295), 1 self-catering cottage for 4 (short breaks from £375): £495–£750 per week.
Meals	Lunch from £5.50.
Closed	Mondays & Tuesdays. Rooms: Fridays & Saturdays only.
Directions	A55, junc.19, then A470 south for 10 miles. House signed left 1 mile south of Llanwst.

Roland Powell & Ralph Sanders
Ffin Y Parc
Betws Road, Llanwst,
Llanrwst, LL26 0PT

Tel	+44 (0)1492 642070
Email	ralph@ffinyparc.co.uk
Web	www.ffinyparc.com

Escape Boutique B&B

A designer B&B with lovely rooms, attractive prices and some seriously fancy bathrooms. The house stands high on the hill, away from the crowds, a short stroll from the buzz of town and its two-mile beach. This is a 19th-century mill owner's villa and its fine old windows, sparkling wood floors and carved fireplace bear testament to its Victorian roots. Other than that it's a clean sweep of funky interiors. Sam and Gaenor scoured Europe for their eclectic collection of colourful retro furniture that fills the rooms – orange swivel chairs, iconic G-plan sofas, beautiful beds wrapped in crisp white linen. You'll find cow-hide rugs, funky wallpapers, big views from rooms at the front. All come with flat-screen TVs, blu-ray DVD players and iPod docks. Bathrooms are excellent: one room has a shower for two, another has a copper bath in the room. Downstairs, there's an honesty bar in the sitting room, while delicious breakfasts are served in an attractive dining room. Good food waits in town – the Seahorse for fish, Mamma Rosa for Italian. Great Orme waits above for big views of the bay. *Minimum stay: 2 nights at weekends*

Rooms	8 doubles, 1 twin/double: £95–£149. Singles from £80.
Meals	Restaurants within walking distance.
Closed	Christmas.
Directions	A55 junc. 19, then A470 for Llandudno. On promenade, head west hugging the coast, then left at Belmont Hotel and house on right.

Sam Nayar & Gaenor Loftus
Escape Boutique B&B
48 Church Walks,
Llandudno, LL30 2HL

Tel	+44 (0)1492 877776
Email	info@escapebandb.co.uk
Web	www.escapebandb.co.uk

Osborne House

Osborne House — originally the summer residence of a Cheshire brewer — dates to 1850, and was one of the first houses to be built on the promenade. It fell into the hands of Elyse's parents in the mid-1980s, who refurbished from top to toe, turning 23 small rooms into seven enormous suites. They didn't hold back — expect a grand Victorian feel with a dash of Belle Époque. You'll find Corinthian columns, crystal chandeliers, noble portraits on the walls, comfy sofas in front of the fire. Downstairs, there's a sitting room at the front with views of the bay, a bar in the middle for the daily papers, then curtains that open theatrically onto a muralled dining room at the back. Suites are huge — big sitting rooms, brass beds, claw-foot baths and walk-in showers. You'll find rugs on wood floors, ornate marble fireplaces, armchairs and sofas to take the strain; all but one have sea views. Bistro food waits downstairs, perhaps seared scallops, a rib-eye steak, baked toffee and chocolate sponge. There's off-road parking, too, and you can use the pool at the Empire, Osborne House's sister hotel. *Minimum stay: 2 nights at weekends.*

Rooms	7 suites for 2: £135–£185.
	Dinner, B&B from £82.50 p.p.
Meals	Lunch from £5. Dinner from £10.95.
	Afternoon tea from £8.50.
Closed	1 week over Christmas
Directions	A55, junc. 19, then A470 in
	Llandudno. At sea, turn left, then right
	at r'bout onto North Parade. On left.

Elyse Waddy
Osborne House
Promenade, 17 North Parade,
Llandudno, LL30 2LP

Tel	+44 (0)1492 860330
Email	sales@osbornehouse.co.uk
Web	www.osbornehouse.co.uk

The Hand at Llanarmon

The Hand sits in glorious country – vast skies, rolling hills, country lanes that deliver you into the middle of nowhere. It's a popular spot with walkers, mountain bikers and wildlife spotters, who spend their days having fun in the hills before rolling down to this 16th-century drovers' inn for the pleasures of a country local. A coal fire burns on the range in reception, a wood fire crackles in the front bar, a wood-burner keeps things cosy in the restaurant. Expect stone walls, low beamed ceilings, old pine settles and candles on the mantelpiece. There's a locals' bar for darts and pool, then a quiet sitting room for maps and books, which doubles as a treatment room. Delicious food draws a crowd, so grab a table and dig into excellent country fare, perhaps Welsh Cheddar brûlée, roast rump of local lamb, sticky toffee pudding with caramel sauce. Airy rooms, all recently refurbished, have a contemporary feel with Welsh woollen throws on good beds and views of village and hill. Those in the main house are a little bigger, a couple have claw-foot-baths, three are dog friendly. Special indeed.

Rooms	11 doubles: £95–£135
	1 suite for 4: £150.
	Singles from £55. Sofabed £25.
Meals	Lunch & dinner £5–£30.
	Sunday lunch from £15.
Closed	Rarely.
Directions	Leave A5 south of Chirk for B4500.
	Llanarmon 11 miles on.

Jackie & Jonathan Greatorex
The Hand at Llanarmon
Llanarmon Dyffryn Ceiriog,
Llangollen, LL20 7LD
Tel   +44 (0)1691 600666
Email   reception@thehandhotel.co.uk
Web   www.thehandhotel.co.uk

Y Meirionnydd

By day you explore the mighty wonders of Snowdonia, by night you return to this lovely small hotel and recover in style. It's one of those places that delivers just what you want; it's smart without being posh, the welcome is second to none, tasty food hits the spot, the bedrooms are excellent. You're in the middle of a small country town with a terrace at the front, so sit outside in summer and watch the world pass by. Inside, soft colours and warm lighting create a relaxed feel. There's a cute bar with armchairs and games, an airy breakfast room for the full Welsh works, then a smart restaurant cut into the rock, which was once the county jail; the food is somewhat better these days, perhaps game terrine with mustard piccalilli, rump of Welsh lamb with rosemary dumplings, Penderyn Welsh whisky and honey ice cream. Bedrooms upstairs fit the bill nicely. Some are bigger than others, but all have the same style: clean lines, cool colours, big beds, beautiful linen. You get the odd stone wall, an armchair if there's room, then super bathrooms. There's secure storage for bikes, too. *Minimum stay: 2 nights at weekends*

Rooms	3 doubles, 2 twin/doubles: £89–£125. Singles £69–£79. Extra bed/sofabed available £20 p.p.p.n.
Meals	Dinner, 3 courses, £25. Not Mondays in low season.
Closed	One week at Christmas.
Directions	In centre of town on one-way system, off A470.

Marc Russell & Nick Banda
Y Meirionnydd
Smithfield Square,
Dolgellau, LL40 1ES

Tel	+44 (0)1341 422554
Email	info@themeirionnydd.com
Web	www.themeirionnydd.com

Penmaenuchaf Hall

This grand old house sits high on the hill with fine views over the Mawddach estuary. It stands in 20 acres of woodlands and formal gardens with daffodils, snowdrops and bluebells running riot in spring and a walled garden that bursts with summer colour. The house has attitude, too. It was built in 1865 for a Bolton cotton merchant, and an open fire crackles in the half-panelled hall, where sofas and armchairs wait. The drawing room is equally grand with mullioned windows that frame the view, cavernous sofas and a grand piano, country rugs on original wood floors. There's an airy restaurant, where French windows open onto a terrace, so eat al fresco in good weather, perhaps seared scallops, Gressingham duck, apple tart and honey ice cream. Bedrooms come in traditional country-house style with big, comfy beds and warm colours. Some are huge, others have balconies or a new bathroom, all have iPod docks and digital radios. Outside, Snowdon waits, there are 13 miles of river to fish and the fabulous mountain biking trails of Coed-y-Brenin for fun at all levels in the forest. *Please ring for enquiries. Children over 6 welcome.*

Rooms	7 doubles, 5 twin/doubles, 1 four-poster: £180-£290. 1 family room for 4: £260-£290. Singles £125-£190.
Meals	Lunch from £6. Dinner, 3 courses, £28.50-£46. Afternoon tea from £7.95.
Closed	Rarely.
Directions	From Dolgellau A493 west for about 1.5 miles. Entrance on left.

Mark Watson & Lorraine Fielding
Penmaenuchaf Hall
Penmaenpool,
Dolgellau, LL40 1YB

Tel	+44 (0)1341 422129
Email	relax@penhall.co.uk
Web	www.penhall.co.uk

Llwyndû Farmhouse

The view here is fabulous — a clean sweep across Cardigan Bay to the Llyn Peninsula beyond. Below, a ten-mile beach runs north to Harlech Point; behind, the Rhinog mountains rise. As for the farmhouse, it sits high on the hill and dates to 1581. It's a small, homespun world — Peter and Paula do it all themselves — a simple retreat with delicious slow food at the end of the day. Inside, you find thick stone walls, comfy sofas and a wood-burner in the inglenook. Bedrooms are scattered about. Those in the main house have a cosy feel with warm colours, low ceilings, perhaps a four-poster. Those in the outbuildings tend to be a little bigger and have painted stone walls, then ceilings open to the rafters. By day you explore the wonders of Snowdonia — you can climb mountains, take to cycle tracks or merely walk in the hills. By night you return to feast on local delights under ancient beams, perhaps Rhydlewis smoked salmon, Welsh Black steak, apple tarte tatin; if you're still hungry after that, excellent Welsh cheeses wait. Don't miss Portmeirion, or links golf at Harlech and Aberdovey. *Minimum stay: 2 nights.*

Rooms	3 doubles, 2 four-posters: £104–£126.
	1 family room for 4: £104–£146.
	Dinner B&B from £82 p.p.
	Singles from £52.
Meals	Dinner £25–£30.
Closed	January.
Directions	A496, 2 miles north of Barmouth when street lights stop. Llwyndû signed on right.

Peter & Paula Thompson
Llwyndû Farmhouse
Llanaber,
Barmouth, LL42 1RR

Tel	+44 (0)1341 280144
Email	intouch@llwyndu-farmhouse.co.uk
Web	www.llwyndu-farmhouse.co.uk

Plas Bodegroes

A glorious house, one of the loveliest in the book, far flung, but worth every second it takes to get here. Outside, six acres of mature gardens include a 200-year-old avenue of beech trees. Inside, a cool elegance roams freely: golden wallpapers, smouldering fires, a quirky bar that appears from thin air. French windows flood the house with light and open on to a veranda that comes wrapped in wisteria in summer – in good weather there are few better places to be. Beautiful bedrooms have chic fabrics, smart beds, crisp linen, super bathrooms – it really doesn't matter which one you get. Some open onto a courtyard where climbing roses flourish. As for Chris and Camille, they took over recently and love their new world. Camille looks after guests with an easy charm, leaving Chris to whisk up delicious food in the kitchen. You eat in a dining room that doubles as an art gallery, perhaps braised pork cheek with crispy ham hock, wild sea bass with lemon and basil, cassis mousse with crème fraîche sorbet. The Llyn Peninsula waits: excellent walking, sandy beaches, towering cliffs. Pure heaven.

Rooms	4 doubles, 3 twin/doubles: £150–£170. 3 suites for 2: £190. Dinner, B&B from £124 p.p. (min 2 nights). Singles from £130.
Meals	Sunday lunch £24.50. Dinner £49.
Closed	Sunday nights & Mondays.
Directions	From Pwllheli A497 towards Nefyn. House on left after 1 mile, signed.

Chris & Camille Lovell
Plas Bodegroes
Efailnewydd,
Pwllheli, LL53 5TH

Tel	+44 (0)1758 612363
Email	info@bodegroes.co.uk
Web	www.bodegroes.co.uk

Plas Dinas Country House

The family home of Lord Snowdon dates to the 1600s and stands in 15 rural acres with an avenue of oak sweeping you up to the house. Princess Margaret often stayed and much of what fills the house belongs to the family: striking chandeliers, oils by the score, gilt-framed mirrors – an Aladdin's cave of beautiful things. There's a baby grand piano in the drawing room, where you find a roaring fire and an honesty bar, but potter about and find masses of memorabilia framed on the walls (make sure you visit the private dining room). Bedrooms – some with views across fields to the sea – mix a graceful past with modern design. You get four-posters, period colours, bold wallpapers, a sofa if there's room. A cute room in the eaves has mountain views, all have hot-water bottles, Apple TVs and excellent bathrooms, some with showers, others with free-standing baths. Good food waits in the restaurant, perhaps fishcakes with lime and ginger, lamb shank with a rosemary jus, chocolate tart with white chocolate ice-cream. Snowdon is close, as you'd expect, so bring walking boots and mountain bikes. *Minimum stay: 2 nights on bank holiday weekends.*

Rooms	5 doubles, 5 twin/doubles: £99–£249.
Meals	Dinner, 3 courses, £25–£35.
Closed	Christmas.
Directions	South from Caernarfon on A487. Through Bontnewydd, signed right after half a mile at brow of shallow hill.

Neil Baines & Marco Soares
Plas Dinas Country House
Bontnewydd,
Caernarfon, LL54 7YF

Tel	+44 (0)1286 830214
Email	info@plasdinas.co.uk
Web	www.plasdinas.co.uk

The Bell at Skenfrith

The position here is magical: an ancient stone bridge, a river snaking through the valley, glorious hills rising beyond, cows grazing in lush fields. It's a perfect spot, not least because providence blessed it with this chic little inn. Inside, you find a locals' bar for the odd game of rugby, sofas in front of a wood-burner in the sitting room, then an airy restaurant for some very good food. In summer, doors fly open and life spills onto a stone terrace with views of hill and wood – a fine spot for lunch in the sun. Elegant country-house bedrooms brim with light. Some are beamed, most are big, you'll find padded bedheads, Farrow & Ball colours, perhaps a walnut bed or a claw-foot bath in your room. Those at the front have river views, those at the back look onto the hills, some have sofas, all have robes in excellent bathrooms. Seven circular walks start at the front door with maps to show you the way. Delicious food awaits your return, perhaps Welsh rarebit with a poached egg, braised beef brisket with dauphinoise potatoes, apple doughnuts with toffee sauce and mulled cider. *Minimum stay: 2 nights at weekends.*

Rooms	5 doubles, 3 twin/doubles, 3 four-posters: £150-£230. Singles £90. Dinner, B&B from £95 p.p. Extra bed/sofabed available £10-£20 p.p.p.n.
Meals	Lunch from £5.95. Dinner, 3 courses, around £35. Sunday lunch from £12.95.
Closed	Rarely.
Directions	From Monmouth B4233 to Rockfield; B4347 north for 5 miles; right on B4521; Skenfrith 1 mile.

Richard Ireton & Sarah Hudson
The Bell at Skenfrith
Skenfrith,
Abergavenny, NP7 8UH

Tel	+44 (0)1600 750235
Email	enquiries@skenfrith.co.uk
Web	www.skenfrith.co.uk

The Whitebrook

Chris and Kirsty came west to do their own thing, refurbishing this popular restaurant with rooms in great style, then winning a Michelin star – all in their first year. It's quite some feat, but no surprise. Chris has a culinary pedigree few can match, including five years with Raymond Blanc at Le Manoir aux Quat'Saisons. As for the house, it sits in a tiny village that's wrapped up in the Wye Valley. Forest rises all around, bluebells carpet the woods in spring, deer amble by in summer. Outside, there's a terrace for lunch in good weather. Inside, a cool, uncluttered elegance runs throughout, a great spot to treat yourself to Chris's ambrosial food. Much is foraged – hogweed, nettles, wild chervil, bitter cress – while most is local with lamb from the valley and beef from Ross. You can eat à la carte or splash out on a seven-course tasting menu, perhaps squab pigeon with rhubarb, Cornish turbot with ground elder, caramelised white chocolate with pink grapefruit. Lovely rooms have colour and style, woollen throws, good beds and fancy bathrooms. Tintern Abbey on the river Wye is close.

Rooms	6 doubles, 2 twin/doubles: £130–£190.
Meals	Lunch from £25.
	Dinner, 3 courses, £54.
	Tasting menu £67. Sunday lunch £35.
Closed	Mondays. Two weeks in January.
Directions	M4 junc. 24, A449/A40 north to Monmouth, then B4293 south. Up hill. After 2.7 miles left for Whitebook. On right after two miles.

Chris & Kirsty Harrod
The Whitebrook
Whitebrook,
Monmouth, NP25 4TX

Tel	+44 (0)1600 860254
Email	info@thewhitebrook.co.uk
Web	www.thewhitebrook.co.uk

32 Townhouse

Narberth is lovely – quirky and colourful, lively and independent. It's wrapped up in Pembrokeshire's rolling hills with the coast and its path waiting ten miles south. As for this stylish restaurant with rooms, it sits on the high street, dates to 1820, and has a smart Georgian exterior with early Victorian bay windows. Inside, the style is hard to miss: Russian red in the bar with a picture of Gorbachev on the wall; then period green in the restaurant, where gilt-framed oils hang by the score. Potter about and find original tiles and ironwork, parquet floors and stained glass windows; the zinc-topped bar was made from a Methodist pulpit. There's a conservatory bistro that opens onto a pretty terrace for strong coffee, homemade quiche and posh burgers. Bedrooms above are soundproofed and come with smart beds, white linen, travertine bathrooms and attractive prices; some interconnect, others in the eaves have the odd beam. Delicious food waits downstairs, perhaps calamari with chorizo and fennel, chicken with braised shallots, toffee apple and blackberry crumble. A great little base.

Rooms	6 doubles, 2 twin/doubles: £85–£115.
Meals	Lunch from £4.95.
	Light bites from £7.45.
	Dinner, 3 courses, about £30.
Closed	Christmas Day.
Directions	M4 west, then A40 past St Clears. After 10 miles, south on A478 for Narberth. On High Street by clock tower.

Dominic Swingler
32 Townhouse
32 High Street,
Narberth, SA67 7AS

Tel	+44 (0)1834 218338
Email	info@32townhouse.com
Web	www.32townhouse.com

Penally Abbey

This beautifully refurbished country-house hotel sits high on the hill with long views over Carmarthen Bay. Outside, there's a small courtyard, then five acres of lawns and woodland, where bluebells run riot in spring. Inside, chic interiors come with cool colours, painted panelling, parquet flooring and the odd Doric column. There's an elegant bar in deep charcoal with fine art on the walls, then a big drawing room with an open fire and huge sea views. Big windows in the main house flood the rooms with light, while doors in the sunroom open onto a gravelled terrace, where you can read the papers, dig into afternoon tea, or fall asleep in the sun. Bedrooms have a stunning new look: off-white walls, beautiful beds, crisp white linen, elegant fabrics. Big rooms in the main house have vast windows to frame the view, all have sublime white marble bathrooms. You eat in style in the restaurant – period colours, grand chandelier – perhaps steamed clams with lemon and ginger, chicken with chestnuts and a pear tarte tatin, a dark chocolate tort with pistachio ice cream. There's fine coastal walking, too.

Rooms	3 doubles, 6 twin/doubles, 2 four-posters: £130-£210. Dinner, B&B from £90 p.p.
Meals	Lunch from £5. Dinner, 3 courses, £30-£35. Sunday lunch from £12.95.
Closed	January.
Directions	From Tenby A4139 for Pembroke. Right into Penally after 1.5 miles. Hotel signed above village green. Train station 5-mins walk.

Melanie & Lucas Boissevain
Penally Abbey
Penally,
Tenby, SA70 7PY

Tel	+44 (0)1834 843033
Email	info@penally-abbey.com
Web	www.penally-abbey.com

AWARD
WINNER

Hotel of the Year

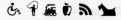

Entry 285   Map 1

Stackpole Inn

This lovely inn sits in a pretty village that's marooned in beautiful country. It's a few miles back from the sea, with Barafundle Bay – one of the finest beaches in Britain – a short walk away. You can pick up the coastal path, too, and follow it round past Stackpole Quay and St Govan's Chapel to the cliffs at Linney Head, then the surfers at Freshwater West. It's pure heaven, one of those sleepy areas you drop into for a couple of days and hardly use your car. As for the Stackpole, it's a great little base – stylish and welcoming with tasty rustic food, perhaps deep-fried whitebait, rib of local beef, almond and hazelnut tart. Outside, the pub is drenched in honeysuckle and there's a small garden to the front for a drop of Welsh ale in summer. Inside, you find low wooden ceilings, exposed stone walls, a hard-working wood-burner and four hand pumps at the slate bar. Super bedrooms have comfy beds, stripped floors, seaside colours and excellent bathrooms. All have sofabeds, two have velux windows for star gazing. Dogs and children are very welcome.

Rooms	2 twin/doubles: £90.
	2 family rooms for 4: £90–£120.
	Singles from £60.
Meals	Lunch from £5.
	Dinner, 3 courses, £25–£30.
	Sunday lunch, 3 courses, £18.95.
Closed	Rarely.
Directions	B4319 south from Pembroke for 3 miles, then left for Stackpole. Through Stackpole Cheriton, up hill, right at T-junction. On right.

Gary & Becky Evans
Stackpole Inn
Stackpole,
Pembroke, SA71 5DF

Tel	+44 (0)1646 672324
Email	info@stackpoleinn.co.uk
Web	www.stackpoleinn.co.uk

Leominster Library
01432 383290

Checkout summary

Date: 29/08/2023   10:25

Loaned today

Title: British hotels & inns
ID: 740007118256
Due back: 19/09/2023

Total item(s) loaned today: 1
Previous Amount Owed: 0.00 GBP
Overdue: 0
Reservation(s) pending: 0
Reservation(s) to collect: 0
Total item(s) on loan 3
Item(s) you already have on loan

Title: Mrs Hudson and the Malabar Rose
Item: 740009827378
Due back: 15/09/2023

Title: Murder for good
Item: 770000062271
Due back: 15/09/2023

For renewals and information
www.herefordshire.gov.uk/libraries

Crug Glas

St Davids is one of the most magical places in Britain. It sits in Pembroke's national park, has an imperious 12th-century cathedral, and is surrounded by magnificent coastline that's dotted with cliffs and vast sandy beaches. As for Janet's wonderful retreat, it's part chic hotel, part farmhouse B&B, stylish yet personal, a great place to stay. The house dates from 1120 and sits in 600 acres of arable and grazing land (they rear cattle and grow cereals). Outside, you find lawns and a small copse sprinkled with bluebells, then field and sky, and that's about it. Inside, there's an honesty bar in the sitting room and a Welsh dresser in the dining room, where Janet serves delicious food: homemade soups, home-reared beef, chocolate mousse with clotted cream. Fancy bedrooms are the big surprise: a vast four-poster, the odd copper bath, old armoires, beautiful fabrics. All have robes in gorgeous bathrooms, bigger rooms come with sofas, one room occupies most of the top floor. Two rooms in an old barn have exposed timbers and underfloor heating. The coast is about five fields to the west.

Rooms	5 doubles, 2 twin/doubles: £150–£190. Singles from £95.
Meals	Lunch, 2 courses, from £18. Dinner, 3 courses, £25–£30. Sunday lunch £22.50. Afternoon tea from £12.50.
Closed	22-27 December.
Directions	South from Fishguard on A487. Through Croes-goch, then signed right after 2 miles.

Janet & Perkin Evans
Crug Glas
Solva,
Haverfordwest, SA62 6XX

Tel	+44 (0)1348 831302
Email	janet@crugglas.plus.com
Web	www.crug-glas.co.uk

The Manor Town House

Fishguard is quirky – arty and friendly with a folk festival in May and a jazz festival in August. You'll find great coastal walks, sandy beaches and magical St Davids a few miles south. In short, it's much more than an overnight stop on your way to Ireland and, with a happy vibe waiting at The Manor Town House, hard to resist. Chris and Helen escaped London and have taken to their new world like ducks to water. Inside, you're greeted by a couple of gorgeous sitting rooms – stripped floorboards, cool colours, local art, and crackling fires in winter. One has an honesty bar, you get fresh flowers, lots of books, and comfy sofas from which to plan your day. Homely bedrooms have lots of charm: bold colours, beautiful fabrics, the odd antique, super-comfy beds. Those at the back have sea views, perhaps a sofa or a padded window seat, while compact bathrooms do the trick. Breakfast is a treat, there's a garden for afternoon tea overlooking the harbour, and it's a one-minute stroll up the road to Bar 5 for cocktails and The Lounge at No. 3 for the best food in town. Pembrokeshire awaits. Brilliant. *Minimum stay: 2 nights at weekends in summer.*

Rooms	2 doubles, 3 twin/doubles: £90-£115. 1 single: £70-£85. Extra beds: adult £20, child under 16, £15.
Meals	Local restaurants within 100 yds.
Closed	23-27 December.
Directions	M4 west, A48 west, A40 north, then A487 into town. Right at roundabout and on left. Parking close by.

Chris & Helen Sheldon
The Manor Town House
11 Main Street, Fishguard, SA65 9HG

Tel	+44 (0)1348 873260
Email	enquiries@manortownhouse.com
Web	www.manortownhouse.com

Llys Meddyg

This cool little restaurant with rooms has a bit of everything: chic bedrooms that pack a punch, super food in a pine-clad restaurant, a cellar bar for cocktails before dinner, a pretty garden for summer. It's a friendly place with happy staff on hand to help, and it draws in the locals, who come for the excellent food, perhaps brown crab brûlée with white crab meat, local pheasant with an oriental consommé, caramelised pear with blue-cheese ice-cream. You eat in style with a fire burning at one end of the restaurant and Welsh art hanging on the walls. Chic bedrooms come as standard. They're split between the main house (cool colours, vast beds, funky bathrooms) and the mews behind (rustic, airy and peaceful). All have the same fresh style: Farrow & Ball colours, lovely art, blond oak beds, fluffy white bath robes. In summer, decant into the garden, where a café/bistro opens up for coffee and cake or pizza from a wood-fired oven. Pembrokeshire's coastal path waits for windswept cliffs and sandy beaches. Don't miss St Davids, or Laugharne for all things Dylan Thomas. Dogs are very welcome.

Rooms	4 doubles, 4 twin/doubles: £100–£180.
	1 suite for 2: £100–£180.
	Singles from £85.
Meals	Lunch from £7. Dinner from £14.
Closed	Rarely.
Directions	East from Fishguard on A487.
	On left in Newport towards eastern
	edge of town.

Louise & Edward Sykes
Llys Meddyg
East Street,
Newport, SA42 0SY

Tel	+44 (0)1239 820008
Email	info@llysmeddyg.com
Web	www.llysmeddyg.com

The Lake Country House & Spa

Deep in the silence of mid-Wales, an old-school country house that looks after you well. Fifty acres of lawns, lakes and ancient woodland wrap around you, there's a spa with an indoor pool, treatment rooms and a tennis court by the lake. Sit in a hot tub and watch guests fish for their supper, try your luck on the nine-hole golf course, saddle up nearby and take to the hills. Come home to afternoon tea in the big, elegant drawing room, where an archipelago of rugs warms a brightly polished wooden floor and chandeliers hang from the ceiling. The hotel opened over a hundred years ago and the leather-bound fishing logs date to 1894. A feel of the 1920s lingers. Fires come to life in front of your eyes, grand pianos and grandfather clocks sing their songs, snooker balls crash about in the distance. Dress for a delicious dinner – the atmosphere deserves it – then retire to cosseting bedrooms. Most are suites: those in the house are warmly traditional, those in the lodge softly contemporary. The London train takes four hours and stops in the village. Resident geese waddle.

Rooms	6 twin/doubles: £195.
	24 suites for 2: £240-£260.
	Singles from £145.
	Dinner, B&B (min. 2 nights) from
	£122.50 p.p.
Meals	Lunch, 3 courses, £22.50.
	Dinner, 4 courses, £38.50.
Closed	Never.
Directions	From Builth Wells A483 west for
	7 miles to Garth. Signed from village.

Jean-Pierre Mifsud
The Lake Country House & Spa
Llangammarch Wells, LD4 4BS
Tel   +44 (0)1591 620202
Email   info@lakecountryhouse.co.uk
Web   www.lakecountryhouse.co.uk

The Felin Fach Griffin

It's quirky, homespun, and thrives on a mix of relaxed informality and colourful style. The low-ceilinged bar resembles the sitting room of a small hip country house, with timber frames, cool tunes and comfy sofas in front of a smouldering fire. Painted stone walls come in blocks of colour, there's live music on Sunday nights, and you dine informally in the white-walled restaurant, with stock pots simmering on an Aga. The food is excellent, perhaps dressed Portland crab, rump of Welsh beef, treacle tart with bergamot sorbet; much of what you eat comes from a half-acre kitchen garden, with meat and game from the hills around you. Bedrooms above have style and substance: comfy beds wrapped in crisp linen, good bathrooms with fluffy towels, Roberts radios, a smattering of books, but no TV unless you ask. Breakfast is served in the dining room; wallow with the papers, make your own toast, scoff the full Welsh. A main road passes outside, but quietly at night, while lanes lead into the hills, so walk, ride, bike, canoe. Hay is close for books galore. Don't miss excellent off-season deals.

Rooms	2 doubles, 2 twin/doubles, 2 four-posters: £130-£170. 1 family room for 3: £170. Dinner, B&B from £92.50 p.p.
Meals	Lunch from £7. Dinner, 3 courses, about £30. Sunday lunch from £20.
Closed	Christmas Eve & Day (evening). 4 days in January.
Directions	From Brecon A470 north to Felin Fach (4.5 miles). On left.

Charles & Edmund Inkin
The Felin Fach Griffin
Felin Fach,
Brecon, LD3 0UB

Tel	+44 (0)1874 620111
Email	enquiries@felinfachgriffin.co.uk
Web	www.felinfachgriffin.co.uk

Gliffaes Hotel

A charming country-house hotel that towers above the river Usk as it pours through the valley below. In summer, doors open onto a large terrace, where you can sit in the sun and soak up the view – red kites circle above, sheep graze beyond. You're in 35 peaceful acres of formal lawns and mature woodland. Inside, interiors pack a punch. Afternoon tea 'on the house' is served every day in the panelled sitting room – family portraits hang on the wall, logs crackle in the grandest fireplace. This is a well-known fishing hotel and fishermen often gather in the bar for a quick drink and a tall tale. Eventually, they spin into the restaurant and dig into lovely seasonal food (the hotel is part of the Slow Food Movement), perhaps goat's cheese soufflé, fillet of halibut, lemon tart with passion fruit sorbet. Country-house bedrooms wait above. Expect smart fabrics, warm colours, crisp linen, fresh flowers. Several have river views, a couple have small balconies, one has a claw-foot bath that overlooks the front lawn. Outside, beautiful gardens include a small arboretum of specimen trees. Wonderful. *Minimum stay: 2 nights at weekends.*

Rooms	19 twin/doubles: £112–£265.
	4 singles: £100.
	Dinner, B&B from £90 p.p.
Meals	Light lunches from £5.
	Dinner, 3 courses, £42.
	Sunday lunch £22–£29.
Closed	January.
Directions	From Crickhowell, A40 west for 2.5 miles. Signed left and on left after 1 mile.

James & Susie Suter
Gliffaes Hotel
Gliffaes Road,
Crickhowell, NP8 1RH

Tel	+44 (0)1874 730371
Email	calls@gliffaeshotel.com
Web	www.gliffaeshotel.com

Milebrook House Hotel

An old-school, country-house hotel with three acres of gardens that run down to the river Teme. You'll find Wales on one side and England on the other, so bring your wellies and wade across; the walking is magnificent. The house was once home to writer Wilfred Thesiger; his friend, Haile Selassie, visited in the 1920s. These days it's informally run by three generations of the Marsden family with Beryl and Rodney leading the way. Step inside and enter a world that's rooted in a delightful past: clocks tick, cats snooze, fires crackle, the odd champagne cork escapes its bondage. Beautiful art hangs on the walls, the sitting room is stuffed with books, the bar comes in country-house style, and there's food to reckon with in the dining room, perhaps local pigeon with caramelised apple, slow-roasted shoulder of Welsh lamb, apple crumble and butterscotch sundae. A kitchen garden supplies much for the table. You can fish, spot deer in the woods, play croquet on the lawn. Red kite, moorhens, kingfishers and herons live in the valley. Homely bedrooms wait. Presteigne and Ludlow are close.

Rooms	5 doubles, 5 twins: £144. 1 family room for 3: £172. Singles from £87.50. Dinner, B&B from £102.50 p.p.
Meals	Lunch, 2 courses, £14.95, not Mon. Dinner, 3 courses, £30–£35. Sunday lunch from £17.
Closed	Rarely.
Directions	From Ludlow A49 north, then left at Bromfield on A4113 towards Knighton for 10 miles. Hotel on right.

Rodney, Beryl & Joanne Marsden
Milebrook House Hotel
Stanage,
Knighton, LD7 1LT
Tel   +44 (0)1547 528632
Email   hotel@milebrookhouse.co.uk
Web   www.milebrookhouse.co.uk

Quick reference indices

Children of all ages welcome

These owners have told us that they welcome children of all ages. Please note cots and highchairs may not necessarily be available.

Channel Islands

Scotland

Wales

Pets

Pets welcome; please let the owner know if you want to bring pets.

England

Quick reference indices

Quick reference indices

Channel Islands

Scotland

Wales

Pool

Swimming pool on the
premises; use may be by
arrangement.

England

Channel Islands

Wales

Bike
Bikes on the premises to hire or borrow.

England
Berkshire 5
Cornwall 14 • 25
Cumbria 34 • 38 • 42
Devon 64 • 66
Dorset 78 • 82 • 83
Essex 91
Gloucestershire 99
Hampshire 100 • 104
Isle of Wight 112
London 134
Norfolk 141
Oxfordshire 150 • 152
Rutland 158
Shropshire 160
Somerset 167 • 171
Suffolk 184 • 187
Sussex 193 • 204
Yorkshire 215 • 217 • 220

Scotland
Argyll & Bute 231 • 232 • 235 • 236
Dumfries & Galloway 239 • 240
Edinburgh 242
Highland 249 • 250
Perth & Kinross 263

Wales
Powys 292

Tennis
Tennis court on the premises; use may be by arrangement.

England
Bath & N.E. Somerset 4
Berkshire 5
Cornwall 13 • 15 • 20
Cumbria 34
Devon 56 • 64
Dorset 85
Essex 90
Hampshire 100
Isle of Wight 111 • 112
Kent 113
Norfolk 136
Northumberland 145
Rutland 158
Sussex 193
Worcestershire 214
Yorkshire 220

Channel Islands
Guernsey 227

Scotland
Argyll & Bute 236

Wales
Powys 290 • 292

Public transport
These places are within 10 miles of a bus/train station and owner can arrange collection, with notice.

Bath & N.E. Somerset 1 • 2 • 3 • 4
Berkshire 5

346

Quick reference indices

Alastair Sawday has been publishing books for over 20 years, finding Special Places to Stay in Britain and abroad. All our properties are inspected by us and are chosen for their charm and individuality. And there are many more to explore on our perennially popular website: www.sawdays.co.uk. You can buy any of our books at a reader discount of 25%* on the RRP.

List of titles:	RRP	Discount price
British Bed & Breakfast	£15.99	£11.99
British Hotels and Inns	£15.99	£11.99
Pubs & Inns of England & Wales	£15.99	£11.99
Dog-friendly Breaks in Britain	£14.99	£11.24
French Bed & Breakfast	£15.99	£11.99
French Châteaux & Hotels	£15.99	£11.99
Italy	£15.99	£11.99

*postage and packaging is added to each order

How to order:
You can order online at: www.sawdays.co.uk/bookshop/
or call: +44 (0)117 204 7810

Photo: 32 Townhouse, entry 284

Photo: The Zetter Townhouse, entry 134

Photo: The Fish Hotel, entry 214

Photo: Sidmouth Harbour Hotel, entry 72